PRIVACY AND PUBLICITY

BEATRIZ COLOMINA

PRIVACY AND PUBLICITY

Modern Architecture as Mass Media

The MIT Press
Cambridge, Massachusetts
London, England

First MIT Press paperback edition, 1996

© 1994 Massachusetts Institute of Technology
All rights reserved. No part of this book may be reproduced in any form by any electronic or mechanical means (including photocopying, recording, or information storage and retrieval) without permission in writing from the publisher.

The book was set in Bodoni by DEKR Corporation, Woburn, Massachusetts, and was printed and bound in the United States of America.

Library of Congress Cataloging-in-Publication Data

Colomina, Beatriz.
Privacy and publicity : modern architecture as mass media / Beatriz Colomina.
p. cm.
Includes bibliographical references and index.
ISBN 0-262-03214-7 (HB), ISBN 0-262-53139-9 (PB)
1. Mass media and architecture. 2. Loos, Adolf, 1870–1933—Archives.
3. Le Corbusier, 1887–1965—Archives. I. Title.
NA2543.M37C65 1994
720'.1'05—dc20 93-36205
CIP

for Andrea and Mark

Contents

Preface

This book has been with me for a long time. I don't know exactly when it all started, but I do know when I first wrote something that one way or another has ended up here. It was 1981. New York. I was writing in Spanish and then translating into English. When, soon after, I tried my hand at English, I was shocked at the extent to which not only the way I was writing had changed but even what I was saying. It was as if with the language, I was also leaving behind a whole way of looking at things, of writing them. Even when we think we know what we are about to write, the moment we start writing, language takes us on an excursion of its own. And if that language is not ours, we are definitely in foreign territory. Lately, I have started to feel that way about Spanish. I have managed to become a foreigner in both languages, moving somewhat nomadically through the discourse on an unofficial itinerary. Traces of this complicated movement can be found throughout this book. The text is somehow suspended between the languages and times in which it was constructed.

Even if the original essay of 1981 on Loos is here rewritten and expanded beyond the point of recognition, the struggle between these different worlds, these different cultures and times, is still there. The changes testify to the abyss that appeared before me when I reopened the text ten years later, during a sabbatical. I could no longer read what I had written without getting a headache. And yet, when trying to reenter it, I found myself ensnared by it, trapped in its complicated mesh of literary references, pulled back into a space in which I had the time and the state of mind to read novels, nostalgic for that space and yet irritated by its testimony, that meandering piece of writing that resists being straightened up, brought into line with the rest of the book. What I anticipated as a cursory labor of editing turned into a lengthy period of writing in which I found myself back in the mood of the first text and, at a certain point, fighting to liberate myself from it but unable to efface it. In the end, the book tracks the evolution of my thinking over the twelve years I have been in the United States.

During this time, I have become indebted to many people and institutions. The research and writing were supported by grants and fellowships from the Caixa de Barcelona, Graham Foundation, Fondation Le Corbusier, SOM Foundation, and Princeton University Committee on Research in the Humanities and Social Sciences. I have also benefited from being a research scholar at the New York Institute for the Humanities, a visiting scholar at Columbia University, and a resident fellow at the Chicago Institute for Architecture and Urbanism. I am grateful to Angela Giral and the staff of Avery Library at Columbia University, to Frances Chen at the School of Architecture Library at Princeton University, to the staff at the Museum of Modern Art library and the archives of the Department of Architecture and Design, and above all to Madame Evelyne Tréhin and her staff at the Fondation Le Corbusier in Paris, who over the years facilitated my research in the extraordinary archives of Le Corbusier.

Earlier versions of parts of this book were published in *9H* no. 6, *Assemblage* no. 4, *Raumplan versus Plan Libre*, *L'Esprit nouveau: Le*

Corbusier und die Industrie, *Le Corbusier, une encyclopédie*, *AA Files* no. 20, *Architectureproduction*, *Ottagono*, and *Sexuality and Space*. I am grateful to the respective editors: Wilfried Wang, K. Michael Hays, Max Risselada, Stanislaus von Moos, Jacques Lucan, Bruno Reichlin, Jean-Louis Cohen, Joan Ockman, Alvin Boyarsky, Mary Wall, and Alessandra Ponte. While the book was in progress, it also benefited from a number of invitations to present it as a small series of lectures: at Harvard University in 1986, Rensselaer Polytechnic Institute in 1987, the Architectural Association in 1989, and Yale University in 1991. Finally, as the book went to press, I was invited to deliver it as the 1993 Preston H. Thomas Memorial Lectures at the School of Architecture at Cornell University, sponsored by Mr. and Mrs. Leonard Thomas. The support of schools of architecture has been invaluable. The extent to which my arguments were sharpened by these exchanges cannot be overestimated.

Perhaps my first thanks should go to my own students. In seminars, first at the School of Architecture at Columbia University and then at Princeton, I ventured the preliminary thoughts. Nothing is more rewarding than the first audience; I will be eternally grateful. In many ways, this book is written for them.

Of course, I am indebted to my friends, all of whom contributed to the project in different ways: Diana Agrest, Jennifer Bloomer, Christine Boyer, Cristina Colomina, Alan Colquhoun, Elizabeth Diller, Mario Gandelsonas, Michael Hays, Jean Leonard, Ralph Lerner, Thomas Leeser, Sandro Marpillero, Margarita Navarro Baldeweg, Irene Perez Porro, Alessandra Ponte, Txatxo Sabater, Ricardo Scofidio, Ignasi de Solá-Morales, Georges Teyssot, and Tony Vidler. I owe a special debt to Roger Conover at the MIT Press, who has been supportive of this project throughout, to Matthew Abbate for his nuanced editing, and to Jeannet Leendertse for the design.

The book is dedicated to Mark Wigley and to my daughter Andrea, who were not there yet when all of this started but without whom it would never have happened.

Archive

25 Beatrixgasse, Vienna. Loos orders all the documents in his office to be destroyed as he leaves Vienna and settles in Paris in 1922. His collaborators Heinrich Kulka and Grethe Klimt-Hentschel gather the few fragments that remain and that will become the basis for the first book on Loos, *Adolf Loos: Das Werk des Architekten,* edited by Kulka and Franz Glück in 1931.[1] Over the years, more documents are found (but almost never complete). This collection of fragments will become the only evidence for generations of scholarship. As Burkhardt Rukschcio put it in 1980: "Today, on the 110th anniversary of Loos' birth, it can truly be said that we are unlikely ever to know more about his work. A sizeable part of his designs and projects has completely disappeared and we know of only some of the hundreds of interiors he did for homes."[2] All investigations of Loos have been marked by his removal of the traces. All of the writing is in, on, and around the gaps. It is even about those gaps, often being obsessed with them.

8–10 square du docteur Blanche, Paris. Le Corbusier decides very early on that every trace of his work, and of himself, should be kept. He saves everything: correspondence, telephone bills, electricity bills, laundry bills, bank statements, postcards, legal documents, court proceedings (he was often involved in lawsuits), family pictures, travel snapshots, suitcases, trunks, filing cabinets, pottery, rugs, shells, pipes, books, magazines, clippings from newspapers, mail order catalogues, samples, mechanical boards, every stage of every manuscript, drafts for lectures, doodles, scribbles, notebooks, sketchbooks, diaries . . . and, of course, his paintings, sculptures, drawings, and all the documentation of his projects. This collection, now housed in the La Roche-Jeanneret house as the Fondation Le Corbusier, has been the basis of a massive research into Le Corbusier culminating, perhaps, in the centennial celebrations of his birth in 1987. The immensity of the materials available has also generated a series of megapublications intended to make the contents of the archive public, including the *Le Corbusier Archive*, 32 volumes containing 32,000 drawings of architecture, urbanism, and furniture, which, as its editor, H. Allen Brooks, describes it, is "the largest architectural publication ever undertaken"; the four volumes of the *Le Corbusier Carnets*, which consist of the 73 notebooks filled with sketches realized between 1914 and 1964 and the transcription of the texts that accompany them; and *Le Corbusier, Viaggio in Oriente*, which chronicles the trip undertaken by Le Corbusier in 1910–1911 and which includes his report "Voyage d'Orient" and all the drawings, photographs, and correspondence of that period.[3] Even the Centre Georges Pompidou's choice of an encyclopedia as the form with which to commemorate the centennial of Le Corbusier's birth is, in this regard, symptomatic.[4] What other architect's work (or artist's) might have lent itself to such a treatment? This kind of exhaustive coverage was anticipated by Le Corbusier when, at the age of 42, he came out with the first volume of his *Oeuvre complète* (covering the years 1910–1929), to which seven further volumes were added over the years, with the last (1965–1969) covering the years after his death in 1965.[5]

Le Corbusier is probably the most written about architect of this century. The writing on Loos, on the other hand, began very slowly. While the first book on him was published in 1931, on the occasion of his sixtieth birthday,[6] the second, *Der Architekt Adolf Loos* by Ludwig Münz and Gustav Künstler (which includes all the documents recovered since 1931 but is otherwise based on the earlier one), did not appear until 1964.[7] Soon translated into English, it became the most influential source on Loos. In 1968, the Graphische Sammlung Albertina bought the documents from the estate of Münz and started the Adolf Loos Archive. And it was not until 1982 that Burkhardt Rukschcio and Roland Schachel came out with the monumental monograph *Adolf Loos, Leben und Werk*,[8] which includes a complete catalogue of the work of Loos based on the Archive in the Albertina and on documents in three private collections. The authors of this book describe their enterprise as having been "truly the work of a detective": the endless search for documents (which, they insist, is by no means finished, and how could it ever be?), a sweeping "raid" on the press of Loos's time, conversations with Loos's friends, clients, and colleagues. These last, they warn us, can not be trusted entirely: "Even in his closer collaborators and his most intimate friends, reality is often deformed by interpretations." Consequently, these "subjective" and "anecdotal" contributions have been included only "after verification."[9] In a sense their book with all its gaps *is* the Adolf Loos archive (even in the police sense of "archive").

If the research into Loos is organized by the gaps in the archive, the research into Le Corbusier is organized by archival excesses. Loos vacates a space and destroys all traces behind him. Le Corbusier fills a space ahead of him, but not just any space: a domestic space, literally a house. To think about Loos one has to occupy a public space, the space of publications, his own and others', but also the space of word of mouth, hearsay, gossip, tips; the enigmatic space of circumstantial evidence. To think about Le Corbusier is necessarily to enter a private space. But what does private mean here? What exactly is this space? And how does one enter it?

Square du docteur Blanche, a small cul-de-sac in Paris-Auteuil, an invaginated space, a street folded upon itself, a space halfway between a street and an interior, a private road. At the end of this dead-end street, number 8–10, Maison La Roche-Jeanneret, a double house, *deux maisons accouplées*, that Le Corbusier designed for Lotti Raaf and his brother Albert Jeanneret[10] and for his patron the art collector Raoul La Roche in 1922, the same year that Loos arrived in Paris. Is 8–10 square du docteur Blanche private or public? A house or an exhibit, an archive or a library, an art gallery or a museum? The dilemma was already present in the original program, since La Roche had an art collection to display in the house; indeed the building was commissioned to "house" the paintings, and visitors used to sign in in a book by the door. Soon the issue of whether visitors were signing in for the paintings or for the house became blurred, at least for Le Corbusier, who would later recommend to Madame Savoye to leave a "golden book" by the entrance to her house too (even if she did not have an art collection displayed there): "You will see how many fine autographs you will collect. This is what La Roche does in Auteuil, and his Golden Book has become a veritable international directory."[11]

But where is this entrance?

No traditional entry presents itself. The house is L-shaped. The "pavillon La Roche," behind a mesh security fence, closes the cul-de-sac, but since it is on pilotis the space of the street flows under the house. To the right, two small identical doors almost flush with the facade have a way of saying that we have nothing to look for in them. The protruding belly of La Roche's gallery pushes the visitor away, back into the space of the street, while at the same time its curve points to the corner, to the hinge of the house where the fence has a small built-in door. Pass through it. Now you see the driveway sweeping toward you. Perhaps the entrance was not clear because we were expected, as in the other houses of Le Corbusier, to arrive by car (in a way, leaving an "interior," the car, for another, the modern house, in its turn inspired by the car). On the right the wall recedes, creating an entrance space. In the middle, hidden from the street view, you finally see the door.

In the *Oeuvre complète*, Le Corbusier goes out of his way to describe the entry into this house. It turns out to be all a matter of vision:

> **You enter: the architectural *spectacle* at once offers itself to the *eye;* you follow an itinerary and the *views* develop with great variety; you play with the flood of *light* illuminating the walls or creating *half-lights.* Large *windows* open up *views* on the exterior where you find again the architectural unity. In the interior the first attempts at polychromy . . . allow the *"camouflage architectural,"* that is, the affirmation of certain volumes or, the contrary, their effacement. Here, reborn for our *modern eyes,* are historic architectural events: pilotis, the horizontal window, the roof garden, the glass facade.**[12]

To *enter* is to *see*. But not to see a static object, a building, a fixed place. Rather, architecture taking place in history, the events of architecture, architecture as an event. It is not so much that you enter architecture as that you see architecture's entrance. The elements of modern architecture (pilotis, horizontal window, the roof garden, the glass facade) are seen being "born" in front of your eyes. And in so doing they make these eyes "modern."

Modern eyes move. Vision in Le Corbusier's architecture is always tied to movement: "You follow an itinerary," a *promenade architecturale*. About this Le Corbusier will become more explicit in his Villa Savoye at Poissy (1929–1931):

Arab architecture gives us a precious lesson. It is appreciated by walking, on foot; it is by walking, by moving, that one sees the order of the architecture developing. It is a principle contrary to that of baroque architecture, which is conceived on paper, around a fixed theoretical point. I prefer the lesson of Arab architecture. In this house it's a question of a real architectural promenade, offering constantly changing views, unexpected, sometimes astonishing.[13]

The point of view of modern architecture is never fixed, as in baroque architecture,[14] or as in the model of vision of the camera obscura, but always in motion, as in film or in the city. Crowds, shoppers in a department store, railroad travelers, and the inhabitants of Le Corbusier's houses have in common with movie viewers that they cannot fix (arrest) the image. Like the movie viewer that Benjamin describes ("no sooner has his eye grasped a scene than it is already changed"),[15] they inhabit a space that is neither inside nor outside, public nor private (in the traditional understanding of these terms). It is a space that is not made of walls but of images. Images as walls. Or as Le Corbusier puts it, "walls of light."[16] That is, the walls that define the space are no longer solid walls punctuated by small windows but have been dematerialized, thinned down with new building technologies and replaced by extended windows, lines of glass whose views now define the space.[17] The walls that are not transparent now float in the space of the house rather than produce it. "Interrogated by Rasmussen about the entrance hall of the La Roche house, Le Corbusier answers that the most important element of the hall is the big window and that for that reason he had prolonged the upper edge of the window to match the parapet of the library."[18] The window is no longer a hole in a wall, it has taken over the wall. And if, as Rasmussen points out, "the walls give the impression of being made out of paper," the big window is a paper wall with a picture on it, a picture wall, a (movie) screen.

Le Corbusier's basic definition of the primordial idea of the house—"The house is a shelter, an enclosed space, which affords protection against cold, heat *and outside observation*"—would have been commonplace if it had not included the question of the view. Seeing, for Le Corbusier, is the primordial activity in the house. The house is a device to see the world, a mechanism of viewing. Shelter, separation from the outside, is provided by the window's ability to turn the threatening world outside the house into a reassuring picture. The inhabitant is enveloped, wrapped, protected by the pictures. But how constrained these early windows were! laments Le Corbusier: the window is the "most restricted *organ* of the house." (Significantly, he says "organ" rather than element, because the window is thought of first and foremost as an eye.) Today the facade, no longer "constricted" by the old building technologies that made the wall responsible for bearing the load of the building,

> **fulfills its true destiny; it is the provider of light. . . . From this emerges the true definition of the house: stages of floors . . . all around them *walls of light.***
>
> ***Walls of light!* Henceforth the idea of the window will be modified. Till now the function of the window was to provide light and air and to be looked through. Of these classified functions I should retain one only, that of being looked through. . . . *To see out of doors, to lean out.***[19]

The modern transformation of the house produces a space defined by walls of (moving) images. This is the space of the media, of publicity. To be "inside" this space is only to see. To be "outside" is to be *in* the image, to be seen, whether in the press photograph, a magazine, a movie, on television, or at your window. It no longer has so much to do with a public space, in the traditional sense of a public forum, a square, or the crowd that gathers around a speaker in such a place, but with the audience that each medium of publication reaches, independent of the place this audience might actually be occupying. But, of course, the fact that (for the most part) this audience is indeed at home is not without consequence. The private is, in this sense, now more public than the public.

Privacy is now what exceeds the eyes. That doesn't include what we used to think of as the private. As Roland Barthes put it: "The age of photography corresponds precisely to the irruption of the private into the public, or rather, to the creation of a new social value, which is the publicity of the private: the private is consumed as such, publicly (the incessant aggressions of the press against the privacy of stars and the growing difficulties of legislation to govern them testify to this movement)."[20] The private has become consumable merchandise. Maybe that explains why Baudelaire writes: "Your eyes lit up like shop windows." Even to look into the eyes, traditionally the only way to see into the private space of the mind, is now but to look at a public display. The eyes are no longer a "mirror of the soul" but its carefully constructed advertisement. As Nietzsche saw it: "No one dares to appear as he is, but masks himself as a cultivated man, as a scholar, as a poet, as a politician. . . . Individuality has withdrawn within: from without it has become invisible."[21]

If modern eyes are lit up like shop windows, so too are the windows of modern architecture. The picture window works two ways: it turns the outside world into an image to be consumed by those inside the house, but it also displays the image of the interior to that outside world. This shouldn't be confused with exposing one's privacy. On the contrary, we have all become "experts" on our own representation. In the same way that we meticulously construct our family history with snapshots, equally skillfully we represent our domesticity through the picture window.

The traditional sense of privacy is now not only scarce but endangered, under attack. It is better protected legally than with walls. This situation may be traced back to the debates over the ownership of the image that developed with photography. The right to privacy has become the right to remain "out of the picture," which means not only out of the press photograph, of the gossip column, but also of the credit report and, most urgently, out of the disclosed medical record. That is, out of public view (or "access").[22]

Modernity, then, coincides with the publicity of the private. But what kind of space results from this redrawing of boundaries? The space of the archive is very much affected by this transformation. In fact, this new reality is first and foremost a question of the archive. The archive has played an important role in the history of privacy, even in the history of history. The archive is private, history is public (the fact that today archives function mainly as clearinghouses for copyrights of the documents they hold only confirms this distinction). "Out" of the archive history is produced, but when writing history the utmost care is traditionally placed on producing a seamless account of the archive,[23] even though all archives are fractured and partial. The messy space of the archive is thus sealed off by a history. History then is a facade. Already in 1874, Nietzsche writes in "The Uses and Abuses of History":

> **The most characteristic quality of modern man [lies in] the remarkable antithesis between an interior which fails to correspond to any exterior and an exterior which fails to correspond to any interior—an antithesis unknown to the people of earlier times. . . .**
>
> **We moderns [have become] walking encyclopedias. . . . With encyclopedias, however, all the value lies in what is contained within, in the content, not in what stands without, the binding and cover; so it is that the whole of modern culture is essentially interior; on the outside the bookbinder has printed some such thing as "Handbook of Interior Culture for Exterior Barbarians."**[24]

Significantly, the antithesis between interior and exterior is expressed by Nietzsche in terms of the home, what he calls "the disorderly, stormy and conflict-ridden *household*" that results from "memory" either trying to accommodate "these strange guests" which are our excessive historical knowledge, "a huge quantity of indigestible stones of knowledge,"[25] or alternatively memory "tidily storing away in its coffers" the "things worth knowing." History is a public representation of this household.

"Forgetting is essential to action of any kind," Nietzsche immediately goes on to argue. Loos seem to have understood as much when he destroyed all the documents in his studio. In a lecture given in 1926, he says:

> **Human works can be summed up in two actions: destruction and construction. And the bigger the destruction, the more human work is nothing other than destruction, the more it is truly human, natural, and noble. The concept of *gentleman* cannot be explained otherwise. The *gentleman* is a man who only carries out work with the help of destruction. The gentleman comes from the peasant class. The peasant only produces destructive work. . . . Who has never desired to destroy something?**[26]

Destruction is construction. Loos's destruction of his traces has generated a massive work of reconstruction, an endless campaign for their recovery. A campaign into which, at first, only his closest friends and collaborators were drawn, but that would soon pass into the hands of another generation of compatriots equally devoted to the enterprise.[27] In this sense, Kulka's book was the first stone in the building of Loos's archive. If with Loos we go from the book into the archive, Le Corbusier follows the opposite strategy. He stores away everything. His obsession with filing cabinets is well known and well documented (in fact, even his filing cabinets have themselves been filed away in the Fondation Le Corbusier). But is not this filing away another way of "forgetting"?

What in the end makes Le Corbusier's archive private is its capacity to hide things. Sometimes the best way to hide something is in full sight. Commenting on the choice of an encyclopedia as the form with which to celebrate Le Corbusier's centennial, Jacques Lucan, the director of the work, writes:

> **The books, the articles, the studies devoted to Le Corbusier are almost innumerable. . . . This abundance finds a justification in the fact that perhaps no other artist has left to posterity, in a foundation created with that purpose, such an enormous number of documents concerning all his activity [public and private]. One would have thought that with the mass of documents available the task of historians and biographers would have been facilitated . . . that it would be possible to retrace his life . . . , the itineraries of his architectural and urban reflections. . . . Paradoxically, perhaps neither is possible.**[28]

The immensity of the traces makes the research a never-ending process, with new traces, or rather new ways of looking at these traces or even seeing them as traces for the first time, always producing new interpretations that displace the old. The encyclopedia, Lucan goes on to argue, does not enclose Le Corbusier precisely because each entry can send the reader through other entries "as in a chain without end," in a way as if offering a "*promenade* through the articles."[29]

The space of Le Corbusier's houses and the space of the histories of Le Corbusier would then have something in common. They are less about enclosure than about the entanglement of inside and outside, less about a traditional interior than about following an itinerary (no matter how many times redrawn, no matter how nonlinear), the enclosure resulting from the collage of fleeting images assembled as the reader moves through too much material, too many images, too many stimuli. And isn't this precisely the experience of the modern city? The archive allows the scholar to wander through the material as the flaneur wanders through the arcades of Paris, which are neither interior nor exterior.

Such a promenade necessarily involves a transformation of our sense of architecture. The way we think about architecture is organized by the way we think about the relationships between inside and outside, private and public. With modernity there is a shift in these relationships, a displacement of the traditional sense of an inside, an enclosed space, established in clear opposition to an outside. All boundaries are now shifting. This shifting becomes manifest everywhere: in the city, of course, but also in all the technologies that define the space of the city: the railroad, newspapers, photography, electricity, advertisements, reinforced concrete, glass, the telephone, film, radio, . . . war. Each can be understood as a mechanism that disrupts the older boundaries between inside and outside, public and private, night and day, depth and surface, here and there, street and interior, and so on.

What is "strange" about the "big city" to which, as Benjamin argues, people now have to "adapt" is the speed, the continuous movement, the sense that nothing ever stops, that there are no limits. Trains, traffic, films, and newspapers use the verb *run* to describe their very different activities. As in to "run" an ad in a newspaper. Even meeting somebody has become running into somebody. With this restless movement that effaces boundaries comes a new mode of perception that has become the trademark of modernity. Perception is now tied to transience.[30] If photography is the culmination of centuries of efforts to arrest the image, "to fix fleeting reflections," to use Benjamin's words, is it not somewhat paradoxical that once the fleeting image is fixed, the mode of perception is what becomes fleeting? Now the observer (the flaneur, the train traveler, the department store shopper) is what is transient. This transience, and the new space of the city in which it is experienced, cannot be separated from the new forms of representation.

For Benjamin, film is the form where these new conditions of perception, which "are experienced on an individual scale by the man in the street in big city traffic," find their "true form of exercise." The city will turn out to be a good stage for the movies. *The Man with the Movie Camera* by Dziga Vertov (1929), for example. This movie is often understood by film theorists to be about the way in which meaning is fabricated in film. In conventional film, the point of view is represented as "neutral," not visible, turning what you see into "reality." But with Vertov's movie there is seen to be a reversal of view and point of view. The subject's point of view comes after the view, making the viewer aware that what s/he sees is but a construction. But what all of this does not yet explain is why Vertov had to demonstrate this transformation with the city.

Realism in film is sometimes defined as a "window on the world." This is an architectural model, a traditional model of an interior with an unmediated view. But the space of the big city had already displaced the model of the room with a view, the model of the camera obscura. It is not by chance that Vertov will choose the city. His film makes clear that it is not just that the new space of the city is defined by the new technologies of representation; those technologies are also transformed by the city.

To think about modern architecture must be to pass back and forth between the question of space and the question of representation. Indeed, it will be necessary to think of architecture as a system of representation, or rather a series of overlapping systems of representation. This does not mean abandoning the traditional architectural object, the building. In the end, it means looking at it much more closely than before, but also in a different way. The building should be understood in the same terms as drawings, photographs, writing, films, and advertisements; not only because these are the media in which more often we encounter it, but because the building is a mechanism of representation in its own right. The building is, after all, a "construction," in all senses of the word. And when we speak about representation we speak about a subject and an object. Traditionally, architecture is considered as an object, a bounded, unified entity established in opposition to a subject that is presumed to have an existence independent of it. Within modernity the object defines a multiplicity of boundaries between inside and outside. Inasmuch as these boundaries undermine each other, the object calls into question its own objecthood and therefore the unity of the classical subject presumed to be outside of it. It is in these terms that this book questions the ideological assumptions underlying our view of modern architecture.

The conventional view portrays modern architecture as a high artistic practice established in opposition to mass culture and to everyday life. It has focused on the internal life of the supposedly autonomous, self-referential object made available to a detached viewing subject, an art object. In so doing, it has neglected the overwhelming historical evidence of modern architecture's continuous involvement with mass culture. It is actually the emerging systems of communication that came to define twentieth-century culture—the mass media—that are the true site within which modern architecture is produced and with which it directly engages. In fact, one could argue (this is the main argument of this book) that modern architecture only becomes modern with its engagement with the media. Banham noted that the modern movement was the first movement in the history of art based exclusively on "photographic evidence" rather than on personal experience, drawings, or conventional books.[31] While he was referring to the fact that the industrial buildings that became icons for the modern movement were not known to the architects from "direct" experience (only from photographs), the work of these architects themselves has become known almost always through photography and the printed media. This presupposes a transformation of the site of architectural production—no longer exclusively located on the construction site, but more and more displaced into the rather immaterial sites of architectural publications, exhibitions, journals. Paradoxically, those are supposedly much more ephemeral media than the building and yet in many ways are much more permanent: they secure a place for an architecture in history, a historical space designed not just by the historians and critics but also by the architects themselves who deployed these media.

This book attempts to trace some of the strategic relationships between modern architecture and the media by looking at the work of the two canonic figures that articulate our view of the modern movement, one marking the threshold of this historical space but not crossing it, the other occupying and dominating the space. To rethink their work will necessarily be to rethink the architecture of that space. Perhaps no other modern architects have aroused so much speculation. If Loos destroys all traces and Le Corbusier accumulates too many, both hide. In so doing they have succeeded in generating an extraordinary amount of critical work. This book is not so much concerned with replacing the old space of modern architecture produced by this mountain of work. Rather it is a preliminary attempt to think about that old space and its limits, and to follow certain openings, tracing some leads but not to any single conclusion. Throughout its various trajectories, the book is not so much concerned with the relationship between architecture and the media as with the possibility of thinking of architecture as media.

City

During long periods of history, the mode of human sense perception changes with humanity's entire mode of existence. The manner in which human sense perception is organized, the medium in which it is accomplished, is determined not only by nature but by historical circumstances as well.

Walter Benjamin, "The Work of Art in the Age of Mechanical Reproduction"

Wall Street, 1864.

Wall Street, 1915. Photograph by Paul Strand.

I

The excessive weight attached to the question of where one is, goes back to nomadic tribes, when people had to be observant about feeding-grounds.

Robert Musil, *The Man without Qualities*

Things, like ourselves, were losing their qualities with astonishing ease. Vienna, for instance, might well have been a city, but this alone did not make it a place. One cannot say that the condition was intolerable, only that the epoch of closed questions, of fixed places, of the objects in themselves had ended, and the period of relationships had begun. A wholly different way of protesting against the natural. A thing made sense only in relation to something else. And this something else did not even have to be real. "If there is such a thing as a sense of reality," says Musil's central character Ulrich, "then there must also be something that one can call a sense of possibility," which "might be defined outright as the capacity to think how everything could 'just as easily' be, and not to attach more importance to what is than to what is not."[1]

All this had occurred before Musil wrote his *Man without Qualities*, although it corresponds to the time in which he brings Ulrich to life. It was not important *where* one was; ever since the railway conveyed us impassively through the "emporium of the world,"[2] place as such no longer permitted any differentiation. Just as in department stores, where things are not differentiated by the place they occupy. Everything occupies one place.[3] In traditional terms, the department store is not even a place. In such a placeless world, even talking about travel had ceased to make sense, since despite the frenetic movement it was as if one did not move. Or to put it another way, one could say, with Huysmans, that it was only possible to travel if one did not move.[4] It did not even matter where one was, which city. For Ulrich, to ask of "something so infinitely complicated such as the city in which one happens to be . . . exactly what particular city it is [is to] distract attention from more important things."[5] While Musil's Diotima states that "the real Austria is the whole world." Everywhere contained everything outside it. Everywhere was without place, without where.

If Vienna was no longer a place and if the question of place was, anyway, already indifferent, what could one do in order to differentiate oneself? What could one separate oneself from in order to gain an identity? Not from nature, which was now a confusing mesh of cables and rails that entangled everything. Surviving let alone inhabiting the city became a question of defining limits, limits much more complicated than the clear lines that established the traditional city.

"After all," says Musil's character, "each thing exists only by virtue of its limits, in other words, by virtue of a more or less hostile act against its environment." City life is a battle for limits rather than a life within limits. A concern with such provisional limits pervaded metropolitan discourse. For Ludwig Wittgenstein, the setting of limits "will signify what cannot be said by presenting clearly what can be said."[6] And Georg Simmel, in his "Metaphysics of Death," quotes Nietzsche's claim that "the secret of form is that it is a boundary; it is the thing itself and, at the same time, the cessation of the thing, the circumscribed territory in which the Being and the non-Being of the thing are only one thing."[7]

The setting of limits is what allows both survival and knowledge within the urban scene. All of so-called fin-de-siècle Vienna revolved about a search for form, the almost desperate quest for limits in order to establish identity. But this identity was neither fixed nor unitary. Identity itself became fragmented, multiplied. In *The Notebooks of Malte Laurids Brigge*, R. M. Rilke writes: "I dream, for example, I have not yet gained consciousness of how many different faces there are. There are quantities of people, but there are even more faces, for each person has several."[8] Each face is a mask.

Vienna, Operngasse and Friedrichstrasse with the Café Museum.

II

Modernity is bound up with the question of the mask. The mask was a very common theme in Vienna. This does not mean that it was always of the same order. If, according to Ulrich, "a civilian has at least nine characters: a professional one, a national one, a civic one, a class one, a geographical one, a sex one, a conscious, an unconscious, and perhaps even a private one," then this individual must also have as many masks. Freud spoke of the mask of "civilized" sexual morality, opposing to it the analysis of the depths of the psyche; an opposition that was to become of great interest to the twentieth-century man, preoccupied with his mental "health." In "'Civilized' Sexual Morality and Modern Nervous Illness" (incidentally, a text where Freud refers to Karl Kraus), the prevailing morality is presented as the cause of madness, particularly in woman.[9] The mask becomes responsible for, rather than simply veiling, "interior" disorders. The mask produces what it hides.

Karl Kraus, in *Die Fackel*, objected to the mask of journalism, which, unlike the storytelling of former times, he accused of concealing rather than revealing what has happened. In his essay "In These Great Times," Kraus recognized that only facts were now able to speak, and that news was, in itself, apart from the event it purports to represent, a fact: "If one reads a newspaper only for information, one does not learn the truth, not even the truth about the paper. The truth is that the newspaper is not a statement of contents but the contents themselves and more than that, it is an instigator."[10] The mask then was a fact, able to speak of itself. Only that which was behind it, "that which is only thought," as Kraus put it, "is unutterable."[11] But the split between thought and speech is not just understood as a property of journalism. For Hugo von Hofmannsthal, for example, it is the condition of language itself. In "The Letter of Lord Chandos," the word is already incapable of revealing anything, it is a mask: "The language in which I might be able not only to write but to think is neither Latin nor English, neither Italian nor

Sigmund Freud's study in Berggasse 19, Vienna, 1938.

Karl Kraus's study in Lothringerstrasse 6, Vienna, 1912.

Spanish, but a language none of whose words is known to me, a language in which inanimate things speak to me and wherein I may one day have to justify myself before an unknown judge."[12]

Architecture participates fully in this pervasive logic of the mask. Adolf Loos recognized Vienna as a city of masks when he compared, in the pages of *Ver Sacrum,* the buildings of the Ringstrasse to the villages erected by Potemkin: "Who does not know of Potemkin's villages, the ones that Catherine's cunning favorite built in the Ukraine? They were villages of canvas and pasteboard, villages intended to transform a visual desert into a flowering landscape for the eyes of Her Imperial Majesty. But was it a whole city which that cunning minister was supposed to have produced? Surely such things are only possible in Russia!"[13] But Loos neglected to tell us that Catherine perhaps thought she saw cities where there was only canvas and cardboard because she was only passing by. Likewise, Vienna started to wear a mask at the time that the railway became a fact of life. In a city where the reality was not the place itself but its displacement, in a place that was not a place because everything was fluid, to stop was to mask oneself, to cease to be real, to cease to have meaning. It was like "posing for a photograph," as Camillo Sitte would say of those who dared to sit in a "modern" square, or like being an "object in an exhibition."[14] Musil put the same thought the other way around when he wrote that "cities could be recognized by their pace, just as people can by their gait."[15] This is how the carrier of a mask can be recognized; while immobile he is indecipherable, becomes part of the space. His mask becomes juxtaposed with those of the buildings. Only the masks (of the immobile people and buildings) *speak,* but this speaking is not about what is behind them. Only when the mask moves is something given away; and, even then, it is somewhat cryptic. This cryptic movement or rhythm is the only trace of identity left.

The real difference in a city of canvas and cardboard is not between the different facades representing their supposedly different interiors. On the contrary, contiguities, relations, and so forth all contribute to presenting the city of masks as a unitary whole, a screen without fissures. The difference is *in* this very screen, with its two faces. The one facing "outside," ostensibly the mask, is different from the one facing "inside." The relation between what the mask says on one side and the structure that supports it on the other is "arbitrary." But in the middle is the screen itself, the mechanism of difference. It is at precisely this time that philosophers are thinking of language as a system of differences, in which the sign is divided into signifier and signified, even using the metaphor of a screen to make their point.[16] In a sense, all the Viennese writers of modernity are "philosophers" of language.

But how can architecture set limits in a city such as this, where the limit cannot have anything to do with the enclosing and bounding of a place? There is no place in "the capital of decoration," to use Hermann Broch's description of Vienna. At first, it would seem that the limit can only reside in the wall that is its mask. But then, the new sense of limit questions the status of the wall. The problem is no longer whether one is here or there, but whether one is on one side of the wall or on the other. And, to be sure, we have not yet said that one side is "inside" and the other "outside." In fact, this distinction, which would seem so irreducible, would soon become the explicit target of a sustained critique by an international architectural avant-garde responding to the same sense of metropolitan life.[17] The wall is at once displaced and given an unprecedented importance. Architecture resides within the wall itself but this residing, this residence, can never take the form of a traditional inhabitation. The wall is a limit, but not simply the limit of a place.

So what is this wall, what limit does it establish? It was no longer possible to think of Vienna in terms of place, of public or private spaces, for the same reason that one could no longer think of the press as the messenger of public opinion. "Opinions are a private matter," Benjamin wrote, speaking about Kraus.[18] Then, too, the press had its other matter: not opinions but facts, news as facts. The same could be said about architecture. On the public side of the wall another language was spoken, the masking language of information. On the other side lay the unspeakable. But this unspeakable domain beyond the public is also beyond the private.

The Viennese attention to the mask ends up focusing on an *inner* space even further removed, the space of "intimacy." This space, unlike traditional private space, cannot simply be located, even by way of opposition to public space. "The intimacy of the heart," writes Hannah Arendt, "unlike the private household, has no objective tangible place in the world, nor can the society against which it protests and asserts itself be localized with the same certainty as the public space."[19] When the city is no longer a place, and all systems of representation that define the city become masks, there is a new concern for the intimate. Indeed, one might say that it is the mask that allows this space its content, that makes it "intimate." Or rather, that it is this obsessive concern with the surface that constructs the intimate. The intimate is not a space but a relationship between spaces.

Take, for example, Saussure. The radical division he establishes between the spoken and the written word rests on a spatial opposition between inside and outside, where writing is the image, the representation, the outside, the clothing, the facade, the mask of speech:[20] "Writing *veils* the appearance of language, it is not a guise for language, but a *disguise*."[21] But, in the end, the written and spoken word turn out to be intermingled. In a passage mysteriously omitted from the English translation, Saussure writes: "The written word is so *intimately* mixed with the spoken word of which it is its image that it ultimately takes over the principal role; we end up giving as much or more importance to the representation of the vocal sign as to this sign itself. *It's as if we believed that, to know someone, it would be better to look at his photograph than at his face*."[22] Strange example of a disguise! A photograph? In what way is a photograph a disguise? How does a person hide behind a

Karl Kraus after his Abitur
(university qualifying examination).

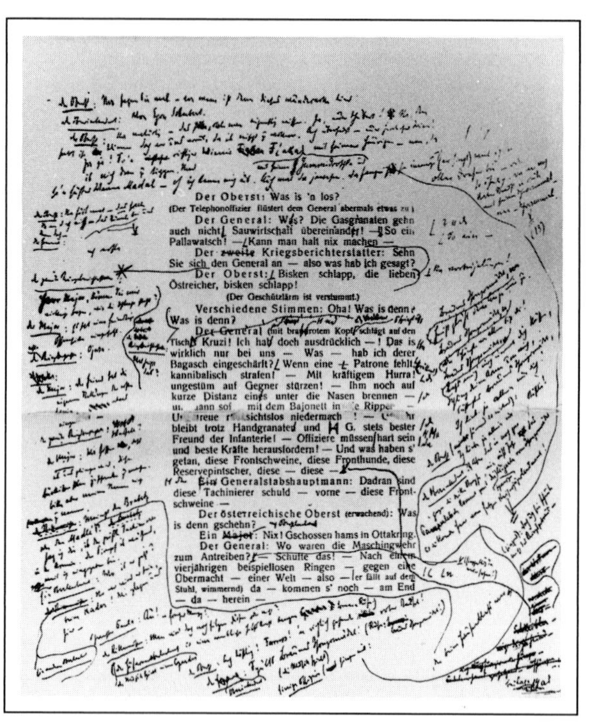

Der Oberst: Was is 'n los?

(Der Telephonoffizier flüstert dem General abermals etwas zu.)

Der General: Was? Die Gasgranaten gehn auch nicht! Sauwirtschaft übereinander! — So ein Pallawatsch! — Kann man halt nix machen —

Der ~~zweite~~ Kriegsberichterstatter: Sehn Sie sich den General an — also was hab ich gesagt?

Der Oberst: Bisken schlapp, die lieben Östreicher, bisken schlapp!

(Der Geschützlärm ist verstummt.)

Verschiedene Stimmen: Oha! Was is denn? Was is denn?

~~Der General~~ (mit braunrotem Kopf, schlägt auf den Tisch) Kruzi! Ich hab doch ausdrücklich —! Das is wirklich nur bei uns — Was — hab ich derer Bagasch eingeschärft? Wenn eine Patrone fehlt, kannibalisch strafen! — Mit kräftigem Hurra! ungestüm auf Gegner stürzen! — Ihm noch auf kurze Distanz eins unter die Nasen brennen — u. [illegible]ann sof[illegible] mit dem Bajonett in [illegible]e Ripper[illegible] — U[illegible]treue r[illegible]sichtslos niedermach[illegible]! — [illegible]hr bleibt trotz Handgranaten und H G. stets bester Freund der Infanterie! — Offiziere müssen hart sein und beste Kräfte herausfordern! — Und was haben s' getan, diese Frontschweine, diese Fronthunde, diese Reservepintscher, diese — diese —

~~Ein~~ Generalstabshauptmann: Dadran sind diese Tachinierer schuld — vorne — diese Frontschweine —

Der österreichische Oberst (erwachend): Was is denn gschehn?

Ein ~~Major~~: Nix! Gschossen hams in Ottakring.

Der General: Wo waren die Maschingwehr zum Antreiben? — Schuften das! — Nach einem vierjährigen beispiellosen Ringen — gegen eine Übermacht — einer Welt — also — (er fällt auf den Stuhl, wimmernd) da — kommen s' noch — am End — da — herein —

Corrections in a page of Kraus's **Die letzten Tage der Menschheit.**

photograph of his face? But Saussure's example is not coincidental. The problematic status of photography can never be detached from the thinking about space, language, and culture of the time. It is perhaps for that reason that Loos insists, in a passage also mysteriously omitted from the English translation of his famous text "Architektur," that the interior is that which cannot be photographed: "The inhabitants of my interiors do not recognize their own house in photographs."[23] The interior is disguised by the photograph in the same way that, for Saussure, the photograph that is writing veils speech.[24]

What is "intimate" in the deleted passage from Saussure is not the "inside" that the written word inadequately represents on the outside, that is to say the thought faithfully presented by the spoken word, but the intermingling itself between spoken and written word. Saussure here identifies writing not only with an outside, the exterior image of thought or its sound, but, precisely, with a photographic image. It is curious to note how close Saussure's and Loos's argument comes to Sitte's. Sitte is advocating a form of town planning that derives its principles from the observation of the "use" of traditional (preindustrial) public space, as against the "regularizing," "geometrical" tendencies of the urban planner (in clear parallel to Saussure's appreciation of the oral tradition of language and its "independence" from writing). It is in this context that Sitte attacks "modern" public space for being only suitable as the stage for a photograph: "Who will try to relax there, seated perhaps on a lonely bench?—in the middle of a square surrounded by heavy traffic, sitting there in isolation *as if to be photographed or as if on exhibit*."[25]

Modern urban space, as opposed to traditional "place," cannot be understood in experiential terms. The "exterior" is not only image but a picture, a photographic image. If, for Saussure, writing is the photograph of speech, and for Loos the interior is that which cannot be photographed, for Sitte "modern" urban space is the photograph of "place." The "outside" is a photographic image. The mask is first and foremost a picture.

III

Depth must be hidden. Where? On the surface.

Hugo von Hofmannsthal, *Buch der Freunde*

Of a terrain I see only the swamps, of their depth I see only the surface, of a situation I see only its manifestations, of these I see only a reflection, and even of that I see only the outlines.

Karl Kraus, "In These Great Times"

When Loos writes, "The house does not have to tell anything to the exterior; instead, all its richness must be manifest in the interior,"[26] he seems to be echoing Nietzsche's claim that modern man is modern by virtue of an unprecedented split between his interior and exterior—the "remarkable antithesis between an interior which fails to correspond to any exterior and an exterior which fails to correspond to any interior."[27] Loos may not have known this text of Nietzsche, but the problematic is similar to his own in more than one way. When Nietzsche goes on to say that we moderns have become "walking encyclopedias" whose cover reveals nothing of the inside except for the label "interior," he, like Loos, is using a linguistic example for a spatial condition. The outside is only the "cover" of the book, it is clothing, it is mask. The "value" is "contained within." But, once more, this inside cannot exist without the outside. The cover of an encyclopedia, no matter how anonymous or unmarked, constructs it as an interior. But what is the interior of an encyclopedia but a continuous outside-inside-outside? Not only is every word an "entry" defining an inside, a space, but then each word refers to other words and other concepts, entangling the space like a labyrinth or a weave. This is not a traditional "interior." If, as Nietzsche says, "modern culture is essentially internal" in this sense, and the old order of the city has been somehow displaced indoors, this "interior" is a much more convoluted space than that established by simple opposition to the exterior. Is it this radical complication of the interior that Loos is talking about? And if so, what would it be to inhabit this space?

When Loos writes that "the house does not have to tell anything to the exterior," he recognizes a limit to architecture in the metropolis, the difference between *dwelling* in the interior and *dealing* with the exterior, but at the same time he formulates the very need for this limit, which implies the need for a mask. The interior does not have to tell anything to the exterior. This mask is not, naturally, the same as the one he had identified as being fake in the facades of the Ringstrasse; the face of equivocal, fictitious language implying that behind the walls was where the nobility were living, whereas in reality those spaces were inhabited by "deracinated upstarts." To be uprooted, Loos believed, was nothing to be ashamed of; it was part of the modern condition. The silence that he prescribed is no more than the recognition of a schizophrenia in metropolitan life: the inside has nothing to tell to the outside because our intimate being has split from our social being. We are divided between what we think and what we say and do.

Loos realized that modern life was proceeding on two disparate levels, the one of our individual experience and the other of our existence as society. For that reason he renounced both the delusion of masks and the invention of *esperantos*. For Loos it was hopeless to try to render the outside in the experiential terms of the inside. They are two irreducible but interdependent systems. The interior speaks the language of culture, the language of the experience of things; the exterior speaks the language of civilization, that of information. The interior is the other of the exterior, in the same way as experience is the other of information, culture the other of civilization.[28] Thus, on the other hand, public buildings could calmly speak of what was going on behind their walls: "The courthouse must make a threatening impression on the furtive criminal. The bank building must say: 'Here your money is securely safeguarded by honest people.'"[29] There is no contradiction between doing and informing.

Adolf Loos, brass fittings from sideboard of Stoessl apartment, Vienna, 1900.

The house's silence vis-à-vis the outside represents the impossibility of communication; but it is also this very silence that protects its incommunicable intimacy. At this moment, silence is also its mask. It is a Simmelian mask, that mask of which Simmel writes in his essay "Fashion" that it allows the interior to be *intimate*. "Over an old Flemish house," writes Simmel in this text, "there stands the mystical inscription: There is more within me."[30]

It is precisely in Simmel's terms that Loos speaks about fashion: "The person who runs around in a velvet suit is no artist but a buffoon or merely a decorator. We have become more refined, more subtle. Primitive men had to differentiate themselves by the use of various colors, *modern man needs his clothes as a mask*. His individuality is so strong that he cannot express it any longer by his clothing. *The lack of ornament is a sign of intellectual power*. Modern man uses the ornament of past and foreign cultures at his discretion. He concentrates his own power of invention on other things."[31] Loos draws a line relating mask not only to individuality but also to creation: "The *Critique of Pure Reason* could not have been created by a man wearing five ostrich feathers on his hat, the Ninth Symphony did not spring from one wearing a ring around his neck the size of a dish."[32] But where is he who has assumed the condition of the modern (the displaced person, the dissident, the traveler, the exile, the foreigner, the melancholic, or the man without qualities) to find an identity? No longer protected by the fixed and the permanent, by the things that *speak*, modern man now finds himself surrounded by objects without meaning. In no way, Loos said, can he make use of these things, force them to speak an invented language or construct a false pedigree (precisely what he was accusing the artists of the Secession of attempting). The modern, like the artist and the primitive, could only restore an order in the universe and find a place in it by reaching within himself and his own creation.[33] But the modern, like the primitive, needs a mask to make this possible.

Adolf Loos, Rufer house, Vienna, 1922.

Modernity implies a return to the function of the mask. But as Hubert Damisch has noted, whereas in primitive societies the mask gave social identity to its bearer, modern man (and the very artist) uses the mask to conceal any difference, to protect his identity.[34] Loos generalizes for "modern man" what Kraus specifies for the artist: "No doubt, the artist is other. But precisely for that reason, in his external appearance he must comply with the others. He can only remain alone when he disappears into the crowd. If he calls attention to himself through some sort of particularity, he renders himself common and directs his pursuers to his trail. The more the artist is justified in being other, the more necessary it is for him to employ the costume of the average as a sort of mimicry."[35] For Loos, every member of the crowd is an "artist"; everyone is complying on the surface but masking his interiority, his sexuality, but also his creativity, his "power of invention." In the end everyone is a new "primitive," everyone has to wear a mask. But the modern function of the mask is for Loos the reversal of the primitive one. Whereas the primitive mask expressed an identity to the outside, in fact constructed that identity, a social identity, the modern mask is a form of protection, a canceling of differences on the outside precisely to make identity possible, an identity that is now individual.

And what of modern woman? The figure of modernity for Loos, as for most writers of modernity, is emphatically male.[36] Woman, and children, are "primitive," "ignoble savages," as distinct from the heroic figure of modern man as primitive "noble savage." This gendering of the subject cannot be separated from the question of the mask. Loos writes: "Ornament at the service of woman will last forever. . . . The ornament of women . . . answers, at bottom, that of the savage; it has an erotic meaning."[37] The ornament, which for "the child, the Papuan and the woman" is a "natural phenomenon," for modern man is a "symptom of degeneration":

The first ornament that came into being, the cross, had an erotic origin. The first work of art . . . was in order to rid himself of his natural excesses. A horizontal line: the reclining woman. A vertical line: the man who penetrates her. The man who created it felt the same urge as Beethoven. . . . But the man of our time who daubs the walls with erotic symbols to satisfy an inner urge is a criminal or a degenerate.[38]

And when this "degeneration" becomes clearly identified as homosexuality, Loos's raid against ornament is not only gender-loaded but openly homophobic.[39] The main target of Loos's attack becomes the effeminate architect, "the decorator" (the Secession and Werkbund members), Josef Olbrich, Kolo Moser, Josef Hoffmann: all these "dilettanti," "fops," and "suburban dandies" who buy their "pre-tied ties in the woman's fashion displays."[40] The question of modernity cannot be separated from that of gender and sexuality.

IV

Loos's real enemy is not Olbrich, as is commonly believed, or the Secession members, but Josef Hoffmann.[41] This did not escape his contemporaries. As Neutra writes: "Hoffmann was *the professor* whom Loos demolished in my eyes, or had tried to demolish in the eyes of his generation."[42] And Loos himself writes in the foreword to the first edition of his *Ins Leere gesprochen* (Paris, 1921): "Mr. Breuer, who had taken great pains collecting the essays, sent them to the publisher and soon received from the publisher's reader, who is in charge of the art department, a note informing him that the publisher could only carry out the publication if I would agree to alterations and deletions of the attacks against Josef Hoffmann—who, however, was never mentioned by name. Thereupon I took back these articles from the publishing firm of Kurt Wolff."[43]

But despite their animosity, the different attitudes that Loos and Hoffmann reveal in their architecture can be understood as different ways of negotiating the same dilemma: the modern split between private and public and the related difference in the metropolis between the space of the intimate and the space of the social. Hoffmann was also conscious of the split in the modern individual between his private and public being, but he confronted it in a different way. For Hoffmann the house was to be intentionally designed to be in harmony with the "character" of its inhabitants. There is nothing as personal as character. But the client could not add objects to the house on his own account, nor could he hire another artist to do so for him.[44] This was the object of Loos's criticism. Loos believed that the house grows with one, and that everything that goes on inside it is the business of its inhabitants.[45] Hoffmann's idea of character was to be a reason for praise, on the other hand, on the part of Peter Behrens. For Behrens, the house was a work of art. He added that Hoffmann's houses acquire meaning in social life,[46] and this remark clarifies any possible misunderstandings about the "character" with which the house was to be in harmony. Hoffmann was speaking about a *social* character. The individual cannot leave his traces on his own house because the house is in accordance with that part of his character that does not belong to him privately: the forms of social convention.

Both Loos and Hoffmann recognized that being in society involves a kind of schizophrenia between one's private and public self, like being in a meeting where one does not understand what is being said. This happens often in foreign countries, that is to say, everywhere. Both responded to this estrangement by understanding architecture as primarily a social mechanism, like dress or manners, a way of negotiating social situations. The difference is in the particular social strategy. For Loos it is a strategy of silence, but this silence is not merely the silence of one who has nothing to say. The introverted character of Loos's houses, the way in which they close themselves to the exterior, is with the silence of one who has recognized the impossibility of any dialogue in a language that is not his own. It is a silence that speaks. It is not a conventional silence, but the rejection of a convention. As Karl Kraus wrote, "In these times you should not expect any words of my own from me—none but these words which barely manage to prevent silence from being misinterpreted."[47]

In the architecture of Hoffmann too the object closes upon itself, but not with an introverted gesture. In this case, it is more the will to fix in a precise way the object's limits as a monad, as if for fear of allowing it to be absorbed by the indifference of the environment (notice how defined the edges of Hoffmann's houses are, with what deliberateness he has concentrated a tension in them). But once this frontier has been delineated—it is a matter of the distance imposed by social courtesy—the object initiates a dialogue that has no other content beyond a series of adopted conventions. The fact that this speaking does not signify—it cannot signify; it does not conform to the conventions of a language, but speaks the language of what we may call a series of invented conventions[48]—is not important because there is no intention to communicate, only to cover a void with forms.

For Hoffmann life is a form of Art. For Loos, who insists on revealing the void, life is the other of Art. "I am anxious," says Behrens in an article on Hoffmann written for the English-speaking world, "that the buildings here illustrated should be considered from the right point of view: that the 'different' element in them shall not mislead anyone into thinking that it is due to affectation or to a desire deliberately to create something unusual." No, what is different here is not intended to shock you. No transgressions-as-knowledge, no avant-gardes. On the contrary, Behrens asserts, there is a "close connection between his great architecture and the easy and harmonious charm of a well-ordered life in beautiful surroundings."[49]

Art, for Hoffmann as for Olbrich, is *education:* "For the artistically inclined, to offer spaces corresponding to their individuality, and for the rest, education through the artistic interior." In other words, leveling, social integration, self-legitimation. Once again, Ulrich, Musil's character in *The Man without Qualities,* offers a strikingly Loosian critique of this state of affairs:

> **Over his head hung the menacing proverb: "Tell me what your house is like and I'll tell you who you are," which he had often read in art journals. After intensive study of these journals he came to the conclusion that he preferred, after all, to take the architectural completion of his personality into his own hands.**[50]

V

Loos and Hoffmann were born in the same year, 1870, only a month apart, and in the same place, Moravia, then part of the Austro-Hungarian empire; after the war to become part of Czechoslovakia. Both were to end up in Vienna.

Then, if one takes the press as a mirror (something that can only be done with care), Hoffmann's and Loos's paths took on a kind of inverse symmetry. Loos, not Hoffmann, is the Viennese figure who has occupied the greater number of pages of recent criticism on both sides of the Atlantic. This attention corresponds to that paid by the architectural press to the figure of Hoffmann in his own time, when Loos was more or less ignored.[51] All this coincides, naturally, with Hoffmann's more powerful position in the various societies for the production and reproduction of architecture and with the related fact that he was extraordinarily successful in building his designs.[52]

The decline of Hoffmann as a public figure[53] virtually coincides with the beginning of Loos's recognition, which—like all prophets'—arose not in Vienna but in Paris, in the circles close to *L'Esprit nouveau*. In 1912 Herwarth Walden published five articles by Loos in the magazine *Der Sturm*. To have access to the pages of *Der Sturm*, as Reyner Banham argues, was to have access to a limited but international audience. It was through this channel that Loos's words arrived in Paris, where his writings were republished and where he was appreciated by the dadaists. Distance in space gave Loos the role of a protagonist, as later would distance in time; but between one moment and the other there is more than a coincidental relation, for where is Loos recognized today but in the intellectual circles? Again a limited but international audience, in a certain sense the inheritors of the earlier avant-garde.[54]

The nature of a certain increase in interest in Hoffmann is also clear—in the market of cultural recuperations his reputation briefly grew again in the 1980s—but I shall go no further than this observation.[55] The *symmetry* between Hoffmann and Loos interests me because it points to the theme of how the press—the architectural magazines—initiated a means of *producing* architecture with words, drawings, and photographs; as well as to the consequences that this could have in a profession that is structurally linked to permanent things and materials of substance. This theme did not escape Loos, who repeatedly attacked the manipulations of the magazines, offering as an ultimate argument the immortality of the work. In yet another passage remarkably omitted in the first English version of his text "Architektur" (1910), Loos writes:

> **It is my greatest pride that the interiors which I have created are totally ineffective in photographs. I have to forego the honour of being published in the various architectural magazines. I have been denied the satisfaction of my vanity. And thus my efforts may be ineffective. Nothing is known of my work. But this is a sign of the strength of my ideas and the correctness**

> **of my teachings. I, the unpublished, I whose efforts are unknown, I, the only one of thousands who has a real influence. . . . Only the power of the example has had an influence. The very power with which the old masters had been effective and faster in reaching the farthest corner of the earth although, or especially because, post, telegraph, or newspapers were not yet in existence.**[56]

Architecture then is to be opposed to the other means of communication, which are more abstract, more synchronized with the times. Architecture communicates itself in spite of them. But why does Loos not mention the printed word? I shall return to this question later. What interests me here about Loos's argument on publishing and architecture is the way it parallels his much better known one about ornament.

For Loos, ornament is that which makes art a commodity. By "ornament" he means something "invented," not something that had its origins in a genuine erotic impulse or in a *horror vacui*, emotions that we overcome today by other, more sophisticated means. But where, asks Loos, will Hoffmann's work be in ten years' time?[57]

Publishing, like ornament, by absorbing architecture into the universe of merchandise, by fetishizing it, destroys its possibility of transcendence. Architectural magazines, with their graphic and photographic artillery, transform architecture into an article of consumption,[58] making it circulate around the world as if it had suddenly lost mass and volume, and in this way they also consume it. It is not a question of the ephemeral character of the medium (obviously Loos does not object to writing). The problem for Loos is that photography is not able to interpret architecture; otherwise the latter could live in the former. When Loos writes, "Good architecture can be described but not drawn," and even "Good architecture can be written. One can write the Parthenon,"[59] he is acknowledging, well before Benveniste, that the only semiotic system capable of interpreting another semiotic system is language. Leaving aside the difficulties of language interpreting architecture, what Loos realized was that photography makes architecture something *other*, transforms it into a news item. And the news item is, in itself and apart from the fact to which it is referring, an event, what Kraus would call a "fact."

As the work of art is different from the useful object, architecture is different from its news. Trying to disguise the limits that exist between the two is, for Loos, to make "decoration."

VI

When Loos arrived in Paris, writes Banham, he was already famous, but his fame was due to his writings, some of which had been published in France, rather than to his buildings, which seem to have been known only by hearsay. Loos would have liked this comment: his architecture was passing by word of mouth like that of "the ancient masters in the times when there was no post, telegraph, or newspaper." But why is it that Loos, who opposed architecture to all the other means of communication that make an abstraction of place, did not also condemn the printed word? Why should this technology be able to transmit an experience of things when it is precisely printing that first prepared us "to act without reacting,"[60] when it is printing that provided the basis for the takeoff from place that ended by turning the world into nothing more than a landing strip?

For Loos, the printed word could only communicate by recuperating "common sense," by deintellectualizing writing, by giving language back to culture. The habit in the German language of beginning nouns with capital letters Loos saw as symptomatic of "the abyss that opens up in the German mind between the written and the spoken word": "When

A LA SORBONNE
Amphithéatre Michelet
46, rue Saint-Jacques à 8 h. 45

Quatre conférences
en langue Allemande

ADOLF LOOS

"Der Mensch mit den modernen Nerven"

Vom Gehen, Stehen, Sitzen, Liegen,
Schlafen, Wohnen, Essen und
Sich-Kleiden

1926

Mercredi, le 17 Février
Lundi, le 22 Février
Jeudi, le 25 Février
Lundi, le 8 Mars

ENTRÉE LIBRE

Poster for Loos's lecture series at the Sorbonne, Paris, 1926, entitled "The Man with Modern Nerves."

the German takes a pen in hand, he can no longer write as he thinks, as he speaks. The writer is unable to speak; the speaker cannot write. And in the end the German can do neither."[61]

Still today Loos is more famous for his writings than for his buildings, which nobody dares to interpret without relying on the former. This hardly happens with any other architect. But do these writings really explain his buildings or him as a figure? Benjamin writes:

> **The replacement of the older narration by information, of information by sensation, reflects the increasing atrophy of experience. In turn, there is a contrast between all these forms and the story, which is one of the oldest forms of communication. It is not the object of the story to convey a happening *per se,* which is the purpose of information; rather, it embeds it in the life of the storyteller in order to pass it on as experience to those listening. It thus bears the marks of the storyteller much as the earthen vessel bears the marks of the potter's hand.**[62]

Loos's writings share something of this ancient form; like those of Benjamin, they have an almost biblical structure. They are writings in which one can start reading at any point and still sense the totality of the message. As in oral communication, the problem and its solution are touched upon at the beginning of the discussion, and then the message is conveyed again and again as in the concentric rings of a spiral.[63] In spite of the seeming redundancy, one can read this type of writing over and over without tiring of it because one never understands exactly the same thing on subsequent readings. It is writing that requires *entry*. By entering, one extracts from every reading an experience that is unique. Such writing is always *modern,* just like Loos's houses, because it requires that someone *enter* in order to make sense of it, that someone make it his or her own.

VII

Anyone [can] observe how much more easily . . .
architecture can be grasped in photographs than in reality.

Walter Benjamin, "A Small History of Photography"

What can an architecture for magazines be when the magazine uses photography as its medium? Does the photographic transformation of architecture do no more than present it in a new vision, or is there a deeper transformation, a sort of conceptual agreement between the space this architecture comprehends and the one implicit in photography? Does the fact that its relation with the masses is transformed through its reproduction not also presuppose a modification in the *character* of architecture, in the Benjaminian sense?

Photography was born at almost the same time as the railway. The two evolve hand in hand—the world of tourism is the world of the camera—because they share a conception of the world. The railway transforms the world into a commodity. It makes places into objects of consumption and, in doing so, deprives them of their quality as places. Oceans, mountains, and cities float in the world just like the objects of the universal exhibitions. "Photographed images," says Susan Sontag, "do not seem to be statements about the world"—unlike what is written, or hand-made visual statements—"so much as pieces of it, miniatures of reality that anyone can make or acquire."[64] Photography does for architecture what the railway did for cities, transforming it into merchandise and conveying it through the magazines for it to be consumed by the masses. This adds a new context to the production of architecture, to which corresponds an independent cycle of usage, one superimposed upon that of the built space.

But in addition to all this, the railway turns places into nonplaces because it poses itself as a new limit, whereas previously the built object

The 1,400-pound camera of George R. Lawrence, 1895.

Accident at the Montparnasse Station, Paris.

had done so; but since the railway is a fluid limit, it actually nullifies the old differences between inside and outside. It is often said of railway stations that they are a substitute for the old gates of the city, but what they do in fact is to displace the notion of *frontier;* not only do they fail to demarcate the edge of the urban fabric, but they ignore the city as such, as fabric. The railway, which knows only of departure and arrival points, turns cities into *points* (as Arturo Soria y Mata understood when he called the cities of "the past," those which existed, "points" rather than "stains," which was more what they looked like), connected to the diagrammatical railway network that is now the territory. This notion of space has nothing to do with that of space as an enclosure within certain limits, a notion the Greeks bequeathed to us along with the agora. It is a space that recognizes only points and directions, not the void and that which surrounds it, a space that does not know of limits but of relations.

Photography participates in this spatial conception, and for this reason it is able to represent it (not so with space conceived as a container). Photography shares with the railway an "ignorance" of place,[65] and this has on the objects shot by the camera an effect similar to that of the railway on the points it reaches: it deprives them of their quality as things.

Loos understands this when he writes that the inhabitants of his interiors are not capable of recognizing their own houses in photographs, "in the same way that one who owns a Monet would not recognize his painting in Kastan."[66] Kastan, Schachel tells us in his notes on Loos's writings, is the name of a panopticon in the Vienna waxwork museum.[67] Kastan is therefore nowhere. It is the reproduction of an imaginary place. That is why one who owns a Monet is not able to recognize it there: because for him the Monet that he possesses exists as an object, as a thing, and not as an idea about this object. To separate the object from its place, which is always part of the object itself, implies a process of abstraction in the course of which the object loses its aura, ceases to be recognizable.[68]

For Sitte, who hated photography and other abstractions that led to it, photography signifies that sense of unreality which creates the no-where of place. In his reasoning, Sitte takes a route that is the inverse of Loos's: in a "geometrical" space (geometrical in Sitte's sense) one becomes *unreal* and for that reason suitable only to be a "photographic model" or "an exhibit."[69]

Something of all this must have been intuited by the first photographers, who from the beginning used scenography as if it were the most natural thing. It is clear that with the exposure time then required, their victims needed something to lean on, but this does not explain why columns were resting on carpets, or why, confronted with protests of unreality—"anyone will be convinced that marble or stone columns never rise from the base of a carpet"—the photographers would retire into the studio to reproduce an imaginary universe at leisure.[70] Scenography is now used only by carnival photographers. Otherwise we have no need of props. Anything will do, even reality itself, particularly when it is little more than a prop, when it no longer matters where one is.[71]

Photography, which for Benjamin finds itself at home in "carnivals" and in the "interpreted world," has a hard time—Loos recognized—representing space as *Raum,* depicting a space that, while endlessly complicating the difference between inside and outside, is still dependent on this difference. Sitte's plaza and Loos's *Raumplan* are spaces defined by the perception of the person whom they enclose, not by that of the one who trespasses their limits.

Whereas Loos's unphotographable architecture is conceived from inside out, Hoffmann's architecture is conceived from outside in. Giedion, always so perceptive, says laconically of the Stoclet Palace that "the flat surfaces of this banker's home are made up of white marble slabs, but they are treated like framed pictures."[72]

Franz Kafka, c. 1888.
Photographer unknown.

Adolf Loos holding a Thonet chair, undated photograph.

Kafka and others on an airplane, in the Prater, Vienna, 1913.

Josef Hoffmann "flying" with his collaborators (right to left) Camilla Birke, Hilde Polsterer, Christa Ehrlich, Paris, 1925.

The most notable thing about this (very photogenic) house of Hoffmann when one looks at it in magazines—and one is obliged to look, because it is also there, on the page, that his architecture is produced—is the moment of doubt as to whether what one is seeing is a built thing or a model. It does not have weight; it floats; it lacks corporeal existence; it is a box, walls surrounding space, which is not an empty hole dug out of building material. There is nothing—to use a concept of that moment—"sculptural" about it.[73]

The confusion with the cardboard model involves more than a conception of space. With this house, something occurs that is similar to what happens with those cutouts that are used to make paper architecture. More important than whether a wall is internal or external, than whether a surface corresponds to the roof or to the kitchen floor, than the differences in the materials covering those surfaces, more important than whether an element is supporting or supported, are the contiguities between the cutouts. One can understand this very clearly when they are still on the paper, before being cut out. Everything is related to what is adjacent, as in a line of writing where a word relates to the one following it. Everything appears to be sewn, just like a treacherous narrative that links the most disparate things, and which in the cutouts is represented by a seam of black dots marking the line where the paper is folded.

In the Stoclet Palace, the "narrative" is the metallic cable molding that tirelessly follows the border of every plane it recognizes, indifferent to whether it is ascending an edge or turning a corner (therefore sewing together two right-angled planes); whether it is crowning a facade as a sort of cornice engaging en route every single window it encounters, windows that are in turn also framed by this banding; whether this ubiquitous cable surrounds the well of the staircase and in so doing stitches up the superimposed plans like a pocket sewn to a jacket, or, alternatively, descends until it recovers a horizontal datum, thereby implying the suggestion of a skirting board. All this suggests another game: how can one form such a figure without ever taking the pencil off the paper?

In the Stoclet interior a whisper made itself felt. Peter Behrens remarked that it was the hall that impressed him most, that it made him feel "as though one must not speak too loudly within its walls. Here, notwithstanding the diversity of their origin, a thousand lines, forms and colours were combined to form a uniform whole."[74] Here again the same banding goes up and down piers, dividing the balcony into compartments and making it look as if it were not a balcony but slabs hovering between the piers (Sekler). The same rhetoric appears in the hanging lamp; could anything have been further from the way Wittgenstein did it? The same approach appears in Hoffmann's carpeting of the floor with square tiles, which, even more than indicating the way one should move, end up giving the impression that it is not oneself who is moving but that which is underneath one's feet. Nothing is left to be itself. Furniture is made to take on the same quality as spaces themselves; there is nothing "sculptural" about it, nothing that reveals any contrast between the space and its occupant (the subject was to preoccupy Le Corbusier). For Hoffmann, space and furniture are part of the same whole. They *are* its inhabitants. One is one's mask.

The walls of the Stoclet Palace are like Giedion's "framed pictures"; they are flat surfaces, independent in the sense that their "frames" delimit them as elements. But since in these walls the frame coincides with the edges that delimit them as planes, differentiating them from adjacent planes, they are at once independent and yet linked to those that are contiguous with them. The same molding, the same metal band that gives them their existence by framing, also links them to adjacent surfaces, thereby forming a three-dimensional object; a box.

Josef Hoffmann, Stoclet Palace and Avenue de Tervueren, Brussels, photograph c. 1911.

Stoclet Palace, detail of the molding.

Stoclet Palace, design for kitchen.

All this creates a tension at the edges of the box, and in so doing weakens the whole and produces in the observer the impression that the walls could well unfold, losing the condition of stability that had been guaranteed to them by the cube that they formed; a premonition of unfolding by which they would recover their original condition as cut-outs. (The same impression is given by one of Hoffmann's chairs, namely that it has been designed without taking the pencil off the paper.) On the very same plane or sheet of paper are now to be found at once wall, roof, and floor plans. Each one corresponds to its opposite on the paper. Across from the interior is the exterior.[75] It is a notion of space that is in accordance with the universe of technics—the railway, photography, electricity, reinforced concrete. It is a space that neither closes nor opens, but establishes relations between points and directions.

Citing the art historian August Schmarsow's observations, Peter Behrens argues that "architecture is the art of defining space and is achieved with sparse geometrical forms, while sculpture, the art of volume and spatial occupation, provides its plastic counterpart."[76] When Behrens says this, he is also reflecting—it was always a favorite theme with him—upon the impact of technological means of transportation on visual perception and on the necessity of adapting architecture to this new way of seeing. For him, simple forms composed of undetailed planes correspond to an age of rapid movement.[77]

Under a photograph of Otto Wagner's Karlsplatz Station of 1894, Giedion reiterates Wagner's prophecy: "The new architecture will be dominated by slablike tabular surfaces and the prominent use of materials in a pure state" (*Moderne Architektur*, 1895).

Detail of the cabin of the* Assanpink, *American locomotive, 1855.

Otto Wagner, Karlsplatz Station, Vienna, 1894.

VIII

> ***The sign of a* truly felt *architectural work is that in plan it lacks effect.***
>
> Adolf Loos

Hoffmann's architecture conveys its strongest impression not only in plans but also in the photographed record of itself. Not only is it an architecture conceived to be experienced primarily in visual terms, but because of the emphasis on the flat, two-dimensional aspect it seems conceived to be experienced through the monocular, mechanical eye of the camera lens. Perhaps Loos was thinking about Hoffmann when he wrote: "There are designers who make interiors not so that people can live well in them, but so that they look good in photographs. These are the so-called graphic interiors, whose mechanical assemblies of lines of shadows and light best suit another mechanical contrivance: the camera obscura."[78]

By "truly felt" Loos means a perception of space involving not only the sense of sight (human sight, two eyes) but also the rest of the senses. It is a way of perceiving that, Loos insists, corresponds to a time prior to the epoch of mechanical reproduction in architecture. In his view, this is the only criterion by which space can be considered *architectural*. Of all the senses, Loos privileged the sense of touch: "Photography renders insubstantial, whereas what I want in my rooms is for people to feel substance all around them, for it to act upon them, for them to know the enclosed space, to feel the fabric, the wood, above all, to perceive it sensually, with *sight and touch*, for them to dare to sit comfortably and feel the chair over a large area of their external bodily senses. . . . How can I prove this to someone by means of a photograph?"[79]

For Loos the relationship between drawing and architecture, architecture and photography is one of translation. Neither drawing nor photography can translate architecture adequately. "Every work of art obeys such strong internal laws that it can take only one form." An architecture that exists "already in drawing," as architects like Boullée and Hugh Ferriss would have liked, was not possible, in Loos's view: "What has been conceived in one art does not reveal itself in another." Drawing and architecture are irreducible systems: "If I were able to erase from the minds of my contemporaries that strongest of architectural facts, the Pitti Palace, and let the best draughtsman present it as a competition project, the jury would lock me in a lunatic asylum." The reverse is not possible either: "But it is a terrible thing when an architectural drawing, itself a graphic work of art, is built in stone, steel, and glass, for there are truly graphic artists amongst architects."[80]

For Loos, the architectural drawing can be no more than a technical language: "The true architect is a man who in no way needs to know how to draw; that is, he does not need to express his inner state through pencil strokes. What he calls drawing is no more than the attempt to make himself understood by the craftsman carrying out the work."[81] (Note again the similarity with Saussure's formulation: "Language and writing are two distinct systems of signs. The second exists for *the sole purpose of representing the first*.")[82] Architecture is a concrete means of communicating the experience of space. Architectural drawing is an abstract, that is to say, technical, means of communication: "The *architect* first senses the effect he wishes to produce, then he visualizes the spaces he wishes to create."[83] Only the social division of labor, then, makes it necessary for the architect to draw. The fact that such a division exists—and with it a kind a bilingualism: the language of information is severed from the language of experience—does not sanction impossible pseudo-translations. For Loos, we are living in an absurd tower of Babel; what we can understand as abstract minds, that is as collective beings, we can no longer understand privately.

Architecture, then, if we take Loos's thinking to its logical conclusion, can do nothing but reflect upon the disjunctive character of modern culture. It must not attempt impossible syntheses. Information is the other of experience, life is the other of art ("Everything that serves a purpose should be excluded from the realms of art"), culture is the other of civilization, the individual is the other of society, the interior is the other of the exterior. But as we have seen, none of these crucial distinctions are simple. They may appear so at first, but on closer view they are endlessly complicated. We have to explore these complications in detail, as they are architectural from the beginning.

Take for example a linguist that Loos admired, Jacob Grimm, from whom he adopted the idea of dropping the practice of capitalizing German nouns. In his introduction to *Ins Leere gesprochen*, Loos quotes a passage from Grimm in which he not only identifies the capital letters with "ornament" but puts the removal of that ornament in architectural terms: "If we have rid our houses of their gables and their projecting rafters, and removed the powder from our hair, why should we retain such rubbish in our writing?"[84] If Grimm, and Saussure, speak of language in architectural terms, almost all of Loos can be read in a linguistic key. The house by the architect is, for Loos, an undesirable "scream" that alters the tranquillity of the mountain lake. And the scream, as in Munch, is the impossibility of uttering words. "The architect comes from the city. He possesses no culture, he is an upstart. I call culture that balance of inner and outer man which alone can guarantee reasonable thought and action."[85]

Loos realized that objects in his culture had lost their immediate meaning. The use by the artists of the Secession of objects as symbolic expressions of inner states confirmed this. But if objects had lost their meaning, for Loos it was not a matter of trying to make them speak Esperanto but of making an effort to distinguish them. Karl Kraus gave form to this thought in his famous statement: "All that Adolf Loos and I have done, he literally and I figuratively, is to show that there is a difference between a chamber pot and an urn, and in that difference there is a small margin left for culture. But the others, 'the positive ones,' are to be distinguished between those who would use a chamber pot for an urn and those who would use an urn for a chamber pot."[86]

Culture and difference: here is the main thrust of Loos's thinking. Ornament can only be read as metaphor. It is all that tries to confuse limits, all unnecessary words, "all words that exceed their condition for meaning,"[87] even all unnecessary vowels: "Twenty-six years ago I stated that with the evolution of humanity the ornament will disappear from the articles of consumption, . . . evolution that is as natural as the disappearance of the vowels from the final syllables in colloquial [German] language."[88] This transformation in the status of ornament involves a transformation in the status of knowledge: "Art comes from know-how [in German, *Kunst* from *Können*.] But as for those dilettantes who from their comfortable studios want to prescribe and trace out for the artist, for the man who produces, just what he should do, let them keep to their field—that of graphic art."[89]

To know, in the civilization of indifference, is to transgress. Disjunction is a form of knowledge. The narrative of a graphic art is for Loos disknowledge (ignorance); it is decoration. Loos's interiors are conservative and at the same time disjunctive. They are conservative because they conform to a traditional idea of comfort. In his houses it is easy to imagine many places where one would like to ensconce oneself, depending on one's mood, the hour of the day, what one desires the space to provide, to communicate, to protect. With the houses of Hoffmann one can think immediately of how to move through them, but it is very difficult to imagine actually using these spaces. It is not that one feels excluded from them; it is that ritualistic way they have of including one.

IX

Benjamin cites a sentence of Theodor Reik to the effect that "the function of remembrance [*Gedächtnis*] is the protection of impressions, memory [*Erinnerung*] aims at their destruction. Remembrance is essentially conservative; memory is destructive." The question for Benjamin here is how philosophy has tried "to lay hold of the 'true' experience as opposed to the kind that manifests itself in the standardized, denatured life of the civilized masses."[90] Benjamin speaks about two kinds of experience; in fact, he uses two different words, *Erfahrung* and *Erlebnis*. Both mean "experience," but in Benjamin *Erfahrung* is used as "raw experience," so to speak, that is, experience without the intervention of consciousness; *Erlebnis* is "lived experience," an experience to whose development consciousness has, so to speak, "attended." In splitting experience in this way Benjamin is referring here also to Bergson, Proust, and Freud.[91]

In these terms, Reik's distinction between conservative memory and destructive remembrance is exactly the same that interests Loos when, again in "Architektur," he writes, "*The work of art is revolutionary, the house conservative*. . . . The work of art aims at *shattering* man's comfortable complacency." The similarity with Reik's formulation is more than apparent; Loos too was distinguishing between *memory* and *remembrance:* "Does the house therefore," he continues, "have nothing to do with art, and should architecture not be classified as an art? This is so. Only a very small part of architecture belongs to art: the tomb and the monument." The tomb and monument are places of memory: "If we find a mount in the forest, six feet long and three feet wide, formed into a pyramid shaped by a shovel, we become serious and something within us says, 'Someone lies buried here.' This is architecture."[92]

As collective beings, for Loos, we can make architecture only in the tomb and in the monument. Only in these two forms can an experience take place "that includes ritual elements," an experience secluded from crisis, because they evoke a world outside time and therefore beyond reason.

X

"The art that gave the ancient man his basis and the Christian man the curvature of his vaults will now be transferred into boxes and bracelets. These times are much worse than we suppose."

This quotation of Goethe appears at the end of Loos's text "Cultural Degeneracy" (1908), where he criticizes the confusion of Hoffmann and the members of the Werkbund in distinguishing between art and commodities (articles of consumption): "The members of this association are people who are trying to replace our contemporary culture with another. Why they are doing it, I do not know. But what I do know is that they will not succeed. No one has tried to put his podgy hand into the spokes of the turning wheel of time without having had that hand torn off."[93]

With regard to this, Bertolt Brecht writes (in a passage quoted by Benjamin): "If the concept of 'work of art' can no longer be applied to the thing that emerges once the work is transformed into a commodity, we have to eliminate this concept with cautious care but without fear, lest we liquidate the function of the very thing as well."[94] While Benjamin writes: "By the absolute emphasis on its exhibition value the work of art becomes a creation with entirely new functions, among which the one we are conscious of, the artistic function, later may be recognized as incidental."[95]

Mechanical reproduction qualitatively modifies the nature of art in modifying the relation of the masses to it. But what could possibly be meant by transforming architecture into an object? Surely it has to have something to do with the change in sensibility that has induced the masses to desire the proximity of things, to take possession of them. The objects of Hoffmann answer such social conditioning. They are part of the effort of architecture to reach the masses. To present architecture as an object, to assimilate the object within its image, is to make it accessible. "By virtue of their very accessibility objects diminish fears of an apocalyptic future" (G. C. Argan). "In the past, a discontent with reality expressed itself as longing for *another* world. In modern society, a discontent with reality expresses itself forcefully and most hauntingly by the longing to reproduce *this* one" (Susan Sontag), by the compulsive desire to appropriate its fragments. "The desire of contemporary masses to bring the thing 'closer' spatially and humanly . . . is just as ardent as their bent toward overcoming the uniqueness of every reality by accepting its reproduction. Every day the urge grows stronger to get hold of an object at very close range by way of its likeness, its reproduction" (Benjamin).[96]

In Hoffmann every thing is made into an object: "The mother-of-pearl and ebony of a cigarette box invite comparison with the marble cladding and metal moulding of the Stoclet Palace exterior. A jewellery box inlaid with a stylized plant motif has the proportions of a miniature pavilion, its lid projecting as the cornice. . . . It is tempting to view Hoffmann's use of perforated sheet metal for vases and plant-stands as a bold three-dimensional projection of the paper's original grid, making design and object one."[97] For Loos, Hoffmann makes decoration not so much because he makes use of ornament but because he sees continuities where there are differences. The object is confused with its drawing, the house with its model, the model with its photograph, and in the latter one would recognize nothing were it not for the legend that informs us of the material, of the measures, of what it is.

Loos's position, on the other hand, is one of a resistance against the leveling brought about by consumption. "The building stands before posterity, and from that point we can explain to ourselves why architecture, in spite of all the changes of our times, will always be the most conservative of the arts."[98] Or as Walter Benjamin writes:

> **Buildings have been man's companions since primeval times. Many art forms have developed and perished. Tragedy begins with the Greeks, is extinguished with them, and after centuries its 'rules' only are revived. The epic poem, which had its origin in the youth of nations, expires in Europe at the end of Renaissance. Panel painting is a creation of the Middle Ages, and nothing guarantees its uninterrupted existence. But the human need for shelter is lasting. Architecture has never been idle. Its history is more ancient than that of any other art, and its claim to being a living form has significance in every attempt to comprehend the relationships of the masses to art. Buildings are appropriated in a twofold manner: by use and by perception—or rather, by touch and sight. Such appropriation cannot be understood in terms of the attentive concentration of a tourist before a famous building.**[99]

This should not be confused with nostalgia for a time before tourism, for a "wholesome" experience, for an experience whereby what is experienced *is* experienced. Benjamin seems to express the opposite sentiment to Loos when he writes: "Anyone will have noticed how much more easily a painting, and above all a scuplture, or architecture, can be grasped in photographs than in reality."[100] The tourist-detached camera now produces the only "authentic" sense of architecture. Architecture is placed by the placeless medium. And in his most explicit architectural text, "Erfahrung und Armut" (Experience and Poverty), he says: "Poverty of experience; it should not be understood as if men longed for a new experience. *No; they long to liberate themselves from experiences*" (emphasis added). And yet it is precisely in this text, dealing with experience, that Benjamin quotes Loos, this "forerunner of modern architecture [who writes]: 'I write only for men who possess a modern sensibility. For the others I do not write.'"[101]

XI

For Benjamin architecture provides the model of an (ancient) art whose reception occurs collectively and in a state of distraction. A form of reception that "finds in the film its true form of exercise." The "distracting element" in film is also "primarily tactile." It "hits" the spectator like a "bullet." Unlike a painting, "which invites the spectator to contemplation," the spectator before the "movie frame" can no longer do that: "No sooner has his eye grasped a scene than it is already changed. It cannot be arrested." This is what makes film tactile.

This is the form of perception in big cities, in department stores, in trains . . . and perhaps even in modern architecture, but not in traditional architecture: "The film is the art form that is in keeping with the increased threat to his life which modern man has to face. Man's need to expose himself to shock effects is his adjustment to the dangers threatening him."[102] Shock is what characterizes modern experience (*Erfahrung*). And the word *Erfahrung* is etymologically linked with danger. "What characterizes experience" in Benjamin, writes Eduardo Cadava, "experience understood in its strict sense as the traversal of danger, the passage through a peril—what characterizes experience is that it retains no trace of itself: . . . an experience whereby what is experienced is not experienced."[103]

This is above all the experience of war. "A generation that from 1914 to 1918 had one of the most atrocious experiences of universal history," writes Benjamin, "came back from the battlefield dumb. Not enriched, but poorer in communicable experience. And what ten years after was spilled in the avalanche of books about the war, was anything but experience that flows from mouth to ear."[104]

"Mass movements are usually discerned more clearly by a camera than by the naked eye," writes Benjamin, but isn't this remarkably the same formulation he uses when he comments on how much easier it is "to grasp architecture in photographs than in reality"? We should therefore pay close attention to the way Benjamin goes on to say: "This means that mass movements, including war, constitute a form of human behavior which particularly favors mechanical equipment."[105] Are we to conclude then that architecture is a form that favors mechanical equipment? And what relationship does architecture have to war? Surely, one look at the architectural avant-garde in these terms suggests that modern architecture becomes "modern" not simply by using glass, steel, or reinforced concrete, as is usually understood, but precisely by engaging with the new mechanical equipment of the mass media: photography, film, advertising, publicity, publications, and so on. And furthermore, this engagement cannot be thought outside of war. Indeed, it is a military engagement from the beginning. The avant-garde is precisely that, the advance guard in a campaign, a campaign that is at once one of publicity and a military one. Modern architecture has to be rethought as war architecture. In these terms, the historians and critics of modern architecture whose work is being rethought here would have been first and foremost war reporters. The battlefield was the marketplace, and the weapons, as in every modern war, were the new technologies of communication. As Karl Kraus puts it in "In These Great Times," the (war) reporter is a "traveling salesman who examines battlefields for their suitability as markets": "What the traveling salesmen must do now is keep putting out their feelers and feeling out their customers! Mankind consists of customers."[106]

Joh. Exinger. ***The only photograph that Loos published in his journal*** **Das Andere.**

Photography

The Mechanical Eye

There is a still from Dziga Vertov's movie *The Man with the Movie Camera* in which a human eye appears superimposed on the reflected image of a camera lens, indicating precisely the point at which the camera—or rather, the conception of the world that accompanies it—disassociates itself from a classical and humanist episteme.

The traditional definition of photography, "a transparent presentation of a real scene," is implicit in the diagram instituted by the analogical model of the camera obscura—a model that would pretend to present to the subject the faithful "reproduction" of a reality outside itself. In this definition, photography is invested in the system of classical representation. But Vertov has not placed himself behind the camera lens to use it as an eye, in the way of a realistic epistemology. He has employed the lens as a mirror: approaching the camera, the first thing the eye sees is its own reflected image.

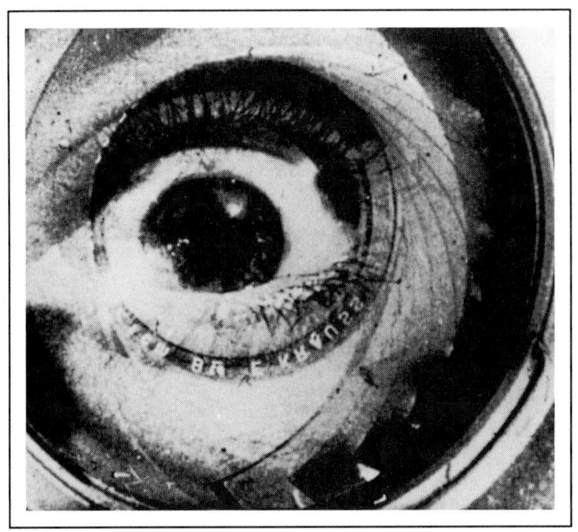

Still from Dziga Vertov's The Man with the Movie Camera, *1928–1929.*

Camera obscura, 1646.

In film, light leaves its traces on the sensitive emulsion, imprinting on it permanent shadows. The manipulation of two realities—the superimposition of two stills, both traces of material realities—produces something that is already outside the logic of "realism." Rather than *represent* reality, it *produces* a new reality.

Photography and cinema seem, on first reflection, to be "transparent" media. But that which is transparent, like the glass in our window, also reflects (as becomes evident at night) the interior and superimposes it onto our vision of the exterior. The glass functions as a mirror when the camera obscura is lit.

Freud hangs a framed mirror against the window of his studio, right next to his work table. As Marie-Odile Briot notes: "The mirror (the psyche) is in the same plane as the window. The reflection is also a self-portrait projected onto the outside world."[1] Freud's mirror, placed in the frontier that separates interior from exterior, undermines its status as a fixed limit. This is not without architectural consequences. The frontier is no longer a limit that separates, excludes, dissociates, a Cartesian limit; rather it is a figure, a convention, its aim is to permit a relation that has to be defined continuously. It is what Franco Rella would call a "shadow line."[2]

The diffusion of photography coincides with the development of psychoanalysis. Between the two there is more than one relation. Benjamin writes that it is through photography that "one first learns of the optical unconscious, just as one learns of the drives of the unconscious through psychoanalysis."[3] And Freud himself explicitly sees the relation between unconscious and conscious in terms of photography:

> **Every mental process . . . exists to begin with in an unconscious stage or phase and it is only from there that the process passes over into the conscious phase, just as a photographic picture begins as a negative and**

Sigmund Freud's study, Berggasse 19, Vienna, 1938. Note the mirror in the window near his work table.

> **only becomes a picture after being formed as a positive. Not every negative, however, necessarily becomes a positive; nor is it necessary that every unconscious mental process should turn into a conscious one.**[4]

The unconscious and the conscious, the invisible and the visible, like the negative enclosed within the camera and the print of the exterior developed from it, cannot be thought of independently of one another. Furthermore, both photography and the unconscious presuppose a new spatial model in which interior and exterior are no longer clear-cut divisions. In fact, photography represents a displacement of the model of the camera obscura, and with it, as Jonathan Crary notes, the figure of an "interiorized observer," a "privatized subject confined in a quasi-domestic space, cut off from a public exterior world," into a model in which the distinctions between interior and exterior, subject and object, are "irrevocably blurred."[5] Likewise, psychoanalysis forever complicates the relationship between inner psyche and its exterior manifestations. The simultaneous and interrelated arrival of psychoanalysis and photography marks the emergence of a different sense of space, indeed of a different architecture.

The Photographic Fetish

In the rare cases when criticism has addressed the subject of Le Corbusier and photography it has done so from within the position that holds photography as a transparent medium of representation, oscillating constantly between a realistic interpretation of the medium and a formalist interpretation of the object. Significantly enough, the subject is addressed as either Le Corbusier the photographer or the photographs of Le Corbusier's work. The place of photography in Le Corbusier's process of production is conspicuously missing. Giuliano Gresleri's fascinating book *Le Corbusier, Viaggio in Oriente* shares in this critical oversight, particularly at the delicate point where it takes on the connotations of a nostalgic album by the amateur photographer Le Corbusier.[6] The subtitle of this book, *Gli inediti di Charles-Edouard Jeanneret fotògrafo e scrittore,* is indicative. First, "inediti," unpublished, hitherto unheard of: this term maintains the commonsense notion that because the "originals" have not yet been published they have a higher value than any circulating images. Then "Charles-Edouard Jeanneret photographer and writer": the use of these terms projects onto Le Corbusier's work a grid that divides knowledge into watertight compartments, presenting him as some sort of multitalented individual capable of producing valuable work in different, specialized branches of knowledge. Le Corbusier as photographer, writer, painter, sculptor, editor, these divisions—often encountered in standard academic criticism—mask Le Corbusier's fundamentally nonacademic method of working.

This nonacademic method is particularly manifest in Le Corbusier's travels, which played an essential part in his formation (I am not referring here to what is conventionally understood as the "formative period" but to his entire lifework). A journey represents the possibility of an encounter with "the other." During Le Corbusier's first trip to Algiers, in the spring of 1931, he made drawings of naked Algerian women and acquired postcards of naked natives surrounded by accoutrements from the Oriental bazaar. Jean de Maisonseul, who as an eighteen-year-old boy had guided Le Corbusier through the Casbah, will later recall their tour: "Our wanderings through the side streets led us at the end of the day to the rue Kataroudji where he [Le Corbusier] was fascinated by the beauty of two young girls, one Spanish and the other Algerian. They brought us up a narrow stairway to their room; there he sketched some nudes on—to my amazement—some schoolbook graph paper with colored pencils; the sketches of the Spanish girl lying both alone on the bed and beautifully grouped together with the Algerian turned out accurate and realistic; but he said that they were very bad and refused to show them."[7] The guide also describes his astonishment at seeing the architect buying such "vulgar" postcards. The Algerian sketches and postcards are a rather ordinary instance of the ingrained mode of a fetishistic appropriation of women, of the East, of "the other."[8] But Le Corbusier, as Samir Rafi and Stanislaus von Moos have noted, turned this material into preparatory studies for a projected monumental figure composition, "the plans for which seem to have preoccupied Le Corbusier during many years, if not his entire life."[9]

From the months immediately following his return from Algiers up to his death, Le Corbusier seems to have produced hundreds and hundreds of sketches on yellow tracing paper by laying it over the original sketches and retracing the contours of the figures. He also studied exhaustively Delacroix's famous painting *Femmes d'Alger,* producing a series of sketches of the outlines of the figures in this painting, divested of their "exotic clothing" and the "surrounding decor." Soon the two projects merged; he modified the postures of Delacroix's figures, gradually making them correspond to the figures in his own sketches. He said that he would have called the final composition "Femmes de la Casbah." But, in fact, he never finished it. He kept redrawing it. That the drawing and redrawing of these images became a lifetime obsession would have been enough of an indication that something was at stake. This becomes even more obvious when in 1963–64, shortly before his death, Le Corbusier, unhappy with the visible aging of the yellow tracing paper, copies a selection of these sketches onto transparent paper and—symptomatically, for someone who kept everything—burns the original sketches.[10]

But the obsessive process of drawing and redrawing had already reached its most intense, if not hysterical, moment when Le Corbusier's "Femmes de la Casbah" studies found their way into a mural that he completed in 1938 in E.1027, the house that Eileen Gray had designed and built for Jean Badovici in Cap-Martin in 1927–1929. Le Corbusier called the mural *Graffite à Cap-Martin*. According to von Moos (who is quoting the new owner of the house, Frau Dr. Schelbert): "Le Corbusier explained

Eugène Delacroix, Les Femmes d'Alger, *oil on canvas, 1833. Paris, Louvre.*

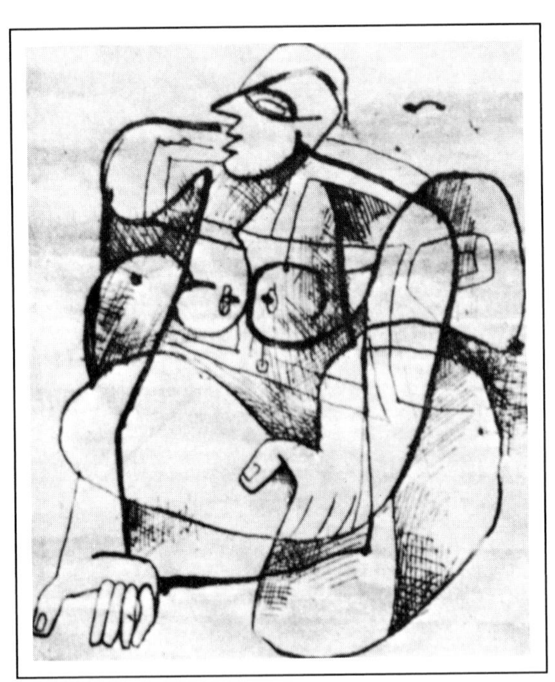

Le Corbusier, crouching woman, front view (after Delacroix's **Les Femmes d'Alger*****), watercolor on transparent paper, 49.7 × 32.7 cm. Unsigned (n.d.). Milan, private collection.***

*Le Corbusier, three women (*Graffite à Cap-Martin*). Mural in Eileen Gray's house E.1027, Roquebrune–Cap Martin, 1938.*

to his friends that 'Badou' was depicted on the right, his friend Eileen Gray on the left; the outline of the head and the hairpiece of the sitting figure in the middle, he claimed, was 'the desired child, which was never born.'" This extraordinary scene, a defacement of Gray's architecture and perhaps even an effacement of her sexuality, is clearly a "theme for a psychiatrist,"[11] as Le Corbusier's *Vers une architecture* says (in a passage curiously omitted from the English translation) of the nightmares with which people invest their houses. Particularly if we also consider Le Corbusier's strange relationship to the couple and to this house, as manifested, for example, in his quasi-occupation of the site when he built after World War II a small wooden shack for himself at the very limits of the adjacent property, right behind Eileen Gray's house. He occupied and controlled the site by overlooking it, the cabin being little more than an observation platform. The violence of this occupation had already been established when Le Corbusier painted the murals in this house (there were eight altogether) without the permission of Eileen Gray, who had already moved out. She considered it an act of vandalism, indeed, as Peter Adam has put it, "it was a rape."[12] When Le Corbusier published the murals in *L'Architecture d'aujourd'hui* (1948), Eileen Gray's house is referred to as a house in Cap-Martin; her name is not even mentioned. Le Corbusier will end up, later on, getting credit for the design of the house and even for some of its furniture.[13]

Le Corbusier's fetishization of Algerian women is consistent with his abuse of Eileen Gray. One might even argue that the child in the mural reconstitutes the missing (maternal) phallus, whose absence, Freud argues, organizes fetishism. In these terms, the endless drawing and redrawing is the scene of a violent fetishistic substitution that in Le Corbusier would seem to require the house, domestic space, as prop. Violence is organized around or through the house. In both circumstances (Algiers or Cap-Martin) the scene starts by an intrusion, the carefully orchestrated occupation of a house. But the house is in the end effaced (erased from the Algiers drawings, defaced at Cap-Martin).

Le Corbusier, cabanon, Cap-Martin, 1952.

Significantly, Le Corbusier describes drawing itself as the occupation of a "stranger's house." He writes: "By working with our hands, by drawing, we enter the house of a stranger, we are enriched by the experience, we learn."[14] Drawing, as has often been noted, plays an essential part in Le Corbusier's process of "appropriation" of the exterior world. He repeatedly opposes his technique of drawing to photography: "When one travels and works with visual things—architecture, painting or sculpture—one uses one's eyes and draws, so as to fix deep down in one's experience what is seen. Once the impression has been recorded by the pencil, it stays for good—entered, registered, inscribed. The camera is a tool for idlers, who use a machine to do their seeing for them."[15] Certainly statements such as this (which accompanies some of Le Corbusier's drawings of his journey through the Orient published in his late work *Creation Is a Patient Search*) have gained him the reputation of having a phobia of the camera—a reputation so strong as to make the discovery of the stock of photographs that he took while traveling in the East a "surprise," as Gresleri describes it. Yet it is difficult to understand how this view of Le Corbusier could ever have been established, let alone sustained, given such evident manifestations of a unique sensibility for the photographic image as his own printed works.

But before that, what is the specific relation between photography and drawing in Le Corbusier? After all, the sketches of the Algerian women were not only redrawings of live models but also redrawings of postcards. In fact, one could argue that the construction of the Algerian women in French postcards, widely diffused at the time, would have informed Le Corbusier's live drawings, in the same way that, as Zeynep Çelik notes, Le Corbusier precisely reproduces in his physical entrance to foreign cities (Istanbul or Algiers, for example) the images of these cities constructed by postcards and tourist guides.[16] In these terms, not only did "he know what he wanted to see," as Çelik says, but he saw what he wanted to see, what he had already seen (in pictures). He "enters" those pictures. He inhabits the photographs. The redrawings of the *Femmes d'Alger* are also more likely to have been realized, as von Moos points out, from postcards and reproductions than from the original painting in the Louvre. So what, then, will be the specific role of the photographic image as such in the fetishistic scene of the "Femmes de la Casbah" project?

The fetish is always about "presence," writes Victor Burgin: "and how many times have I been told that photographs 'lack presence', that paintings are to be valued *because of their presence*!"[17] Clearly this separation between painting and photography is what organizes the dominant understanding of Le Corbusier's relation to photography. And while Le Corbusier's writings, in some passages like the one quoted above, may lead the reader to similar conclusions, what these accounts seem to ignore is what happens when the drawing, the hand-crafted artistic meditation, is done "after" the photograph: the art reproduction, the postcard, even the architect's own photographs. Photography too has been read, in more than one sense, in terms of the fetish. Victor Burgin writes:

> **In fetishism, an object serves in place of the penis with which the child would endow the woman (her "incompleteness" threatening the child's own self-coherence). Fetishism thus accomplishes that separation of knowledge from belief characteristic of representation; its motive is the unity of the subject. . . . The photograph stands to the subject-viewer as does the fetishized object. . . . We know we see a two-dimensional surface, we believe we look through it into three-dimensional space, we cannot do both at the same time—there is a coming and going between knowledge and belief.**[18]

So if Le Corbusier "enters the house of a stranger" by drawing, could "the house" be standing in here for the photograph? By drawing he

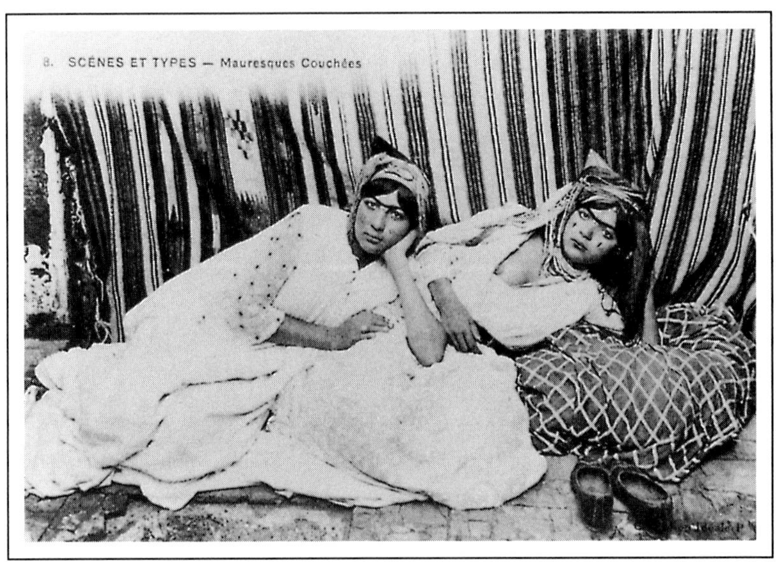

French postcard of Algerian women:
Scenes and types—Reclining Moorish women.

enters the photograph that is itself a stranger's house, occupying and reterritorializing the space, the city, the sexualities of the other by reworking the image. Drawing on and in photography is the instrument of colonization.

In fact, even the early material from his trip to the Orient, which Gresleri collected in *Le Corbusier, Viaggio in Oriente,* reveals the existence of drawings—such as the cathedral of Esztergom viewed from the Danube—that have obviously been realized "after" photographs.[19] This practice of drawing an image after it has already been fixed by the camera appears throughout Le Corbusier's work, recalling his no less enigmatic habit of sketching his own projects again and again, even long after they have been built. He redrew not only his own photographs but also those he encountered in newspapers, catalogues, postcards. The archives of *L'Esprit nouveau* hold numerous sketches on tracing paper that are obvious reworkings of found photographs. These depict such unlikely subjects as *horreurs* (as Le Corbusier would have said) like "Khai Dinh, the present emperor of Annam" or "The opening of the English Parliament. The king and queen" (taken from *L'Illustré* and reproduced in *L'Art décoratif d'aujourd'hui*), side by side with a portrait of Gaston Doumergue, President of the French Republic.[20]

While these drawings were ostensibly done to indicate which image was to be published on which page, they are not simply minimal outlines. Rather they resemble Le Corbusier's purist drawings in their careful reduction of everyday objects to essential forms. In this sense, they seem to indicate Le Corbusier's resistance to a passive intake of photography, to the consumption of images occurring in the world of tourism and mass media. In the face of an explosion of information in the illustrated newspapers, industrial catalogues, and advertisements—with their pretense of representing reality by extensive documentation, by the addition of "facts"—Le Corbusier operates by exclusion. In the terms conditioned by the logic of mass media, a photograph does not have

View of the cathedral of Esztergom: photograph by Charles-Edouard Jeanneret, 1911.

Charles-Edouard Jeanneret, drawing of the cathedral of Esztergom, 1911.

***Photograph of President Gaston Doumergue, from* L'Illustré.**

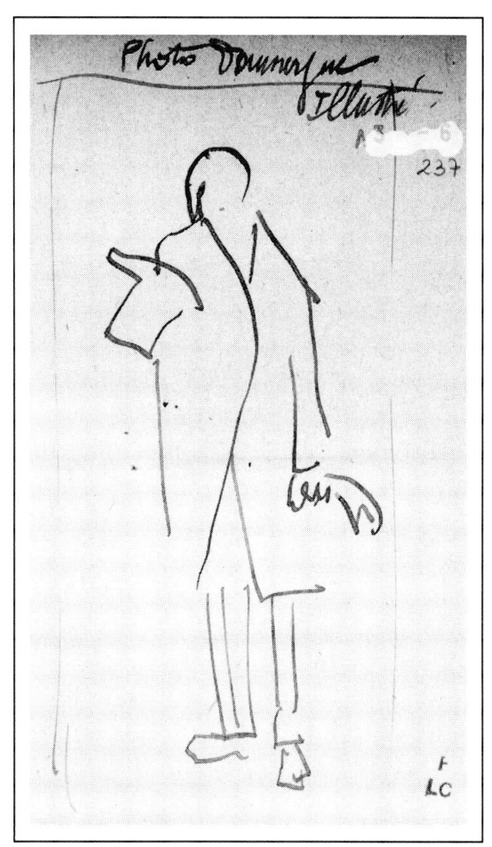

Le Corbusier, sketch realized after the photograph of Gaston Doumergue.

Photograph of Emperor Khai Dinh, from L'Illustré.

Le Corbusier, sketch after the photograph at left.

specific meaning in itself but rather in its relationship to other photographs, the caption, the writing, and the layout of the page. As Roland Barthes puts it: "All images are polysemous; they imply, underlying their signifiers, a floating chain of signifieds, the reader able to choose some and ignore others. Polysemy poses a question of meaning. . . . Hence in every society various techniques are developed intended to *fix* the floating chain of signifieds in such a way as to counter the terror of uncertain signs."[21] While photography as constituted in the mass media is most often uncritically received as a fact, Barthes further makes clear that "the press photograph is an object that has been worked on, chosen, composed, constructed."[22] Le Corbusier takes pleasure in reconstructing the images thus "constructed," isolating, for instance, some of them from their original context, an illustrated magazine or a mail order catalogue, and drawing sketches after them. Again, the sketch learns from what the photograph excludes. By drawing he is obliged to select, to reduce to a few lines the details of the image. The preformed image thus enters Le Corbusier's creative process, but interpreted. As he himself would put it:

> **To draw oneself, to trace the lines, handle the volumes, organize the surface . . . all this means first to look, and then to observe and finally perhaps to discover . . . and it is then that inspiration may come. Inventing, creating, one's whole being is drawn into action, and it is this action which counts. Others stood indifferent—but you saw!**[23]

Drawing is an instrument of the *recherche patiente*. It is a technique to overcome the obsessive closure of the object, to reincorporate it into the process, a process of "no beginning and no end." For Le Corbusier the process is more important than the product. This also accounts for the form of his writings, constantly combining the bits and pieces of his thoughts in different contexts, reworking them, as if resisting a final form. As Peter Allison once put it, in spite of the "apparent repetitiveness, . . . he seldom ever repeated himself exactly."[24]

Reflection and Perception

During his first trip to Italy and Vienna in 1907–1908, Le Corbusier became aware of the difference between architecture and its photographic representation. This reflection on representation became a constant subject of his letters. In Vienna, to which Charles L'Eplattenier had directed Le Corbusier and his companion Léon Perrin, the travelers could not find their way to houses they had previously seen in architectural magazines. Le Corbusier wrote to L'Eplattenier asking for the addresses of modern houses published in *Innen Architektur* and *Deutsche Kunst:* "Illogisme, se faire indiquer de La Chaux-de-Fonds des addresses pour Vienna; tant pis c'est ainsi." L'Eplattenier sent them reproductions of Hoffmann interiors and included some of the music room designed by one of his students for the Mathey-Doret house in La Chaux-de-Fonds.[25]

The photographs of the music room disappointed Le Corbusier: "They are well done, but how pitiful is the effect! Yes, Perrin and I were really upset at what photography gives of the beautiful things we know."[26] They consoled themselves by considering that their photographs of Florence and Siena taken a few months earlier, in the fall of 1907, had also been a disappointment: "From our stock of photographs from Italy, we do not have a good one of the beautiful architectural things [we saw], because the effect of photography is always distorted and offensive to the eyes of those who have seen the originals."[27] The opposite was true for the *épatant* reproductions of Hoffmann interiors; at first they seemed impressive, but they did not withstand a close inspection:

> **Look at the photographic effect of these halls and dining rooms of Hoffmann: how much unity it has, how sober, simple, and beautiful it is. Let's examine it closely and analyze it: what are these chairs? This is ugly, impractical, boring, and juvenile. These walls? of taped gypsum, like in**

Music room of the Mathey-Doret house, La Chaux-de-Fonds, interior by pupils of Charles L'Eplattenier, 1908.

Josef Hoffmann, house for Dr. Friedrich V. Spitzer, hall, 1902.

the arcades of Padua. This fireplace, a nonsense. And this dresser and these tables and everything? How cold, surly, and stiff it is. And how the devil is it built?[28]

The atectonic quality of "modern Vienna" shocked and disgusted Le Corbusier, who had been educated in a vernacular crafts tradition. "All the construction is masking and trickery [masquée et truquée]," he wrote to L'Eplattenier. "The German movement is in search of originality to the extreme, not occupying itself with construction, logic, or beauty. No point of support in nature."[29] He faulted L'Eplattenier for having misdirected him ("you have sent us to Italy to educate our taste, to love what is [well] built, what is logical, and you want us to renounce all this because of some impressive photographs in art magazines"),[30] and suggested that he spend fifteen days in Vienna instead of relying on magazine pictures. As for himself, Le Corbusier had decided to leave Vienna for Paris to learn construction: "c'est qu'il me faut, c'est ma technique." Not surprisingly, he did very little drawing during his stay in Vienna.

It is interesting how close these letters come to Adolf Loos's criticism of photography and its shortcomings in representing architecture. In 1910 Loos wrote in "Architektur": "It is my greatest pride that the interiors which I have created are totally ineffective in photographs. . . . I have to forego the honour of being published in the various architectural magazines."[31] Loos was reacting to the confusion between architecture and the image of architecture so characteristic of the overfed journals of the Jugendstil. Le Corbusier was to go a step further than Loos. In Paris, more precisely with the experience of *L'Esprit nouveau,* he came to understand the press, the printed media, not only as a medium for the cultural diffusion of something previously existing but also as a context of production with its own autonomy. His encounter with the metropolis produced a break with L'Eplattenier's crafts forma-

Charles-Edouard Jeanneret, engraved watchcase, c. 1902.

Omega advertisement in L'Esprit nouveau *2.*

tion where the object is identified with the world, where the material carries the traces of its maker. Such continuity between hand and object is inside a classical notion of the artifact and of the relationship between producer and product. With industry, mass production, and reproduction this continuity is broken, inverting the relationship between producer and product. Production in a "consumer society" develops, as Adorno and Horkheimer noted, according to a logic completely internal to its own cycle, to its own reproduction. The main mechanism by which this is accomplished is the "culture industry," the vehicles of which are mass media: cinema, radio, publicity, and periodical publications.[32] Le Corbusier engages fully with this industry. Indeed, it is arguably only through such an engagement that architecture could itself become industrialized.

Faked Images

In *L'Esprit nouveau* 6, Le Corbusier published the only work he ever recognized from his La Chaux-de-Fonds period: Villa Schwob. (This house, built in 1916, did not appear in the *Oeuvre complète*.) In the accompanying article, Ozenfant, under the pseudonym Julien Caron, remarked on the difficulties of capturing architecture through the eye of the camera: "And photography, already misleading when it reproduces surfaces (paintings), is how much more so when it pretends to reproduce volumes."[33] Ironically, the published photographs of this house are *trompeuse* indeed, they have been "faked."

Le Corbusier air-brushed the photographs of Villa Schwob to adapt them to a more "purist" aesthetic. In the "façade sur la cour," for instance, he masked the pergola in the court, leaving its white trace on the ground, and cleared the garden of any organic growth or distracting object (bushes, climbing plants, and the dog house), revealing a sharply defined

Une Villa DE LE CORBUSIER 1916

Dans ses articles remarquables de l'*Esprit Nouveau*, Le Corbusier-Saugnier, architecte, avec modestie, ne s'est occupé que des rapports de l'ingénieur avec la construction moderne, afin de mettre en évidence les conditions primordiales de l'architecture : le jeu des formes dans l'espace, leur conditionnement par les procédés de construction. Il a montré que le calcul peut introduire à une grande architecture, que les moyens de construire actuels (financiers et techniques) offrent des ressources plus vastes que ceux des époques passées.

Le Corbusier sut, dans ses articles, lui artiste, faire momentanément abstraction des qualités de sensibilité qui font l'artiste, pour dégager, avant tout, les moyens de l'ingénieur,

Charles-Edouard Jeanneret, Villa Schwob, La Chaux-de-Fonds, 1916, as published in* L'Esprit nouveau *6, 1921.

***Villa Schwob*, as published in**
L'Esprit nouveau.

Villa Schwob, detail of the pergola.
Original photograph, c. 1920.

outer wall. He also modified the service entrance to the garden, cutting the protruding vestibule and the angled steps with a straight plane aligned with the door (a difference observable in the original plans published in the same article). The window corresponding to the vestibule became a pure rectangular opening.[34]

Le Corbusier discarded everything that was picturesque and contextual in this house, concentrating on the formal qualities of the object itself. But the most striking modification in the photographs of this house published in *L'Esprit nouveau* is the elimination of any reference to the actual site, which is, in fact, a steep terrain. By eliminating the site, he makes architecture into an object relatively independent of place. This relationship between an ideal object and an ideal site is a constant in Le Corbusier's architecture of the twenties. For example, he designed the small villa for his parents on the shores of Lake Geneva before he knew its specific location.[35] And in Buenos Aires he proposed a suburban development consisting of twenty "replicas" of Villa Savoye.[36]

An analysis of the *Oeuvre complète* uncovers a similar reworking of the photographic image. In the published photographs of Villa Savoye, for example, Le Corbusier masked, by painting them gray, anomalous columns (wet columns perhaps) visible in other photographs of the villa. Interestingly, the published section of Villa Savoye corresponds to an earlier version of the project rather than to the one that was built.[37] It becomes evident that for Le Corbusier any document from the process, which better reflects the concept of the house, takes precedence over the faithful representation of the actual built work. Furthermore, the distinction he makes between real space and the space of the page is equally clear. It is precisely because the latter is necessarily reductive that certain elements—such as wet columns—while innocuous in an experiential reading of the building, are distracting when seen in a photograph.

Villa Schwob, as published in L'Esprit nouveau.

Villa Schwob. Original photograph, c. 1920.

Likewise in the *Oeuvre complète*, Le Corbusier eliminated in the plan for Villa Stein at Garches the two columns that frame the apse of the dining room projection into the living room.[38] The resulting plan conveys the spatial, experiential reading of this house. The absence of the two columns reinforces the diagonal thrust of the villa, further disintegrating the "central axis" into fragments.[39]

Outside his architectural work, Le Corbusier used analogous techniques to reinforce his theoretical arguments. For instance, in *L'Esprit nouveau* and later in *Vers une architecture* he published a photograph of Pisa taken from his own collection of photographs from his first trip to Italy; but prior to its reproduction Le Corbusier traced portions of the print in black ink to stress the purity and clarity of lines in the platform.[40] A page of sketches from the working material of *Vers une architecture* reveals similarly notable instructions for modifications to be applied to the photographs of the church of S. Maria in Cosmedin in Rome.[41] These consist of removing tabernacles, decoration on the arches, leather pillows, columns, windows, and anything else that would distract the reader from seeing Greece in "Byzantine Rome." He writes: "Greece by way of Byzantium, a pure creation of the spirit. Architecture is nothing but ordered arrangement, noble prisms, seen in light."[42]

Stanislaus von Moos has written that for Le Corbusier the relationship of the architectural work to a specific site and its material realization are secondary questions; that for him architecture is a conceptual matter to be resolved in the purity of the realm of ideas, that when architecture is built it gets mixed with the world of phenomena and necessarily loses its purity.[43] And yet it is significant that when this same built architectural piece enters the two-dimensional space of the printed page it returns to the realm of ideas. The function of photography is not to reflect, in a mirror image, architecture as it happens to be built. Construction is a significant moment in the process, but by no means its end product. Photography and layout construct another architecture in

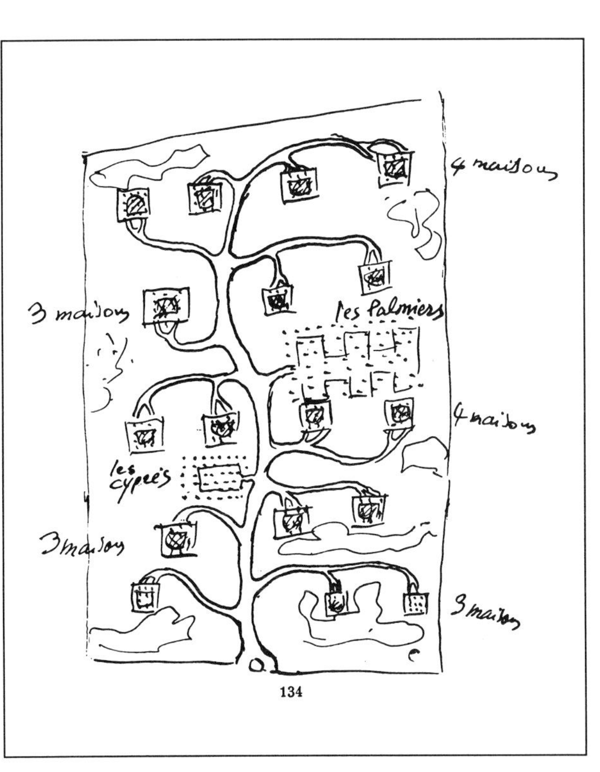

***Replicas of Villa Savoye for the Argentine countryside, proposed by Le Corbusier in a lecture in Buenos Aires, October 1929, and published in* Précisions.**

Le Corbusier, sketches of the interior of S. Maria in Cosmedin, Rome, with instructions for modifying the original photographs before their publication in Vers une architecture.

S. Maria in Cosmedin as published in Vers une architecture, *1923.*

the space of the page. Conception, execution, and reproduction are separate, consecutive moments in a traditional process of creation. But in the elliptic course of Le Corbusier's process this hierarchy is lost. Conception of the building and its reproduction cross each other again.

Continuous Editing

In the division of tasks among the editorial group of *L'Esprit nouveau,* Le Corbusier took as his responsibilities "administration et finances." Amédée Ozenfant and Paul Dermée, coeditors of the magazine, were in charge of the more traditional work of production and editing. But Le Corbusier opted to mix with the world outside the intellectual circles, to participate actively in the world of industry and finance, himself a "producer" rather than an "interpreter"—the classical task of the intellectual—of the new industrial reality.[44] As the magazine was largely financed by advertising, Le Corbusier came in contact with the culture of mass media.

His avid collection of industrial catalogues, department store brochures, and images clipped from newspapers and magazines thus has, in part, a productive explanation. Le Corbusier was in search of publicity contracts for *L'Esprit nouveau*. In fact, many of these catalogues came from companies whose products were ultimately advertised in the magazine. But Le Corbusier also appropriated this material as a source of images for his articles and books.[45]

In *L'Esprit nouveau* photography is not presented as an artistic project, rather as a documentary means. But in Le Corbusier's articles, photographs taken from publicity material coexist with images extracted from art books and photographs of his own work. Within these pages the world of mass culture intrudes into the world of high art, shaking the edifice to its foundations. No matter how often Le Corbusier claims a higher rank for the art object than for the everyday object, his work is continually "contaminated" by the materials of low culture.[46]

On the cover of the publicity brochure that Le Corbusier prepared for *Vers une architecture* he stated: "Vient de paraître / [interrupted by the reproduction of the book's cover] / Ce livre est implacable / Il ne ressemble à aucun autre." Inside he explained the novelty of his book in terms of his use of images: "This book derives its eloquence from the new means; its magnificent illustrations hold next to the text a parallel discourse, and one of great power."[47]

Photography in Le Corbusier's book is rarely employed in a representational manner. Instead it is the agent of a never-resolved collision of images and text, its meaning derived from the tension between the two. In this technique Le Corbusier borrowed much from modern advertising: the association of ideas that can be produced through the juxtaposition of images and of images with writing. A similar sensibility is evident in Le Corbusier's photographs of his early villas, which, as von Moos has noted, often include cars, if not his own Voisin: "Indeed, it is often unclear in these images whether it is the car or the house that supplies the context for an advertisement of the contemporary good life."[48] In Le Corbusier's books, images are not used to "illustrate" the written text; rather they construct the text. Again in the publicity brochure of *Vers une architecture* he wrote: "This new conception of the book . . . allows the author to avoid flowery language, ineffectual descriptions; the facts explode under the eyes of the reader by force of the images."[49]

In fact, Le Corbusier's books were conceived through a continuous editing of found images. The working material of *Vers une architecture* and *L'Art décoratif d'aujourd'hui* reveals as much.[50] It consists of a series of sketches, grouped as vignettes, that correspond to the images to be

Photograph of a turbine from a catalogue of the Swiss company Brown Boveri, c. 1924.

110 1925

Salon d'Automne.

Salon de l'Aéronautique.

Lui, l'ami, n'avait rien à contredire aux enthousiasmes de Paul; il les partageait. Mais il était trop artiste pour n'avoir pas, de longtemps, cherché une explication à l'émoi qu'il avait aussi ressenti et surtout, pour n'avoir pas, depuis longtemps, cherché à vaincre la profonde démoralisation qui l'avait saisi lorsque, par exemple, passant sans transition en 1921 du *Salon d'Automne* à celui de l'*Aéronautique*, dans ce même Grand Palais, il s'était senti écrasé par la splendeur de la machine et n'avait regagné son atelier que dans le doute et la négation. Il avait réagi découvrant le rapport fécond qui pouvait unir l'œuvre d'art qu'il poursuivait à la machine qu'il admirait. Il tenta de donner à Paul la leçon reçue de la machine : la machine est un événement si capital dans l'histoire humaine qu'il est permis de lui désigner un rôle de conditionnement de l'esprit, rôle aussi décisif et combien plus étendu que l'imposèrent dans les âges les hégémonies guerrières remplaçant une race par une autre race. La machine n'oppose pas une race à une autre race, mais un monde nouveau à un monde ancien dans l'unanimité de toutes les races.

La machine, phénomène moderne, opère dans le monde une

LA LEÇON DE LA MACHINE 111

Brown-Boveri.

réformation de l'esprit. Une preuve tangible que nous sommes bien loin du terme de l'évolution commencée, c'est qu'une langue universelle n'est point encore en usage, qui ferait tomber cette haute barrière de carton dressée à l'endroit des frontières désormais subjuguées, barrières de nuit sur un site qui s'éclaire.

Intact, le facteur humain demeure, la machine étant conçue par l'homme pour des besoins humains; là est l'élément solide et efficace : la machine est construite sur le système spirituel que nous nous sommes donné et non sur une fantaisie, système qui nous constitue un univers tangible; ce système, arraché article par article au monde qui nous entoure et dont nous participons, est assez cohérent pour déterminer la création d'organes remplissant des fonctions semblables aux phénomènes naturels. Vérification rassurante.

Le miracle de la machine, c'est donc d'avoir créé des organes

Double-page spread from **L'Art décoratif d'aujourd'hui,** *1925.*

Publicity brochure for Vers une architecture, *1923(?).*

Le Corbusier and Pierre Jeanneret,
Villa Stein-De-Monzie, Garches,
1927.

displayed. Some images come from Le Corbusier's memory ("carte postale, où est la carte postale?" is the footnote to one vignette); others are extracted from machinery catalogues, from Frédéric Boissonnas's albums of Greece, and so forth. Almost invariably Le Corbusier transformed these photographs. Beyond removing them from their original context, he painted on them, erased their details, reframed them; these, then, are images that have been worked on, chosen, composed, constructed.

Though photography makes everything accessible—"distant places, famous people, springtime" (as Benjamin put it)—choice rather than accumulation is its essence. Framing is the issue of photography. The photographs of Greece by Boissonnas that Le Corbusier published in *Vers une architecture* were taken primarily from Maxime Collignon's *Le Parténon* and *L'Acropole*.[51] Some were reframed and bear a resemblance to his own sketches in "Voyage d'Orient." They are "incomplete." They create a tension that pulls toward the missing element. As Stanford Anderson, referring to the sketches, has observed:

> **We hold no vantage point from which we may possess the building objectively. And if we did possess such a vantage point, these drawings tell us we would be missing something else. Experience itself and the knowledge which comes only through experience. . . . At a conceptual level Le Corbusier is concerned with how we correlate experience and knowledge. . . . This insistence on experience is more forceful when made in the presence of a work [the Parthenon] for which we have previously instilled modes of appropriation. . . . Le Corbusier did not repeat or make more precise the earlier researches into the orders . . . he produced a set of sketches which evoke vividly the sequential experience of the ascent of the Acropolis.**[52]

Boissonnas's photographs exemplify the instilled mode of an aestheticized appropriation of the Parthenon. The enormous plates of this book

110 VERS UNE ARCHITECTURE

Photo Albert Morancé. Le Parthénon.

Petit à petit, le temple se formule, passe de la construction à l'architecture. Cent ans plus tard le Parthénon fixera le point culminant de l'ascension.

du guerrier et du prêtre, pour atteindre à ce qu'on appelle justement la culture. La culture est l'aboutissement d'un effort de sélection. Sélection veut dire écarter, émonder, nettoyer, faire ressortir nu et clair l'Essentiel.

Depuis le primitivisme de la chapelle romane, on a passé à Notre-Dame de Paris, aux Invalides, à la Concorde. On a épuré, affiné la sensation, écarté le décor et conquis la proportion et la mesure; on a avancé; on a passé des satisfactions primaires (décor) aux satisfactions supérieures (mathématique).

S'il reste des armoires bretonnes en Bretagne, c'est que les Bretons sont demeurés en Bretagne, bien loin, bien stables, toujours occupés à la pêche et à leur élevage. Il n'est pas séant que les messieurs de la bonne société dorment, en leur hôtel de Paris, dans un lit breton; il n'est pas séant qu'un monsieur qui possède une limousine dorme dans un lit breton, etc. Il suffit de se rendre compte et de tirer les déductions logiques. Posséder une limousine et un lit breton, c'est, hélas, courant.

DES YEUX QUI NE VOIENT PAS... 111

Photo Albert Morancé. Le Parthénon.

Chaque partie est décisive, marque le maximum de précision, d'expression; la proportion s'y lit catégorique.

Tout le monde s'écrie avec conviction et enthousiasme : « La limousine marque le style de notre époque! » et le lit breton se vend et se fabrique toujours chez les antiquaires.

Montrons donc le Parthénon et l'auto afin qu'on comprenne qu'il s'agit ici, dans des domaines différents, de deux produits de sélection, l'un ayant abouti, l'autre étant en marche de progrès. Ceci ennoblit l'auto. Alors! Alors il reste à confronter nos maisons et nos palais avec les autos. C'est ici que ça ne va plus, que rien ne va plus. C'est ici que nous n'avons pas nos Parthénons.

***

Le standart de la maison est d'ordre pratique, d'ordre constructif. J'ai tenté de l'énoncer dans le précédent chapitre sur les avions.

Le programme Loucheur qui comporte 500.000 logements à construire en dix ans fixera sans doute celui de l'habitation ouvrière.

Double-page spread from* Vers une architecture, *1923, with reproductions of photographs by Frédéric Boissonnas taken from Maxime Collignon's* Le Parthénon *and reframed.

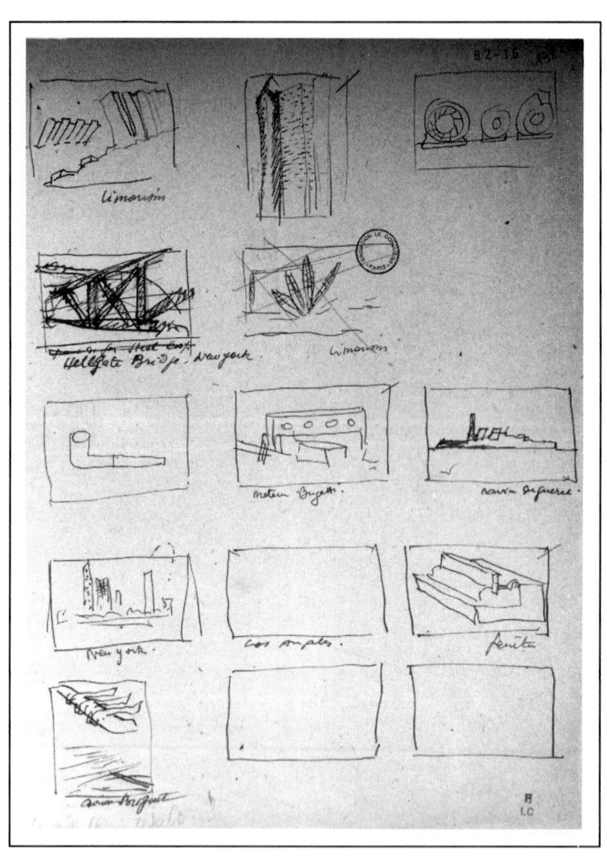

***Original page of sketches from the draft manuscripts of* Vers une architecture.**

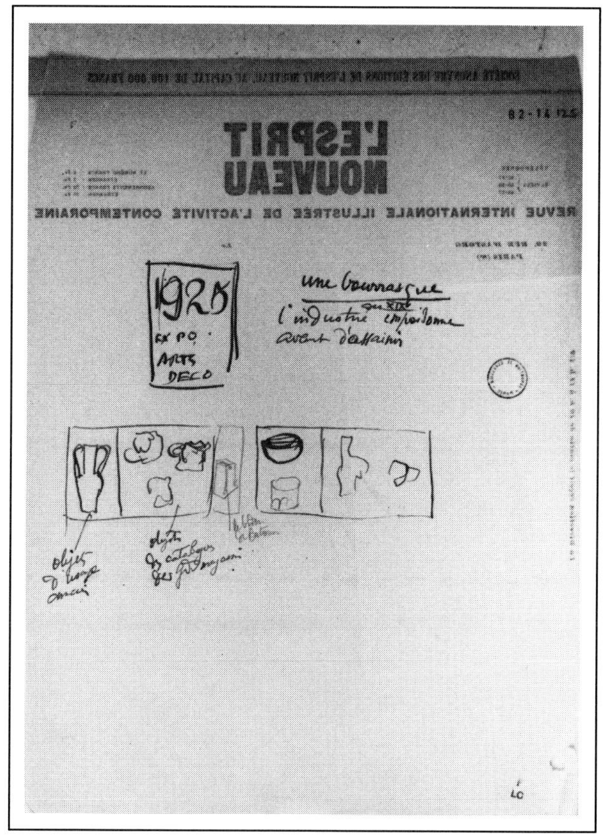

***Sketches on* L'Esprit nouveau *letterhead for* L'Art décoratif d'aujourd'hui.**

force the reader to step back every time a page is turned, presenting each image as an object for contemplative immersion, as a "work of art." Le Corbusier breaks away from his source when he wrenches these images from the sanctuary of high art, reduces their size, and places them next to the everyday images of newspapers and industrial catalogues (which themselves have undergone equivalent transformations). Mass media make everything contiguous and equivalent. Le Corbusier does not pretend to maintain a hierarchical division of the material by genre or type. Instead, he presents the collision of fragments corresponding to the experience of culture in the media. Thus his work becomes a critical comment on the conditions of culture in our time.

This rethinking of culture through a systematic reappropriation of photography transforms the fundamental sense of space in Le Corbusier's work. The transformation is most evident in his thinking of the window. After all, the window like the photograph is first of all a frame. The frame of Le Corbusier's horizontal window, like his photographs of the Parthenon, upsets the classical viewer's expectations, precisely because it cuts something out of the view.

A Window with a View

Nobody was more upset by Le Corbusier's horizontal window than his mentor Auguste Perret. From their initial dispute in the pages of the *Paris Journal* in 1923, they engaged for years in a bitter debate over the *fenêtre en longueur,* about which Bruno Reichlin has made an insightful analysis.[53]

A page of sketches by Le Corbusier with the heading "Ronéo," found in the archives of *L'Esprit nouveau,* appears to have been made when he was in the process of making a publicity brochure for the company

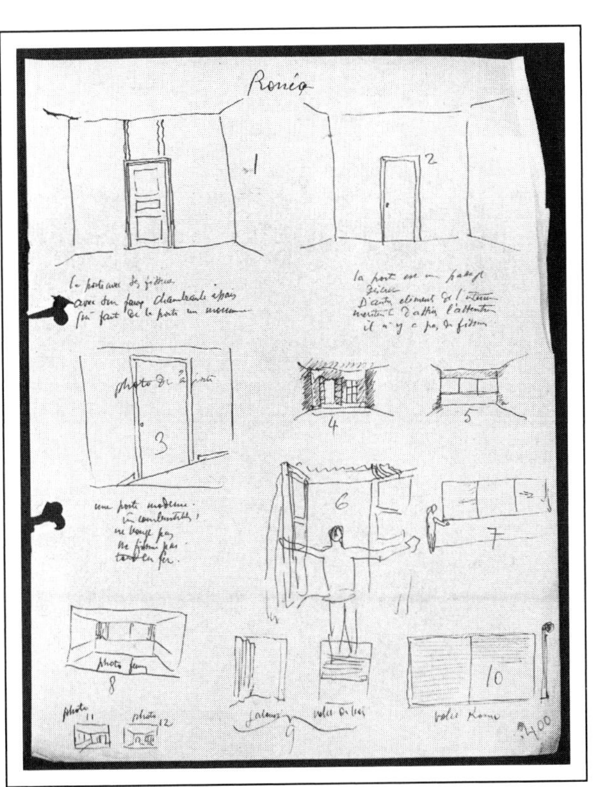

Le Corbusier, "Ronéo" page of sketches, illustrating the polemic between Le Corbusier and Auguste Perret over the **fenêtre en longueur.**

of that name.[54] What the drawings illustrate, however, is that famous controversy between Perret and Le Corbusier. Perret maintained that the vertical window, the *porte-fenêtre,* reproduces an "impression of complete space" because it permits a view of the street, the garden, and the sky, giving a sense of perspectival depth. The horizontal window, the *fenêtre en longueur,* on the other hand, diminishes "one's perception and correct appreciation of the landscape." In fact, Perret argued, it cuts out of view precisely that which is most interesting: the strip of the sky and the foreground that sustains the illusion of perspectival depth. The landscape remains, but (as Bruno Reichlin has put it) as though it were a planar projection "sticking to the window."[55]

In this dispute Perret expresses, with an exceptional clarity, the authority of the traditional notion of representation within a realistic epistemology, representation defined as the subjective reproduction of an objective reality. This is what he means by "complete" space. In these terms, Le Corbusier's concept of the horizontal window, as well as other aspects of his work, undermines this concept of representation. While classical paintings attempted to identify images with their models, purist paintings, built up with shapes and images of recognizable objects—bottles, glasses, books, pipes, and so forth—eschew this identification, as Ozenfant and Jeanneret claim. In *La Peinture moderne* they define the standard objects that they chose to represent in their paintings as "objects of the most perfect banality," which have "the advantage of a perfect readability and of being recognized without effort."[56] Objects on the canvas are therefore like words in a sentence: they refer to recognizable things, but the objects in the world that are represented are less important than the conjunction of differential units within the painting itself, each element being qualified by its place in the ensemble, or in Saussure's words by "differences without positive terms."[57]

The terms of Le Corbusier's "pictorial frontality" have been read by Rosalind Krauss as threefold:

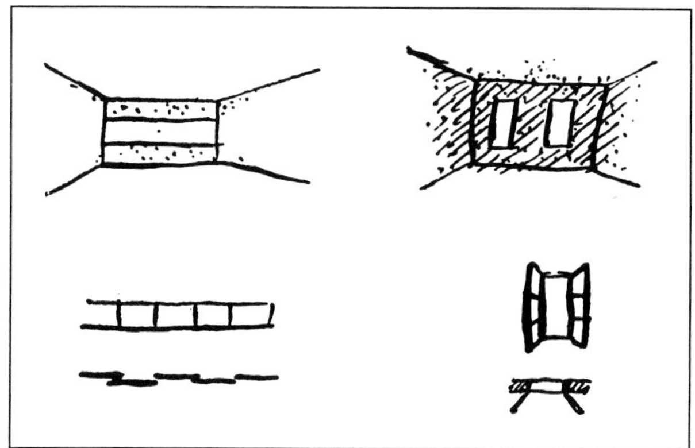

Le Corbusier, sketch of the confrontation between the porte-fenêtre *and the* fenêtre en longueur.

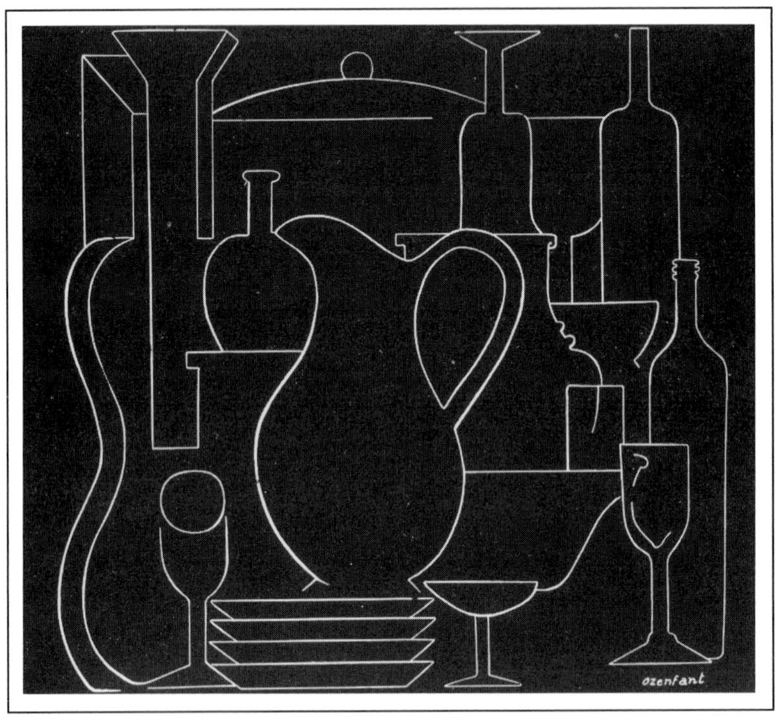

Amédée Ozenfant, drawing, 1925.

> **First, the object is registered as pure extension, as flat shape which never breaks rank with the picture's frontality to suggest a turning of one of its facets into depth. Second, the constellation of objects wedge together in that insistent continuity of edges which the Purist called *mariage de contours*. Third, color and texture are handled in a manner that calls attention to the inherent superficiality of these "secondary qualities"—so that distance or depth in the painting becomes no longer a matter of representing the space separating one object from another in the real world. Instead distance is transformed into a representation of the caesura between the appearance of the object and the object itself.**[58]

Viewing a landscape through a window implies a separation. A "window," any window, "breaks the connection between being in a landscape and seeing it. Landscape becomes [purely] visual, and we depend on memory to know it as a tangible experience."[59] Le Corbusier's horizontal window works to put this condition, this "caesura," in evidence.

Perret's window corresponds, as Reichlin has shown, to the traditional space of perspective representation in Western art. Le Corbusier's window corresponds, I would argue, to the space of photography. It is not by chance that Le Corbusier continues the polemic with Perret in an argument in *Précisions*, demonstrating "scientifically" that the horizontal window illuminates better, by relying on a photographer's chart that gives times of exposure.[60] While photography and film, based on single-point perspective, are often seen as "transparent" media, deriving from the classical system of representation, there is an epistemological break between photography and perspective. The point of view of photography is that of the camera, a mechanical eye. The painterly convention of perspective centers everything on the eye of the beholder and calls this appearance "reality." The camera—particularly the movie camera—implies that there is no center.

Using Walter Benjamin's distinction between the painter and the cameraman, one could conclude that Le Corbusier's architecture is the result of his positioning himself behind the camera.[61] By this I am not referring now to the aforementioned implications, Le Corbusier as "producer" rather than "interpreter" of industrial reality, but to a more literal reading, emphasizing the deliberate dispersal of the eye in Le Corbusier's villas of the twenties, effected through the architectural promenade, together with the collapsing of space outside the horizontal window—the architectural correlative of the space of the movie camera.

On this basis, may we therefore say that Perret's architecture falls within the humanist tradition and Le Corbusier's within the modernist? There is something paradoxical about the Ronéo drawing. While Le Corbusier intends by this drawing to illustrate the superiority of the horizontal window, in fact the intensity and detail with which he draws Perret's *porte-fenêtre*, in contrast to the sketchiness of the horizontal window, show it to be much more emotionally charged.[62] Above all this may be seen in the way Le Corbusier draws the human figure in each. In the *porte-fenêtre*, a carefully drawn man stands at the center of the window, holding it open with wide-stretched arms—recalling Perret's assertion (in an imaginary dialogue published by Le Corbusier in the *Almanach d'architecture moderne*) that "a window is man himself. . . . The *porte-fenêtre* provides man with a frame, it accords with his outlines. . . . The vertical is the line of the upright human being, it is the line of life itself." In contrast, the diminutive man drawn in the horizontal window occupies a peripheral position; the window opens by sliding. Le Corbusier wrote in the *Almanach:* "fenêtre, élément type—élément mécanique type: nous avons serré de près le module anthropocentrique."[63]

Any concept of the window implies a notion of the relationships between inside and outside, between private and public space. In Le Corbusier's work this relationship has to do with the contrast between the infinity of

Le Corbusier and Pierre Jeanneret, Maison Cook, 1926.

space and the experience of the body, a body that has become a surrogate machine in an industrial age. As he writes in *L'Art décoratif d'aujourd'hui:* "Decorative art is the mechanical system that surrounds us . . . , an extension of our limbs; its elements, in fact, *artificial limbs*. Decorative art becomes orthopaedic, an activity that appeals to the imagination, to invention, to skill, but a craft analogous to the tailor: the client is a man, familiar to us all and precisely defined."[64] And in a footnote to the book, Le Corbusier wrote that when the typewriter came into use, anthropocentrism became standardization: "This standardization had considerable repercussions upon furniture as a result of the establishment of a module, that of the *commercial format*. . . . An international convention was established [for paper sheets, magazines, books, newspapers, canvases, photographic prints]."[65] Le Corbusier understands the window in the same terms. Rather than framing the body, it is the body's mechanical substitute.

This can be seen in the evolution of the *fenêtre en longueur*. The one that stretches along the facade of the villa for Le Corbusier's parents in Corseaux on Lake Geneva (1923)—a house that became central to the Perret-Le Corbusier controversy—does not open by sliding. The window is divided into four elements, each of which is divided into three panels. The central panel, a rectangle, opens by pivoting; the two square panels are fixed. There, the occupant of the house still has to go to the center of the window to open it, and is thereby framed. In the Ronéo drawing, the *fenêtre en longueur* is again divided into three panels, but now the central one is square, like the others, and is fixed. This window slides open; and when opened, one glass panel is overlaid on another. The individual no longer occupies the center of the window when opening it, but must stand to one side. More than in Corseaux, the subject is displaced by the equipment.

How important the division of the window into three panels is for Le Corbusier is evident in his sketches of the house: the view outside each

Le Corbusier, small villa for his parents, Corseaux, drawing of the view through the interior overlooking Lake Geneva.

Maison Cook, view showing the fenêtre en longueur *of the opposite wall reflected in the mirror of the buffet.*

panel seems relatively independent of the adjacent view. The grouping of curtains in the side post, also stressed in Le Corbusier's sketches, reinforces the division of this window into four. The panorama "sticking" to the window glass is superimposed on a rhythmic grid that suggests a series of photographs placed next to each other in a row, or perhaps a series of stills from a movie.

We imagine a boat going down the lake. Viewed from a *porte-fenêtre* there would be an ideal moment: the boat appears at the center of the opening directly in line with the gaze into the landscape—as in a classical painting. The boat would then move out of vision. From the *fenêtre en longueur* the boat is continuously shot, and each shot is independently framed.

With Le Corbusier's *fenêtre en longueur* we are returned to Dziga Vertov, to an unfixed, never-reified image, to a sequence without direction, moving backward and forward according to the mechanism or the movement of the figure.

Publicity

Readymade Images

> ***At every moment, either directly or through the medium of newspapers and reviews, we are presented with objects of an arresting novelty. All these objects of modern life create, in the long run, a modern state of mind.***
>
> Le Corbusier, *Vers une architecture*

The archives of *L'Esprit nouveau* in the Fondation Le Corbusier in Paris indicate that throughout the years of the magazine's publication, from 1920 to 1925,[1] Le Corbusier collected a great number of industrial catalogues and manufacturers' publicity brochures lavishly illustrated with photographs of their products. These include not only the automobiles Voisin, Peugeot, Citroën, and Delage, Farman airplanes and Caproni seaplanes, suitcases and trunks from Innovation, office furniture by Or'mo and file cabinets by Ronéo, hand bags, sport bags, and cigarette cases by Hermès, and Omega watches; but also, and perhaps

L'ESPRIT NOUVEAU

REVUE INTERNATIONALE D'ESTHÉTIQUE

PARAISSANT LE 15 DE CHAQUE MOIS

DIRECTEUR : PAUL DERMÉE

ESTHÉTIQUE EXPÉRIMENTALE
PEINTURE SCULPTURE ARCHITECTURE
LITTÉRATURE MUSIQUE
ESTHÉTIQUE DE L'INGÉNIEUR
LE THÉATRE LE MUSIC-HALL LE CINÉMA LE CIRQUE LES SPORTS
LE COSTUME LE LIVRE LE MEUBLE
ESTHÉTIQUE DE LA VIE MODERNE

N° 1

SOMMAIRE

L'Esprit Nouveau		3
L'esthétique nouvelle et la science de l'art,	Victor BASCH.	5
Notes sur l'art de Seurat,	BISSIÈRE.	13
Découverte du Lyrisme,	Paul DERMÉE.	29
Sur la Plastique,	A. OZENFANT et Ch. E. JEANNERET.	38
La Musique Polonaise,	Henry PRUNIÈRES	49
Les deux routes	**	60
Picasso,	André SALMON	61
L'Esthétique du Cinéma,	B. TOKINE	84

DANS CE NUMÉRO

30 photogravures et deux reproduction aux trois couleurs.

Trois rappels à MM. les Architectes,	LE CORBUSIER-SAUGNIER.	9
Le Cirque, art nouveau,	Céline ARNAULD.	9
Notes sur les revues 1914-1920,	G. de LACAZE-DUTHIERS	9
Calligrammes (*Apollinaire*),	Louis ARAGON	10
Les Expositions (Picabia),	G. RIBEMONT-DESSAIGNES	10
La littérature de langue espagnole d'aujourd'hui,	Vicente HUIDOBRO	11
La nouvelle poésie allemande,	Ivan GOLL	11
Échos de l'Hôtel Drouot		11
	etc...	13

Voir au dos les avantages et les primes réservés aux Abonnés.

PRIX NET : 6 francs français
POUR TOUS PAYS

ÉDITIONS DE L'ESPRIT NOUVEAU
SOCIÉTÉ ANONYME AU CAPITAL DE 100.000 FRANCS
13, QUAI DE CONTI
PARIS (VIe)

Front cover of L'Esprit nouveau *1 (1920).*

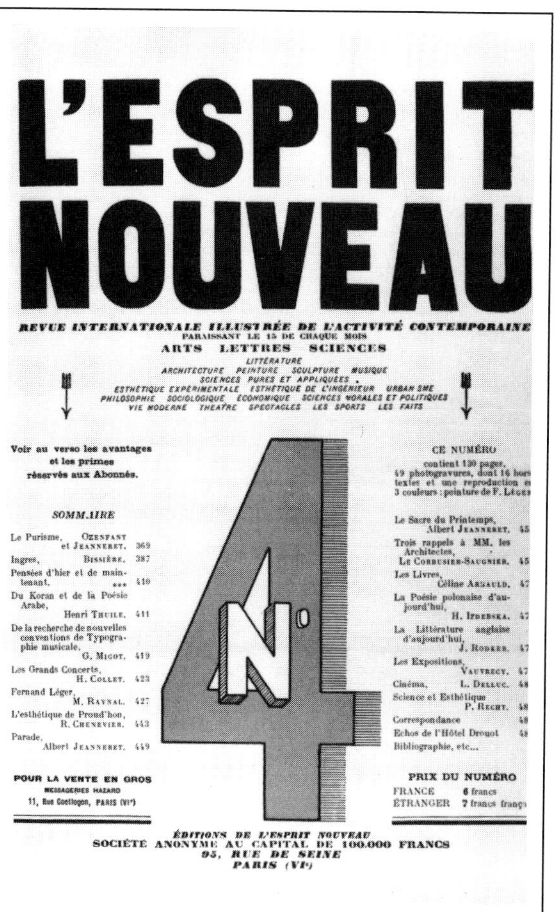

L'ESPRIT NOUVEAU

REVUE INTERNATIONALE ILLUSTRÉE DE L'ACTIVITÉ CONTEMPORAINE
PARAISSANT LE 15 DE CHAQUE MOIS
ARTS LETTRES SCIENCES
LITTÉRATURE
ARCHITECTURE PEINTURE SCULPTURE MUSIQUE
SCIENCES PURES ET APPLIQUÉES .
ESTHÉTIQUE EXPÉRIMENTALE ESTHÉTIQUE DE L'INGÉNIEUR URBANISME
PHILOSOPHIE SOCIOLOGIQUE ÉCONOMIQUE SCIENCES MORALES ET POLITIQUES
VIE MODERNE THEATRE SPECTACLES LES SPORTS LES FAITS

Voir au verso les avantages et les primes réservés aux Abonnés.

N° 4

SOMMAIRE

POUR LA VENTE EN GROS
MESSAGERIES HAZARD
11, Rue Coetlogon, PARIS (VIe)

CE NUMÉRO

contient 130 pages, 49 photogravures, dont 16 hors textes et une reproduction e[n] 3 couleurs : peinture de F. LÉGE[R]

PRIX DU NUMÉRO
FRANCE 6 francs
ÉTRANGER 7 francs franç[ais]

ÉDITIONS DE L'ESPRIT NOUVEAU
SOCIÉTÉ ANONYME AU CAPITAL DE 100.000 FRANCS
95, RUE DE SEINE
PARIS (VIe)

Front cover of* L'Esprit nouveau *4 (1921). Note the change in subtitle in issue 4 and that Paul Dermée is no longer editor.

Proof of an advertisement for Delage prepared for* L'Esprit nouveau *but never published.

Page from a Caproni publicity brochure in the* L'Esprit nouveau *archives.

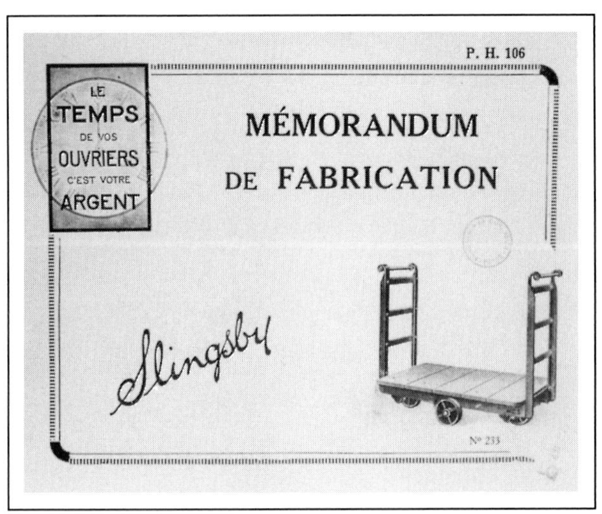

"The Time of Your Workers Is Your Money": front cover of a Slingsby catalogue in the L'Esprit nouveau *archives.*

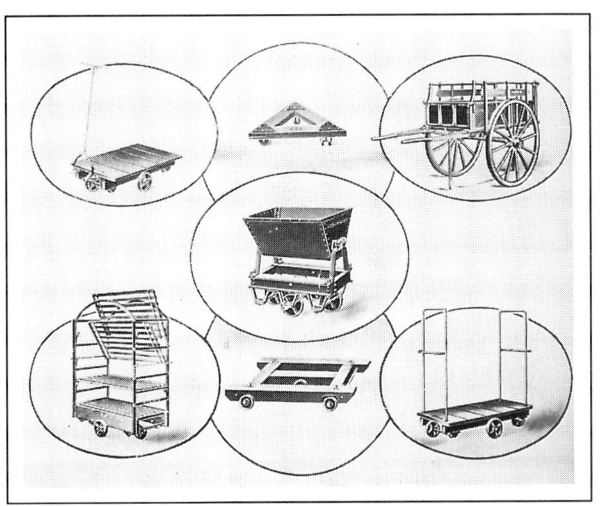

Inside page of Slingsby catalogue.

more surprisingly, turbines by Brown Boveri, high-pressure centrifugal ventilators by Rateau, and industrial equipment by Clermont-Ferrand and Slingsby. Le Corbusier went, in fact, very much out of his way to obtain this material, constantly writing to companies to ask for it. Not only were the catalogues useful in securing advertising contracts for *L'Esprit nouveau* (the products of most of the companies ended up being advertised in the magazine), but they also had an influence on his work.

Along with the catalogues, Le Corbusier collected department store mail order brochures (Printemps, Au Bon Marché, La Samaritaine) and clippings from newspapers and magazines of the time, such as *The Autocar, Science et la vie, Revue du beton armé, L'Illustré*. In fact, he seems to have collected everything that struck him visually, from postcards to the cover of a child's school notebook illustrated with the basic geometric volumes.[2] This material, these "everyday images," are the source of many illustrations in *L'Esprit nouveau* and the five books that came out of that experience: *Vers une architecture, Urbanisme, L'Art décoratif d'aujourd'hui, La Peinture moderne*, and *Almanach de l'architecture moderne*.[3] The illustrations in *L'Art décoratif d'aujourd'hui* especially come from this "disposable" material; here images from department store catalogues, industrial publicity, and newspapers like *L'Illustré* alternate with ones taken from art history and natural science books. One entire page is devoted to a publicity photograph of an industrial lamp that was apparently promised by the manufacturer but never obtained; in its place one reads the story of the abortive attempt: *on ne se comprend pas*.

Le Corbusier's arguments in *L'Esprit nouveau* rely to a great extent on the juxtapositions of image and text. Unlike the "representational" use of imagery in traditional books—whereby the image is subordinate to and consistent with the written text—Le Corbusier's arguments are to be understood in terms of never-resolved collisions of these two elements. In this unconventional manner of conceiving a book, one can

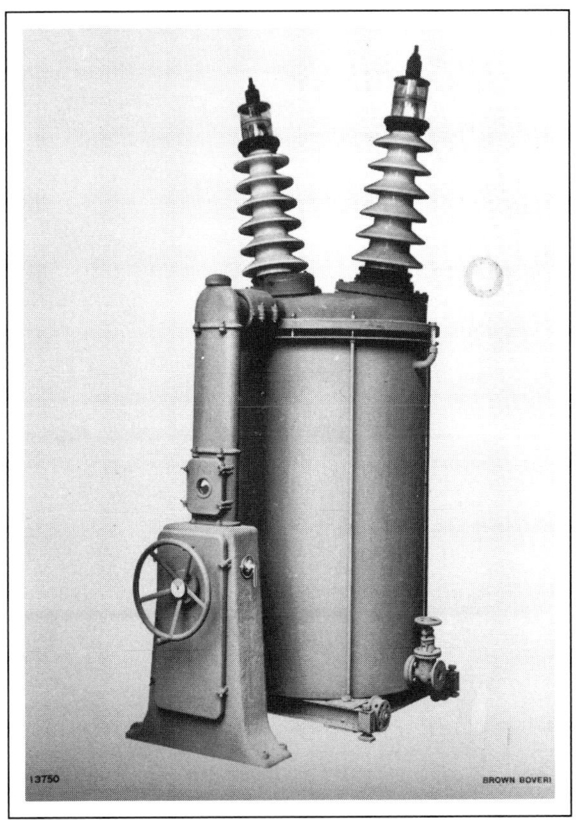

Electric turbine by the company Brown Boveri. Photograph in the L'Esprit nouveau *archives.*

Page entière réservée au

cliché d'un phare des

Anciens Établissements Sauter-Harlé

16, Avenue de Suffren,

PARIS

EXEMPLE D'UNE HISTOIRE DE CLICHÉS :

Mai 1924. Foire de Paris, Stand de l'Électricité : demande d'une photo du grand phare exposé par Sauter-Harlé.

Début Juillet : 1er téléphone pour réclamer le document (pourparlers avec plusieurs chefs de service, exposés de nos buts, moyens, etc..., etc...).

Quelques jours après : second téléphone (mêmes discours).

Quelques jours plus tard : visite d'un des directeurs de L'Esprit Nouveau *aux Établissements Sauter-Harlé ; attente de 1 h. 1/2 dans les antichambres. Premier ingénieur, chef de service : exposé du but de la visite. Deuxième ingénieur : second exposé. Troisième ingénieur (enfin compétent !) : troisième exposé. Accueil plein de réserve : " Écrivez à la direction, à M. W... en exposant votre projet, vos buts, vos moyens et en spécifiant bien que ce sera entièrement gratuit ".*

Le même jour : lettre d'exposé complet avec rappel des... stations du calvaire !

30 Juillet : troisième coup de téléphone ; réponse : " on ne sait pas. "

31 Juillet : quatrième coup de téléphone ; réponse : " on ne sait pas. "

1er Août : cinquième téléphone au patron M. W... Exposé général. M. W... demande qu'on écrive en envoyant un numéro de la revue, car M. R... autre patron, a déclaré qu'il ne donnerait pas la photo pour L'Esprit Nouveau.

Même jour, une demi-heure après, taxi. Visite de l'un des directeurs de L'Esprit Nouveau *à M. W... Pas d'attente d'antichambre. M. W... fait un interrogatoire serré ; exposé éloquent des buts, des moyens, etc. Conclusion de M. W..., sévère : " notre phare n'est pas décoratif, etc... " Coupant court : " Je vous téléphonerai lundi le sort réservé à votre* requête *". M. W... s'en va, sans saluer.*

Depuis 15 jours les Établissements Sauter-Harlé savent que nous tirons notre N° 25 et qu'aujourd'hui est le dernier jour ! Mentalité fréquente de l'ingénieur drapé dans la haute fierté du chiffre. Incompréhension totale de ce qui n'est pas l'étroit champ de ses investigations. Telle est l'histoire d'un cliché, exemple entre tant d'autres, désespérant. On ne se comprend pas.

Page of* L'Esprit nouveau *25 reserved for the photograph of an industrial lamp.

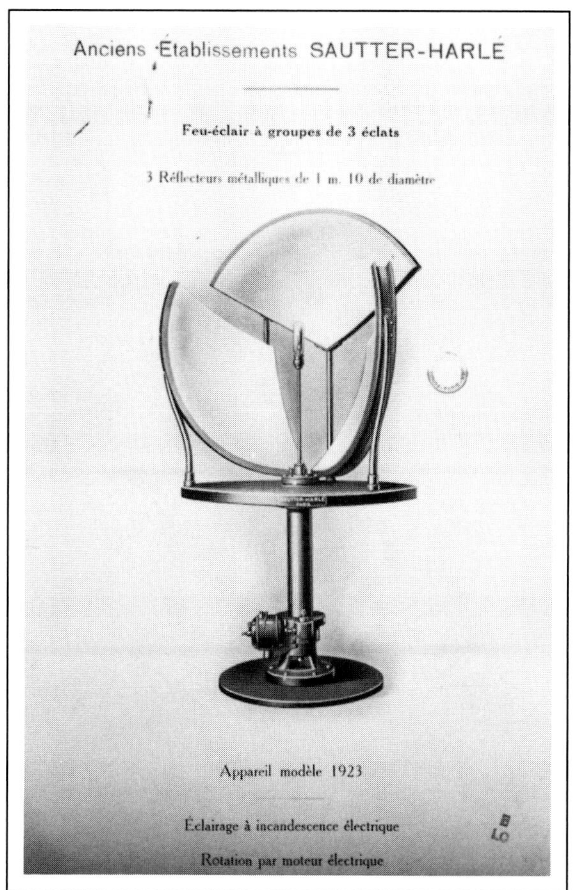

Photograph of a Sautter-Harlé lamp in the* L'Esprit nouveau *archives. The image arrived too late!

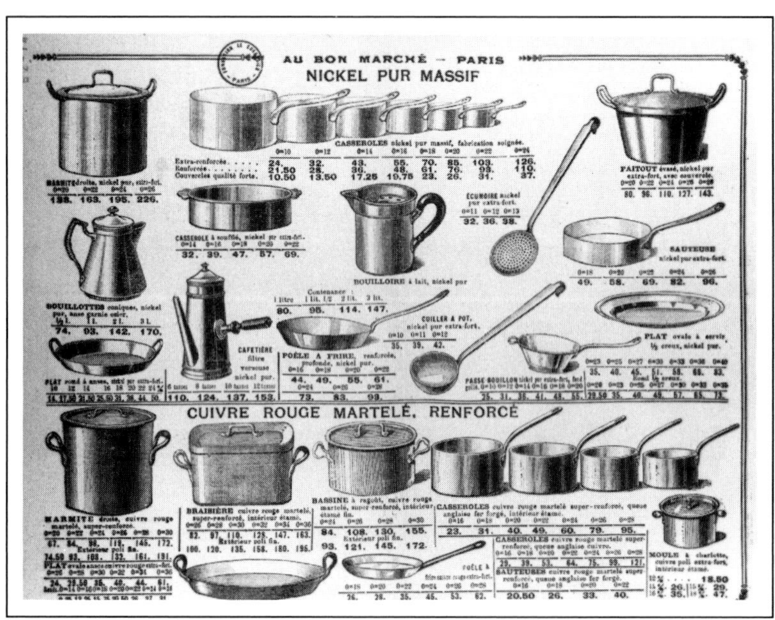

Page from a mail order brochure of the department store Au Bon Marché, Paris, in the **L'Esprit nouveau** ***archives.***

see the influence of advertising techniques. As in advertising, the strongest effect is achieved through the impact of the visual material.

When a low-pressure centrifugal ventilator from the Rateau company is placed on the page opposite the opening of the chapter "Architecture ou Révolution" in *Vers une architecture*, and a turbine from the Centrale électrique de Gennevilliers placed at the head of the chapter, the message derives from the interaction between title and images: it is not social conditions in general that most preoccupy Le Corbusier, it would seem, but the condition of the architect in an industrial society. The Rateau ventilator puns on the meaning of mechanical revolution in a literal sense and industrial revolution. In the article one reads, "modern society does not recompense its intellectuals judiciously, but it still tolerates the old arrangements as to property, which are a serious barrier to transforming the town or the house." Le Corbusier here is defending public property and the need to address the housing problem through mass production—directing his critique, precisely, to where a "revolution" in the position of the architect in an industrial society is at stake.[4]

The imagery derived from advertising is considerably more pervasive in the pages of *L'Esprit nouveau* than that from strictly architectural sources—for example, Le Corbusier's famous borrowing of photographs of American silos from the Gropius article in the *Werkbund Jahrbuch* of 1913. Whereas the Gropius borrowing (and the subsequent traveling of this image through avant-garde journals and publications: *De Stijl*, *MA*, *Buch neuer Künstler*, etc.)[5] might also be read as a "media phenomenon"—as Reyner Banham has noted, none of the architects had seen the silos in question[6]—the presence of this heterodox publicity material in *L'Esprit nouveau*'s pages suggests a shift in the conventional interpretation of that journal: from an internal exchange among avant-garde movements (as if enclosed in their own "magic circle," uncontaminated by the materials of low culture) to a dialogue with an emerging new reality, namely the culture of advertising and mass media.

224 VERS UNE ARCHITECTURE

Conclusion : Il s'agit d'un problème d'époque. Davantage, du problème de l'époque. L'équilibre des sociétés est une question de bâtiment. Nous concluons sur ce dilemme défendable : *Architecture ou Révolution.*

ARCHITECTURE
OU RÉVOLUTION

Double-page spread from* Vers une architecture, *1923, with photographs of a ventilator and a turbine taken from industrial catalogues.

***Page from a Société Rateau publicity brochure in the* L'Esprit nouveau *archives, with the image of the ventilator used by Le Corbusier in* Vers une architecture.**

The modern media are war technology. They evolved from the technical revolution of the post–World War I years in much the same way as the vehicles of speed, automobiles and airplanes, had emerged from the prewar revolution.[7] The media were developed as part of the technology and instrumentation of war. What made possible the involvement of so many distant countries in World War I was communications, which bridged the distance between the battlefield and the places the news was being transmitted, between the fighting and the decision making. The battle of the Marne is said to have been won by *coups de téléphone*.[8] The classic accounts of World War I explain the significant role of propaganda built up among nations, especially through the medium of the newspaper. After the war, this technology was gradually domesticated. Just as regular airline services were being established throughout Europe at the beginning of the twenties, radios and telecommunications had become household items.

In contrast to the amount of attention that has been focused on Le Corbusier's architecture in relation to the culture of the "machine age,"[9] very little has been paid to its relation to the new means of communication, the relation of architecture to the culture of the consumer age. Ironically, the very idea of the "machine age," which served the period as a symbolic concept, was largely induced by the advertising industry.[10] Architecture's relationship to the mechanisms of that industry needs to be analyzed in order to establish architecture's role in that period.

Retrospectively speaking, the concept of the "machine age" has served the critical purpose of sustaining the myth of the "modern movement" as an autonomous artistic practice in which the artist/architect is "interpreter" of the new industrial reality. Critics interested in sustaining this myth are those who under labels such as "machine age" put together such different attitudes toward the industrial reality as, for instance, the futurist, the dadaist, and Le Corbusier's. The differences, however, are more striking than the similarities.

L'Illustration, *15 February 1919.*

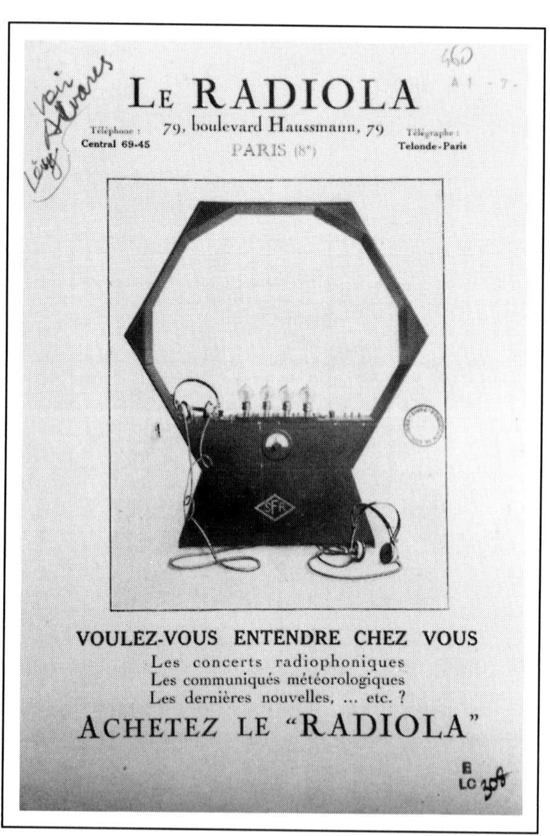

Front cover of a Radiola publicity brochure in the* L'Esprit nouveau *archives.

For example, when Le Corbusier selects images from the airplane catalogues of Farman, Voisin, Bleriot, etc. for the article "Des yeux qui ne voient pas" in *L'Esprit nouveau* (later reprinted as a chapter in *Vers une architecture*), it is important to note that he is not talking here about airplanes but about mass-produced houses. His interest is the insertion of architecture into the contemporary conditions of production. (The futurists, on the other hand, while using the same images, were indifferent to the processes of industrialization.) In fact, Le Corbusier had more than just a philosophical interest. He actually negotiated with leading industrialists like Gabriel Voisin. At the end of the war the Voisin company was trying to keep its aircraft plant occupied by entering the building industry.[11] Voisin produced two prototypes of houses that were published in an article in *L'Esprit nouveau* ("Les Maisons 'Voisin'"), where Le Corbusier and Ozenfant write:

> **Impossible to wait on the slow collaboration of the successive efforts of excavator, mason, carpenter, joiner, tiler, plumber . . . houses must go up all of a piece, made by machine tools in factory, assembled as Ford assembles cars, on moving conveyor belts. . . . Aviation is achieving prodigies of serial production. . . . It is in aircraft factories that the *soldier-architects* have decided to build the houses; they decided to build this house like an aircraft, with the same structural methods, lightweight framing, metal braces, tubular supports.**[12]

Le Corbusier's concern with the contemporary conditions of production is necessarily a concern with the mechanisms that sustained that production: advertising, mass media, and publicity. The images of airplanes that he was deploying were very much part of the popular imagination. Illustrated newspapers, for example, moved from the fetishistic display of images of aircraft in war to images of the new passenger aircraft, such that around 1919 these images appear side by side. Le Corbusier was employing modern publicity techniques: on the one hand he grabs the readers' visual attention through the spectacular image to direct them to the concept he is promoting, the mass production of houses. On the other hand, subliminally inscribed within the images he chooses is the domestication of military technology.

In these terms, Le Corbusier not only had an "intuitive understanding of media and a definite feel for news," as Marie-Odile Briot writes in one of the few existing comments on Le Corbusier and the media.[13] Purist culture, by which I mean Le Corbusier and Ozenfant's project of arriving at a theory of culture in industrialized everyday life throughout the pages of *L'Esprit nouveau,* can be read as a "reflection," in both the specular and intellectual sense of the word, on the culture of the new means of communication, the world of advertising and mass media.

To the first meaning of the word belong Le Corbusier's use of mass media culture, of the everyday images of the press, industrial publicity, department store mail order catalogues, and advertisements, as "ready-mades" to be incorporated in his editorial work. The architect's tracings and sketches on the catalogues suggest that he was not taking these images in a passive manner; these drawings testify to a formal search ultimately directed to his design practice. But there is more, and this is where the second meaning of "reflection" comes in. Le Corbusier identified in the very existence of the printed media an important conceptual shift regarding the function of culture and the perception of the exterior world by the modern individual. In *L'Art décoratif d'aujourd'hui* he writes, "The fabulous development of the book, of print, and the classification of the whole of the most recent archaeological era, has flooded our minds and overwhelmed us. We are in a completely new situation. *Everything is known to us*."[14]

This new condition in which one knows "everything about everything" represents a critical transformation of traditional culture. Paradoxically, the classical, humanist accumulation of knowledge becomes problematic.[15] We can begin to read Le Corbusier's position vis-à-vis this trans-

Cliché Hostache.

MAISONS EN SÉRIE

"Maisons en série." Page from Vers une architecture *(1923).*

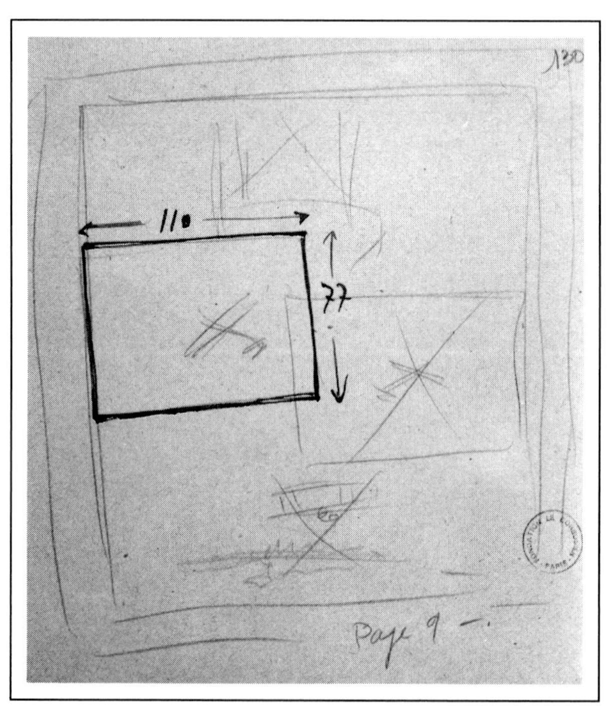

Sketch page indicating image of an airplane to be reproduced from a Farman catalogue.

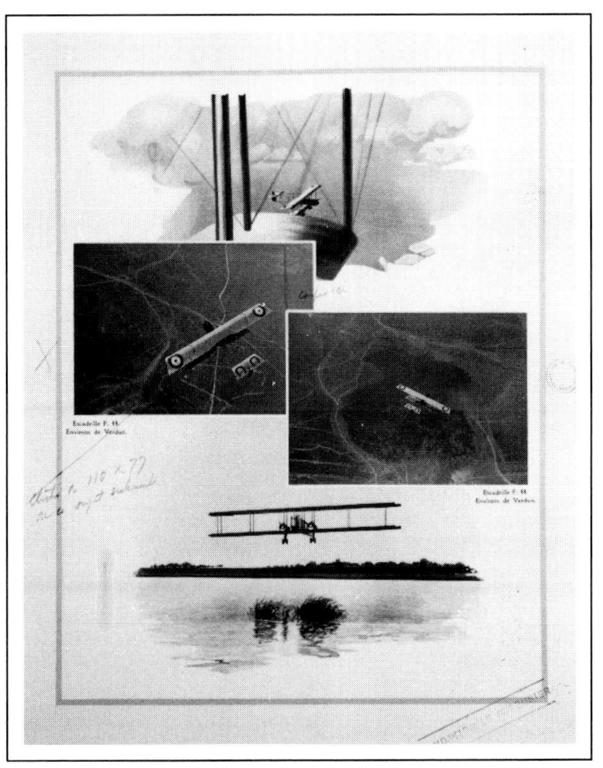

***Annotated page from a Farman publicity brochure. The image chosen will later head the article "Des yeux qui ne voient pas . . . : II Les avions" in* L'Esprit nouveau *9 (1921), reprinted as a chapter in* Vers une architecture.**

Page from Vers une architecture *with image from the Farman catalogue.*

Wing of Farman airplane as seen through the window by a passenger. L'Illustration, *February 1919.*

LES MAISONS " VOISIN "

Il semblait jusqu'ici qu'une maison fut lourdement attachée au sol par la profondeur de ses fondations et la pesanteur de ses murs épais ; cette maison, c'était le symbole de l'immuabilité, la « maison natale », le « berceau de famille », etc. Ce n'est point par un artifice que la maison Voisin est l'une des premières à marquer le contre-pied même de cette conception. La science de bâtir a évolué d'une manière foudroyante en ces derniers temps ; l'art de bâtir a pris racine fortement dans la science.

L'énoncé du problème a fourni à lui seul les moyens de réalisation et, incontinent, s'affirme ici fortement l'immense révolution dans laquelle est entrée l'architecture : lorsqu'on modifie à tel point le mode de bâtir, automatiquement l'esthétique de la construction se trouve bouleversée. Cet énoncé est le suivant ; il fut formulé par des soldats en pleine guerre qui se dirent en voyant tomber tant d'hommes autour d'eux :

"Les Maisons 'Voisin,'"
Le Corbusier-Saugnier, **L'Esprit nouveau** ***2 (1920).***

"Les Maisons 'Voisin.'"

Mockup of layout of Hermès bags for L'Esprit nouveau *24 (1924).*

The equipment of a French soldier during the war.* L'Illustration, *February 1919.

formation by addressing one aspect of it, his view of the status of the artwork in an industrial society.

The role of art in society was, in Le Corbusier's view, radically altered by the existence of mass media. In *L'Art décoratif d'aujourd'hui* he writes, "Now broadly disseminated through books, in the schools, newspapers, and at the cinema is the linguistic form of our emotions, which, in the centuries prior to our own, found expression *in the arts*."[16] And in the introduction to *La Peinture moderne,* he writes with Ozenfant, "Imitative art has been left behind by photography and cinema. The press and the book operate much more efficiently than art relative to religious, moral, or political aims. What is the destiny of the art of today?"[17]

The Uneasy Status of the Object

One question that presents itself in relation to Le Corbusier's use of publicity images as readymades is to what extent this is paralleled by dadaist practices. This question contains a conceptual problem that has become important in recent critical discourse—the difference between modernism and the avant-garde in the context of the first half of this century.[18]

Picabia, for instance, picks up machine images from mail order catalogues and advertisements, redraws them, and endows them with legends to make a series of "objects-portraits," among them: *Voilà Haviland* (portrait of Paul Haviland as a portable electric lamp), *Ici, c'est ici Stieglitz* (Alfred Stieglitz as a folding camera), *Portrait d'une jeune fille américaine dans l'état de nudité* (an American girl as a spark plug), etc., all reproduced in Stieglitz's journal *291*.[19] But, unlike Picabia, Le Corbusier does not remain prisoner of the representative paradigm of a tragic *mise-en-scène*. Le Corbusier juxtaposes images on the page: meaning is in the void, in the silence of the white space between the images and the written text. The mechanical element is not used in a representational manner but as a "disjunctive" element.

A comparison between Le Corbusier and Marcel Duchamp may be more productive. Take the image of a bidet by the manufacturer Maison Pirsoul that Le Corbusier publishes at the head of the article "Autres icones: les musées" in *L'Esprit nouveau,* and Duchamp's *Fountain by R. Mutt* of 1917. (Incidentally, J. L. Mott was, at the time, a prominent manufacturer of ironworks. Aside from plumbing fixtures, Mott produced actual fountains, elaborate objects with mythological themes—very "artistic" indeed. This suggests that *Fountain by R. Mutt* was, among other things, a pun on this manufacturer's name and products that Duchamp must have known through advertisements.)[20]

Fountain by R. Mutt and the bidet by Maison Pirsoul are, if we take representation as a transparent medium, two plumbing fixtures. And both are obviously intended (exploiting the sexual allusions so dear to the dadaists) as assaults on the institution of art. Less evident is the fact that they both exist only as reproductions. The origin of the first is its publication in the pages of *L'Esprit nouveau;* there is no other "original." The second was supposed to have been exhibited in the Salon of the Independents in New York but never was, as it was rejected; what remains is only the photograph of it. Nevertheless, it is this document, together with a piece of contemporary criticism by Beatrice Wood in *The Blind Man,* a New York dada journal, that has assured this piece a place in history. The original object, the actual urinal, has been lost. Thus both of these "objects" exist only as "reproductions." Another aspect of the lack of an original has to do with the objects each reproduction represents. Duchamp's artwork is a mass-produced object turned upside-down, signed, and sent to an art exhibition. Le Corbusier's "raw material" is an advertising image, obviously taken from an industrial catalogue, and placed in the pages of an art journal.

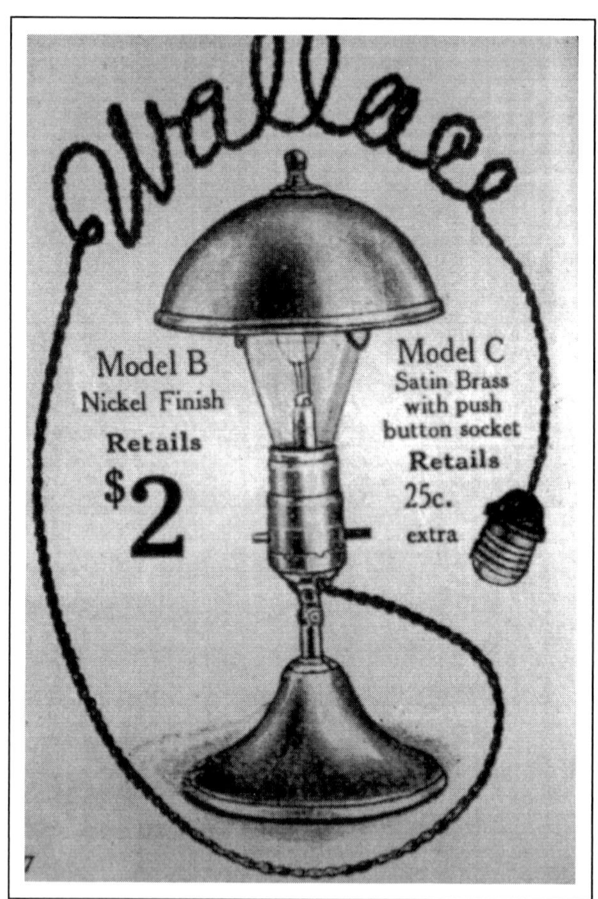

Advertisement for a Wallace portable electrical lamp.

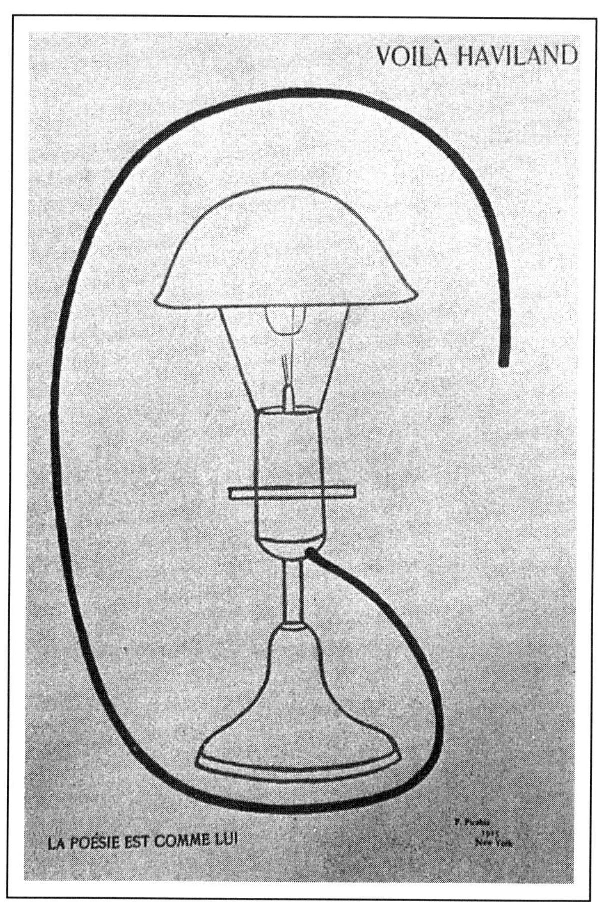

Francis Picabia, **Voilà Haviland: la poésie est comme lui** *(1915)*.

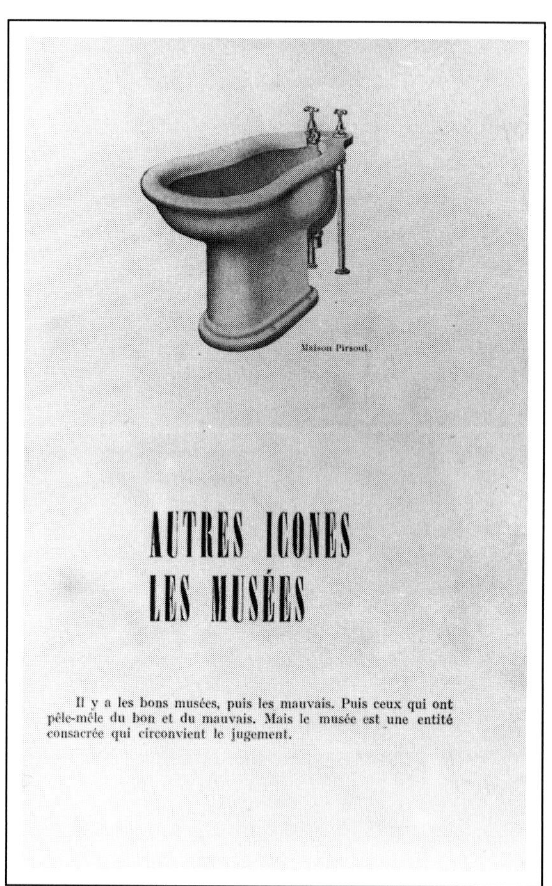
Maison Pirsoul.

AUTRES ICONES
LES MUSÉES

Il y a les bons musées, puis les mauvais. Puis ceux qui ont pêle-mêle du bon et du mauvais. Mais le musée est une entité consacrée qui circonvient le jugement.

Page from* L'Esprit nouveau *20 (1924).

Fountain by R. Mutt

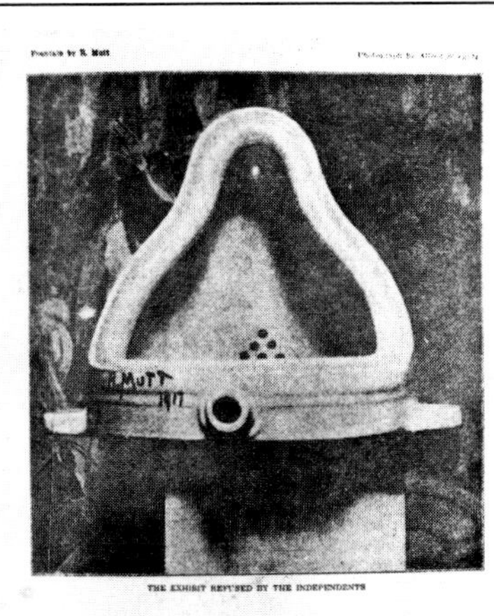

THE EXHIBIT REFUSED BY THE INDEPENDENTS

THE BLIND MAN

The Richard Mutt Case

They say any artist paying six dollars may exhibit.

Mr. Richard Mutt sent in a fountain. Without discussion this article disappeared and never was exhibited.

What were the grounds for refusing Mr. Mutt's fountain:—

1. *Some contended it was immoral, vulgar.*
2. *Others, it was plagiarism, a plain piece of plumbing.*

Now Mr. Mutt's fountain is not immoral, that is absurd, no more than a bath tub is immoral. It is a fixture that you see every day in plumbers' show windows.

Whether Mr. Mutt with his own hands made the fountain or not has no importance. He CHOSE it. He took an ordinary article of life, placed it so that its useful significance disappeared under the new title and point of view—created a new thought for that object.

As for plumbing, that is absurd. The only works of art America has given are her plumbing and her bridges.

"Buddha of the Bathroom"

I suppose monkeys hated to lose their tail. Necessary, useful and an ornament, monkey imagination could not stretch to a tailless existence (and frankly, do you see the biological beauty of our loss of them?), yet now that we are used to it, we get on pretty well without them. But evolution is not pleasing to the monkey race; "there is a death in every change" and we monkeys do not love death as we should. We are like those philosophers whom Dante placed in his Inferno with their heads set the wrong way on their shoulders. We walk forward looking backward, each with more of his predecessors' personality than his own. Our eyes are not ours.

The ideas that our ancestors have joined together let no man put asunder! In *La Dissociation des Idees,* Remy de Gourmont, quietly analytic, shows how sacred is the marriage of ideas. At least one charming thing about our human institution is that although a man marry he can never be *only* a husband. Besides being a money-making device and the *one* man that *one* woman can sleep with in legal purity without sin he may even be as well some other woman's very personification of her abstract idea, Sin, while to his employees he is nothing but their "Boss," to his children only their "Father," and to himself certainly something more complex.

But with objects and ideas it is different. Recently we have had a chance to observe their meticulous monogomy.

When the jurors of *The Society of Independent Artists* fairly rushed to remove the bit of sculpture called the *Fountain* sent in by Richard Mutt, because the object was irrevocably associated in their atavistic minds with a certain natural function of a secretive sort. Yet to any "innocent" eye

"The Richard Mutt Case," in **The Blind Man** *2 (1917).*

Cover of the publicity catalogue **Fountains**, *issued by the manufacturer J. L. Mott.*

Illustrated page from the* Fountains *catalogue.

les lettres

Cubistes contre Dadaistes

La 3ème Chambre du tribunal civil, présidée par M. Lemoine, a rendu son jugement hier dans l'affaire « l'Esprit Nouveau » contre Mr. Dermee.

MM. Ozenfant et Jeanneret, deux artistes cubistes ultra-modernes, avaient décidé de fonder la Société d'édition en formation « l'Esprit Nouveau », une revue d'art plastique où toutes les idées originales, mais présentant un caractère artistique, étaient largement admises.

Une édition très luxueuse, la revue « l'Esprit Nouveau », était en préparation, et comme il s'était agit de trouver un bon agent de publicité pour alimenter le budget de la revue, MM. Ozenfant et Jeanneret s'adressèrent au Syndicat de la publicité qui leur procura Mr. Dermee.

Celui-ci exigea un contrat de directeur aux appointements de 1.000 francs par mois pendant dix ans.

Au bout de quelques temps, Mr. Dermee, au lieu de se contenter de rester dans le « Cubisme », voulu se lancer dans le « dadaïsme » ; diverses manifestations furent organisées par lui, dont le grotesque et le ridicule ont été signalés en leur temps et ont eu leur écho dans la presse.

MM. Ozenfant et Jeanneret durent empêcher la publication des articles de Mr. Dermee et le mettre en demeure de quitter la direction de la revue Cubiste, l'attitude de leur ancien directeur compromettant le « sérieux » de l'art cubiste et nuisant à la prospérité de la Société d'édition « l'Esprit Nouveau.

Le tribunal estimant que la Société commerciale « l'Esprit Nouveau » n'avait pas ratifié le contrat passé par MM. Ozenfant et Jeanneret, a débouté, purement et sim-

"Cubistes contre Dadaistes." Newspaper clipping from the archives of L'Esprit nouveau.

Postcard in the archives of* L'Esprit nouveau. *Origin unknown.

These are the superficial similarities between the two documents. Their difference, however, resides in the meaning of each gesture and the context in which it is placed. The context of the *Fountain by R. Mutt* is the exhibition space. It does not matter that it was never exhibited there. It has to be thought of in that setting; it cannot be thought outside its interpretation. It doesn't exist outside its interpretation. As Peter Bürger says in his book *Theory of the Avant-Garde*, the meaning of Duchamp's gesture derives from the contrast between mass-produced object on the one hand and signature and art exhibit on the other. In signing a mass-produced object, Duchamp is negating the category of individual creation and unmasking the art market, where a signature means more than the quality of the work. The avant-garde gesture, in Bürger's definition, is an attack on art as an institution.[21]

To what extent can we consider Le Corbusier's bidet an avant-garde gesture? The context of the bidet is *L'Esprit nouveau*. The image heads an article titled "Other Icons: The Museums," which belongs to the series published between 1923 and 1924, reprinted in *L'Art décoratif d'aujourd'hui* in 1925. The series was issued in preparation for the 1925 Exposition des Arts Décoratifs in Paris. In the article Le Corbusier writes, "Museums have just been born. There were none in other times. In the tendentious incoherence of museums the model does not exist, only the elements of a point of view. The true museum is the one that contains everything."

These observations on museums again appear close to Duchamp. The museum viewer can only perform an intellectual operation; contemplation is no longer possible. When the *Fountain by R. Mutt* was rejected by the Independents as "plagiarism, a plain piece of plumbing," Beatrice Wood wrote in *The Blind Man*, "Whether Mr. Mutt with his own hands made the fountain or not has no importance. He CHOSE it. He took an ordinary article of life, placed it so that its useful significance disappeared under the new title and point of view—created a new thought for that object."[22] If the museum transforms the work of art—in fact, creates it as such—and allows the viewer only an intellectual experience of it, Marcel Duchamp's act consists in putting this condition in evidence: creating a new thought for an ordinary product.

The Maison Pirsoul bidet is an everyday object, an industrial product, and Le Corbusier never intended it to abandon this status. His statement that it should be in a museum does not mean he intended to present it as an art object. That the bidet should be in a museum—to be precise, in the museum of decorative arts—means for Le Corbusier that the bidet speaks of our culture, as the folklore of a certain place spoke of that place's culture in other times. But in the places where the railway had already arrived, as Le Corbusier realized, after Loos, folklore could no longer be preserved. The industrial product had become the folklore of the age of communications.[23] Both folklore and industrial production are collective phenomena. Modern decorative art did not have the individual character of artistic creation but the anonymous one of industrial production, of folklore.

While Duchamp was questioning the institution of art and artistic individual production, Le Corbusier, more in line with Adolf Loos (who was also fascinated with sanitary material), was distinguishing between the object of use and the art object. Indeed, Le Corbusier's arguments in *L'Art décoratif d'aujourd'hui* are strongly indebted to Loos, who not only wrote the famous essay "The Plumbers" (1898) but in 1907 wrote another called "The Superfluous." This text is devoted to the architects of the Werkbund. Loos writes:

> **Now they have all gathered together in a congress in Munich. They want to demonstrate their importance to our craftsmen and industrialists. . . . Only the products of industries that have managed to keep away from the**

"Usurpation/Le Folklore," **L'Esprit nouveau** *21 (1924), reprinted in* **L'Art décoratif d'aujourd'hui.**

> **superfluous have attained the style of our times: our automobile industry, our production of glass, our optical instruments, our canes and umbrellas, our suitcases and trunks, our saddles and our silver cigarette cases, our jewelry and our dresses are modern. . . . Certainly, the cultivated products of our time do not have any relation to art. . . . The nineteenth century will pass into history as having effected a radical break between art and industry.**[24]

Contrary to the received view of Loos, it is not only the unselfconscious craftsman, the master saddler, who is "modern." Modern, for Loos, includes everything that we do not know as such: anonymous collective production. Le Corbusier, like Loos, distinguishes between art and life, between the art object and the everyday object. He does not deny the individuality of artistic creation. In *L'Art décoratif d'aujourd'hui* he writes:

> **Permanence of the decorative arts? or more precisely, of the objects that surround us? It is there that we have to pass judgment: the Sistine Chapel first, then chairs and file cabinets—to tell the truth, problems of a second order, as the cut of a man's suit is a second-order problem in his life. Hierarchy. First the Sistine Chapel, that is, works where passion is inscribed. Then, machines for sitting, for classifying, for illuminating, *machine-types*, problems of purification, of cleanliness. . . .**[25]

There are three key words in this passage: *permanence*, *passion*, and *purification*. The first two are associated with art, the third with the everyday object. For Le Corbusier the essential thing about art is its permanence, lastingness. As Banham has noted, Le Corbusier rejected the futurist theory of the *caducità* or ephemerality of the work of art. He distinguishes works of art from works of technology and insists that only the latter are perishable.[26]

Against the products of reason Le Corbusier sets the products of passion, the passion of a creative man, a genius. The capacity of a work of art to provoke an emotion, qualitatively different from the pleasures of a beautiful object, lies in recognizing the passionate gesture of the artist who created it, in any time or place. He thus sets the artwork apart from the everyday object, the artist from all the other "producers" in society.

Finally, *L'Art décoratif d'aujourd'hui* promotes cleanliness and purification. This notion reminds us once again of Loos, when in "The Plumbers," after commenting that "the most remarkable difference between Austria and America is the plumbing" (reminiscent of Duchamp's claim that "the only works of art America has given are her plumbing and her bridges"),[27] he goes on to say.:

> **We don't really need art. We don't even have a culture of our own yet. This is where the state could come to the rescue. Instead of putting the cart before the horse, instead of spending money on art, let's try producing a culture. Let's put up baths next to the academies and employ bath attendants along with professors.**[28]

However, Loos's caustic and irreverent writings should be distinguished from the shock tactics of dada. A comment made by Walter Benjamin in reference to Karl Kraus is applicable here to Loos, who predicted that in the twentieth century a single civilization would dominate the earth: "Satire is the only legitimate form of regional art." "The greatest type of satirist," continues Benjamin, "never had firmer grounds under his feet than amid a generation about to board tanks and put on gas masks, a mankind that has run out of tears but not of laughter."[29] Le Corbusier is a postwar figure, Loos a prewar one. Le Corbusier's architect is, precisely, a "soldier-architect"; Loos's architect is "a mason who knows Latin" (a cultivated craftsman). While it is possible to establish relations between their work, a crucial question remains unanswered: how much does this demarcation line of the war cause them to be such different historical witnesses?

The Architect as (Re)producer

In his books and articles Le Corbusier borrows the rhetoric and persuasive techniques of modern advertising for his own theoretical arguments and manipulates actual advertisements to incorporate his own vision, thus blurring the limits between text and publicity. He does this consciously, arguing that in this way persuasion is most effective: "*L'esprit nouveau*," he announces in the publicity brochure sent to industrialists, "is read calmly. You surprise your client into calmness, far from business, and he listens to you because he doesn't know you are going to solicit him."

In obtaining advertising contracts Le Corbusier often reversed the usual procedure. Once he had incorporated images from industrial catalogues in his articles, or even published actual advertisements in the review, he would send the company a letter with a copy of *L'Esprit nouveau* and request payment for the publicity the company was receiving. Of course, the request was not made so crudely but rather wrapped in Le Corbusier's flattering rhetoric: the product had been singled out as representative of the spirit of the times, and so forth.

The strategy was not always effective: "Les bagages Moynat thank *L'Esprit nouveau*'s administration very much for the free publicity given to them in issues 11 and 13 . . . but we cannot commit ourselves for the moment to an advertising contract." In some cases, however, as with the company Innovation, Le Corbusier obtained not only an advertising contract for *L'Esprit nouveau* but a commission to redesign and publish its catalogue. This type of commission, also pursued with other com-

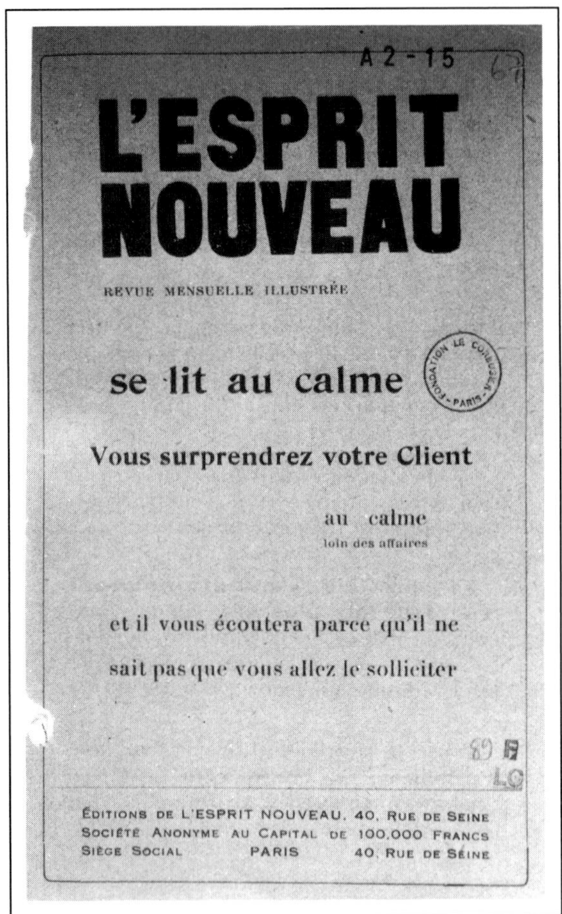
A2-15

L'ESPRIT NOUVEAU

REVUE MENSUELLE ILLUSTRÉE

se lit au calme

Vous surprendrez votre Client

au calme
loin des affaires

et il vous écoutera parce qu'il ne
sait pas que vous allez le solliciter

ÉDITIONS DE L'ESPRIT NOUVEAU. 40, RUE DE SEINE
SOCIÉTÉ ANONYME AU CAPITAL DE 100,000 FRANCS
SIÈGE SOCIAL PARIS 40, RUE DE SEINE

Publicity brochure for L'Esprit nouveau *directed to potential advertisers in the magazine.*

panies such as Ingersoll-Rand and Ronéo, was part of a wider project conceived by Le Corbusier as *Catalogues spéciaux de L'Esprit nouveau:* "We have thus conceived a kind of publicity that is almost editorial, but it can only be applied—this is evident—to products whose fabrication and use are consistent with a certain *esprit nouveau*." (Note that it is not the product itself, its formal qualities, that count, but its fabrication and use.) "*L'Esprit nouveau* itself comments on the product of the advertising firm, and, with respect to the clientele, this will certainly have an effectiveness that is far different from ordinary publicity."[30]

The company was to have a full page with a different text and illustration published in each issue of *L'Esprit nouveau* for a year. At the end of the year, the twelve pages thus constituted would be printed "in an edition of 3,000 (or more) on fine paper" and put together to form a brochure or catalogue called "L'Esprit nouveau" that the advertising firm "will be able to distribute usefully to a certain segment of its clientele."

Innovation's first page of "editorial publicity" appeared in *L'Esprit nouveau* 18. Instead of the conventional text of an Innovation catalogue—"An Innovation armoire holds three times as much as an ordinary armoire. Makes order. Avoids unnecessary folds"—one reads, "Construction in series is necessary to setting up house. . . ." This is followed in *L'Esprit nouveau* 19 by "To construct in series is to dedicate oneself to the pursuit of the element. . . . By analyzing the element one arrives at a standard. We must establish the standards of construction—windows, doors, plans, distribution, and all the interior mechanics that modern man requires for his comfort and hygiene." This tone seems to intensify progressively. A double page in *L'Esprit nouveau* 20, laid out in the shape of an hourglass, starts with "The war has shaken us out of our torpor. Taylorism has been spoken of and achieved. . . ." Throughout those pages specific references to Innovation products are practically nonexistent.

Innovation publicity leaflet in the shape of a wardrobe trunk, from the L'Esprit nouveau *archives.*

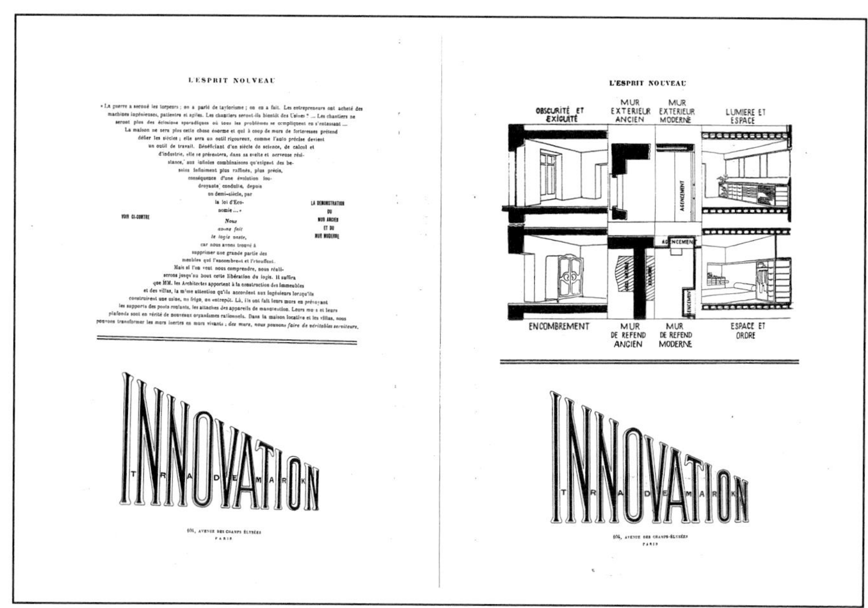

Double-page advertisement for Innovation.* L'Esprit nouveau *20 (1924).

While this is not the place to attempt a complete analysis of these pages of publicity produced by Le Corbusier—an analysis, I should note in passing, that would prove very fruitful not only for an understanding of Le Corbusier's ideology but also for tracing the source of certain of his architectural concepts such as the horizontal window—I shall try to relate this strategy of Le Corbusier's to contemporary advertising strategies.

In his book *The Making of Modern Advertising* Daniel Pope divides the history of advertising into three periods. The third one, the modern era, extends from 1920 to the present, and is defined as the "era of market segmentation." At this point the marketplace begins to be transformed from production for mass consumption—that is, for an undifferentiated group of consumers—to a stratified marketplace characterized by consumers organized into relatively well-defined subgroups. *L'Esprit nouveau*'s special catalogues fall clearly into this category. The audience in this context becomes the "product" to be sold to advertisers. Thus the contract with Innovation states, "Mr. Jeanneret will himself take responsibility for the writing of the text and the choice of images to accompany it, thereby furnishing you with a catalogue that can favorably influence your clientele and especially architects."[31]

Another publicity strategy deployed by Le Corbusier includes the portrayal of his own work in actual advertisements, as often occurs in the *Almanach de l'architecture moderne* (the content of the *Almanach* was originally intended to be issue 29 of *L'Esprit nouveau*, which never appeared). The image used in the text and in the advertisement is the same. Sometimes an image of a built work by the architect is placed in the advertisement of a company that has been involved in its construction (Summer, Euboolith, etc.), a strategy that clearly illustrates the previous point—publicity addressed to a targeted group, in this case architects.

Pavillon de l'*Esprit Nouveau*
Sol en « Euboolith »

« L'EUBOOLITH »

Société Anonyme française
au capital de 600.000 Fr.

PLANCHERS SANS JOINT

Adresse télégraphique : Safolith-Paris
Téléphone : Wagram 2438
R. C. Seine ; 75.932

36 bis, Rue Laugier, PARIS (XVIIe)

Advertisement for Euboolith. **Almanach de l'architecture moderne**, *1925.*

Another dimension is added when the process is reversed, as happens with the Immeubles-Villas. The image in the *Almanach* text and in the advertisement is again the same. But since the Immeubles-Villas do not actually exist, their appearance in an advertisement confers on them a degree of legitimacy (beyond that which publishing already confers). The advertising context conflates the realm of ideas with that of facts. Something of the same order also happens when Le Corbusier associates himself with industrialists for his visionary projects. Le Corbusier, as Stanislaus von Moos has pointed out, tried to involve the Michelin tire company in the Plan Voisin for Paris. The plan was to have been called *Plan Michelin et Voisin du Centre de Paris* (the Michelin and Voisin Plan for the Center of Paris). In a letter to Michelin, Le Corbusier wrote: "Through association of the name 'Michelin' with our plan, the project will acquire considerable mass appeal. It will become possible to motivate public opinion in a much more fundamental way than would be possible through books, for example."[32] As this statement reveals, Le Corbusier's interest in industrial publicity was twofold: on the one hand, the industrialists were to provide economic support for his projects, editorial or otherwise; on the other, the association with such concerns would have a multiplying effect owing precisely to the reputation of their names and products within mass culture. Of course, the blurring of the limits between publicity and content in *L'Esprit nouveau* was more effective not only for the advertised product but also for the dissemination of the review's theories. Every time its readers were confronted in another context with, for instance, a Ronéo advertisement, they would inevitably associate it with Le Corbusier's ideas.

L'Esprit nouveau was effectively used by Le Corbusier to publicize his own work. In the archives of the review in the Fondation, there is a box containing numerous letters from potential clients. These were readers of the magazine or visitors to the L'Esprit Nouveau Pavilion in the Exposition des Arts Décoratifs. As Roberto Gabetti and Carlo del Olmo have noted, the pavilion was used by Le Corbusier not to launch the

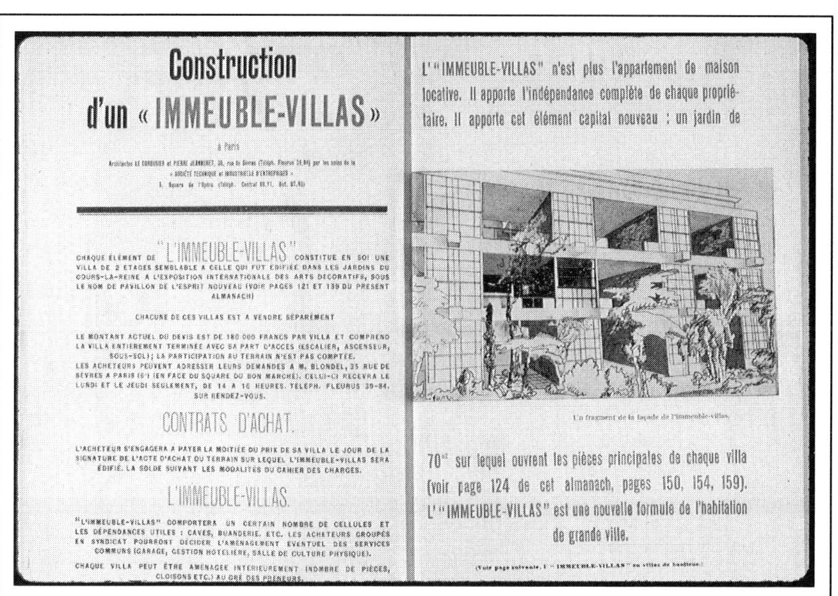

Advertisement for "Immeuble-Villas."* Almanach de l'architecture moderne, *1925.

magazine but to attract a professional clientele.[33] Le Corbusier answered the letters he received, sending sketches and preliminary budgets and, in some cases, proposing an actual site. While this is a subject for detailed study, it is sufficient for our purposes to note that some readers of *L'Esprit nouveau* became actual clients.

When *L'Esprit nouveau* ceased publication in 1925 ("Five years is a lot for a magazine," Le Corbusier declared, "one ought not to repeat oneself continuously. Others, younger people, will have younger ideas"), he emerged from the experience as an established architect. This maturation process was abetted by his production of the review and the nature of the audience it was reaching. Statistics included in a letter to the Ateliers Primavera, a subsidary of the Printemps department store, in an effort to obtain an advertising contract, state that only 24.3 percent of *L'Esprit nouveau*'s subscribers were artists (painters and sculptors). The rest comprised "people occupying active positions in society." Architects, of course, were included in the latter category, together with doctors, lawyers, teachers, engineers, industrialists, and bankers. While these statistics are not entirely reliable—Le Corbusier also asserted that *L'Esprit nouveau* had a circulation of 5,000 copies when the maximum ever reached was 3,500—his statement in the same letter that "*L'Esprit nouveau* finds its most sympathetic response precisely in the active milieu of society" not only was a stratagem to sell *L'Esprit nouveau* readership as a "product" to the Ateliers Primavera, but also reveals Le Corbusier's relentless desire to integrate his work into the contemporary conditions of production. The largest group of subscribers was, as he claims, constituted by industrialists and bankers, 31 percent; architects made up 8 percent.[34] Financing for the magazine, which it was Le Corbusier's responsibility to produce, also came largely from industrialists and bankers, many of Swiss origin.[35]

Le Corbusier's understanding of the media also secured his review a place in the international architectural circuits. A map published in

L'Esprit nouveau 17 shows the distribution of subscribers by country of origin. Le Corbusier and Ozenfant even attempted at one point to come out with an English-language version of the review, but "L'affaire Améri-caine," as they themselves called the project, was never realized.[36] *L'Esprit nouveau* was part of an exchange network with avant-garde magazines such as *MA*, *Stavba*, *De Stijl*, *Veshch/Gegenstand/Objet*, *Disk*, and others. Correspondence in the Fondation illuminates Le Corbusier's relations with El Lissitzy, Ilya Ehrenburg, Walter Gropius, László Moholy-Nagy, Theo van Doesburg, Karel Teige, and others. Perhaps the most telling document in this respect, not only on a symbolic level, is a card Sigfried Giedion wrote to Le Corbusier in 1925 mentioning that he was preparing a book on modern architecture and that Moholy-Nagy had recommended that he visit Le Corbusier.

We can already see in this the network of the avant-garde engaged in its own historical legitimation, something Giedion would carry out full-scale as the first "operative critic" of the modern movement. "What is normally meant by *operative criticism* is," as Tafuri puts it, "an analysis of architecture (or of the arts in general) that, instead of an abstract survey, has as its objective the planning of a precise poetical tendency, anticipated in its structure and derived from historical analyses programmatically distorted and finalised."[37] The relations between "operative criticism" and a "consumerist" culture are clear. Differences are canceled by the process of labeling, and the product in turn becomes marketable. Modern architecture does not simply address or exploit mass culture. It is itself, from the beginning, a commodity. Perhaps nowhere is this made more explicit than with the 1932 exhibition "Modern Architecture" in the Museum of Modern Art and the book that accompanied it, *The International Style: Architecture since 1922*.

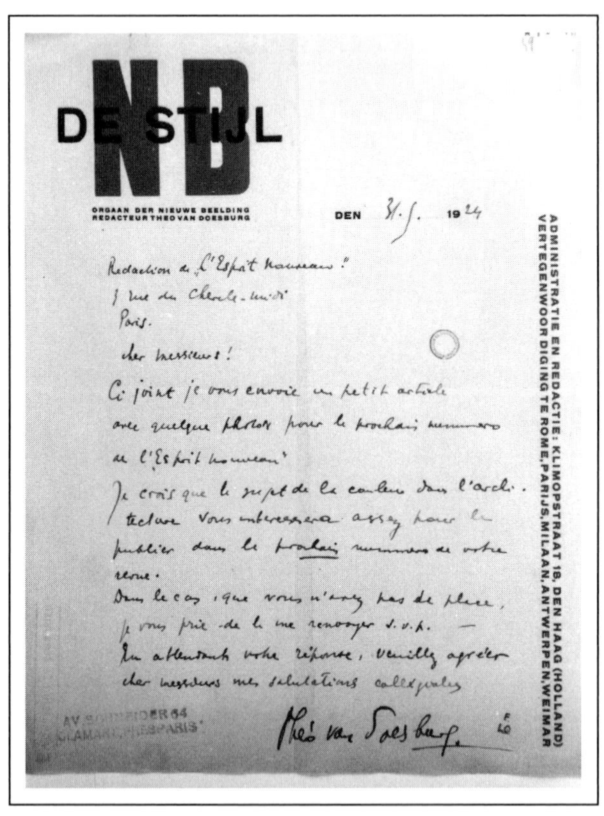
NB
DE STIJL
ORGAAN DER NIEUWE BEELDING
REDACTEUR THEO VAN DOESBURG

ADMINISTRATIE EN REDACTIE: KLIMOPSTRAAT 18, DEN HAAG (HOLLAND)
VERTEGENWOORDIGING TE ROME, PARIJS, MILAAN, ANTWERPEN, WEIMAR

DEN 31.5. 1924

Redaction de „L'Esprit nouveau"
3 rue du Cherche-Midi
Paris.

Cher Messieurs!

Ci joint je vous envoie un petit article avec quelque photos pour le prochain numéro de l'Esprit nouveau.

Je crois que le sujet de la couleur dans l'architecture vous intéressera assez pour le publier dans le prochain numéro de votre revue.

Dans le cas que vous n'avez pas de place, je vous prie de le me renvoyer s.v.p. —

En attendant votre réponse, veuillez agréer cher messieurs mes salutations collégiales

Théo van Doesburg

Letter from Theo van Doesburg to the editors of* L'Esprit nouveau, *10 April 1924.

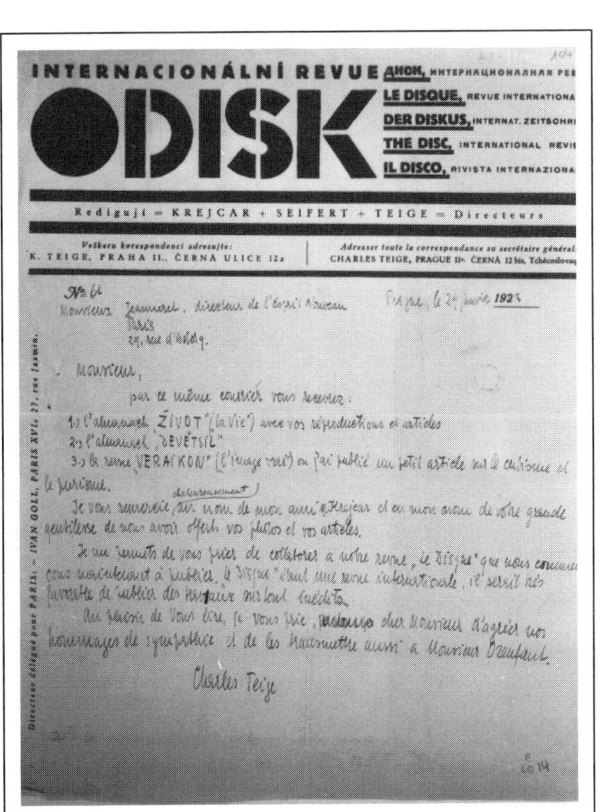

INTERNACIONÁLNÍ REVUE ДИСК, ИНТЕРНАЦИОНАЛЬНАЯ РЕВ

DISK

LE DISQUE, REVUE INTERNATIONA

DER DISKUS, INTERNAT. ZEITSCHRI

THE DISC, INTERNATIONAL REVI

IL DISCO, RIVISTA INTERNAZIONA

Rediguji = KREJCAR + SEIFERT + TEIGE = Directeurs

Veškeru korespondenci adresujte: K. TEIGE, PRAHA II., ČERNÁ ULICE 12a

Adresser toute la correspondance au secrétaire général: CHARLES TEIGE, PRAGUE IIe ČERNÁ 12 bis, Tchécoslovaq

Directeur délégué pour PARIS. – IVAN GOLL, PARIS XVI, 27, rue Jasmin.

№ 61

Monsieur Jeanneret, directeur de l'Esprit Nouveau
Paris
29, rue d'Astorg.

Prague, le 29 janvier 1923

Monsieur,

par ce même courrier vous recevrez:

1.) l'almanach „ŽIVOT" (la Vie) avec vos reproductions et articles
2.) l'almanach „DEVĚTSIL"
3.) la revue „VERAIKON" (l'image vraie) ou j'ai publié un petit article sur le cubisme et le purisme.

Je vous remercie chaleureusement au nom de mon ami Krejcar et en mon nom de votre grande gentilesse de nous avoir offert vos photos et vos articles.

Je me permets de vous prier de collaborer à notre revue „Le Disque" que nous commençons maintenant à publier. Le Disque étant une revue internationale, il serait très favorable de publier des travaux surtout inédits.

Au plaisir de vous lire, je vous prie, cher Monsieur, d'agréer nos hommages de sympathie et de les transmettre aussi à Monsieur Ozenfant.

Charles Teige

Letter from Karel Teige to Le Corbusier, 29 January 1923.

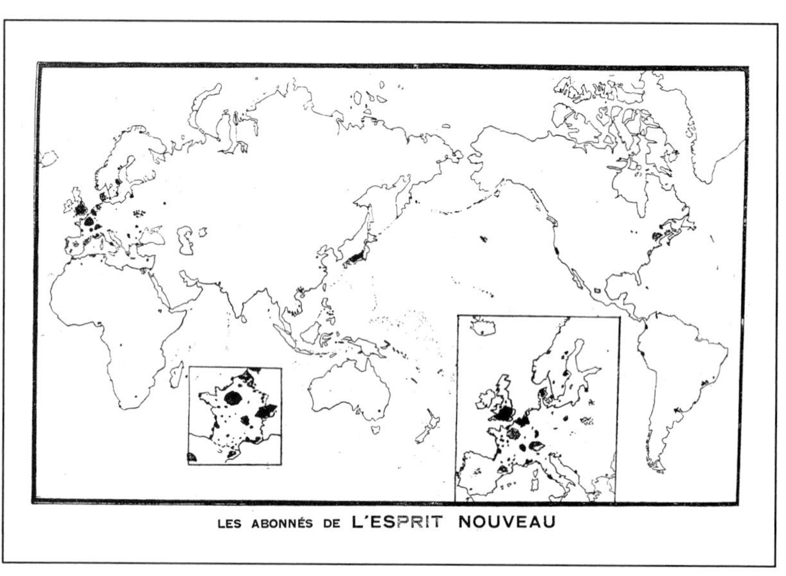

Map of subscribers. L'Esprit nouveau *17 (1922).*

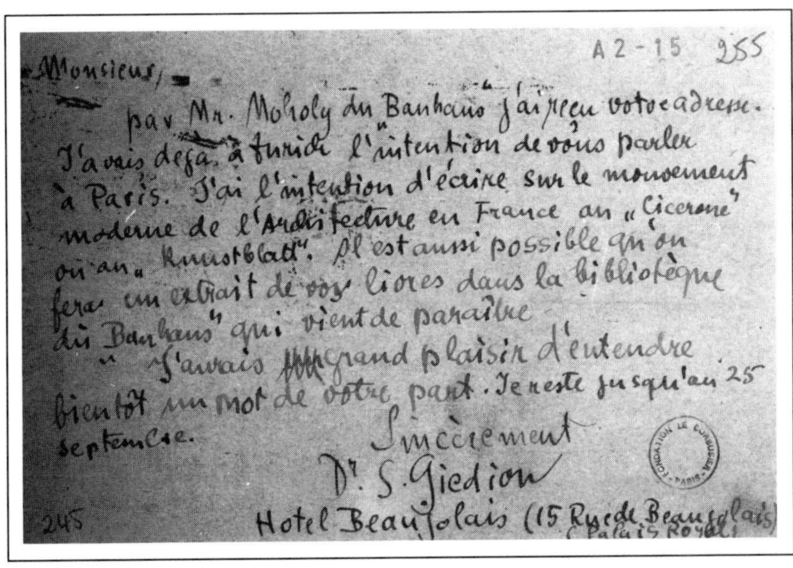
A2-15 255

Monsieur,

par Mr. Moholy du Bauhaus j'ai reçu votre adresse. J'avais déjà à Zurich l'intention de vous parler à Paris. J'ai l'intention d'écrire sur le mouvement moderne de l'Architecture en France au „Cicerone" ou au „Kunstblatt". Il est aussi possible qu'on fera un extrait de vos livres dans la bibliotèque du „Bauhaus" qui vient de paraître.

J'avais grand plaisir d'entendre bientôt un mot de votre part. Je reste jusqu'au 25 septembre.

Sincèrement
Dr. S. Giedion
Hotel Beaujolais (15 Rue de Beaujolais)
(Palais Royal)

Fondation Le Corbusier · Paris

245

Postcard from Sigfried Giedion to Le Corbusier and Pierre Jeanneret.

Museum

The (American) Translation of Le Corbusier

When the modern movement arrived in America with the exhibition "Modern Architecture," curated by Henry-Russell Hitchcock and Philip Johnson, and the subsequent book *The International Style* by the same authors, Le Corbusier's engagement with mass culture would seem to have been erased in the translation. His work, as well as that of other figures of the modern movement, was understood only in aesthetic terms and reduced to a "style" devoid of its social, ethical, and political content.[1] The violence of this translation is by now common knowledge. But the question of "style" needs to be reexamined in terms of the play between high and mass culture that is being followed here.

The museum presented the American public with a cultural reality already long in place. While promoting modernity, the present (Hitchcock and Johnson state repeatedly that "the international style already exists in the present"), the exhibition was in fact a retrospective: "Our book was written looking backward at the preceding ten years." That is, the "present" was actually the recent past, but a past that did not simply project into the future: "The International Style, of course—this is something most people don't realize—was almost over in 1932, but I was not conscious of that. History you can be conscious of, but you can't possibly know what you are doing as you go along."[2] These sentiments are reminiscent of Le Corbusier's: "Our own epoch is determining, day by day, its own style. Our eyes, unhappily, are unable to discern it." But where for Le Corbusier this contemporary style was to be found precisely in the everyday object and the industrial product, that is, in the unselfconscious anonymous design, for Johnson and Hitchcock the International Style was specifically established by a few masters and masterpieces, "the canon of executed works." In their book they write: "The four leaders of modern architecture are Le Corbusier, Oud, Gropius and Mies van der Rohe." And in his foreword to the 1966 edition, Hitchcock congratulates himself on how timely the book had turned out to be and says: "Had we written it several years earlier—as I had my *Modern Architecture* of 1929, . . . the canon of executed works on which our designation of the style was based would have been seriously incomplete, for the two finest houses in the new style—Le Corbusier's Villa Savoye and Mies's Tugendhat house—would not have yet existed."[3]

For Le Corbusier, concerned with the everyday, the new style is everywhere and precisely for that reason difficult to discern. For Johnson, concerned with exclusive moments of high culture, the difficulty is that the International Style necessarily dies in the very moment it is canonized. The International Style was over in 1932 because it never existed outside of its representation: the exhibition and accompanying publications. It both came into being and ended with its consumption in a sea of publicity. The moment the practice of some architects was labeled

"International Style" and identified (by its insertion in the museum) as high art, it necessarily left that domain to be disseminated in and as popular culture.

It is important in this respect to consider the role that the institution, the Museum of Modern Art, played in the construction of the International Style. The museum was obviously collecting as "art" the materials of the architects of the modern movement. The exhibition "Modern Architecture" and the book *International Style* indeed provided the museum with a department of architecture (headed by Johnson) only two years after opening its doors. In these terms, the institution was only able to construct itself by detaching the modern movement from everyday life so that it became available for appropriation by high culture.

The curators established this dichotomy between art and life, the artwork and the everyday object, by maintaining a hierarchy between architecture and building, between "the aesthetic" and the "technical or sociological." In a 1982 interview, Johnson says:

> **The last sentence in our book is the only important one—"We have an architecture still"—because the functionalists denied it. We wrote that book in a fury against the functionalist, German Social Democratic worker's approach to architecture as a part of social revolution. We thought that architecture was still an art; that it was something you could look at; that, therefore, architects should not be worried about the social implications, but about whether the work looked good or not. In that sense, we had only three allies in the Modern movement: Le Corbusier, Oud, and Mies. Talking to Gropius was a dead end because he would still mouth the Giedionesque platitudes of social discipline and revolution; that is, in Corbusier's phrase, "if you have enough glass walls, you become free."[4]**

Against the architects and critics of "functionalism," those who claim that "the modern world has neither the time nor the money required to raise building to the level of architecture" (Hannes Meyer and Giedion), Hitchcock and Johnson contend that these arguments are not valid in the contemporary world outside of Russia: "Whether they ought to or not, many clients can still afford architecture in addition to building."[5] These clients are those who can afford art.

But while the museum distorted modern architecture's engagement with everyday life, there is another sense in which it understood that engagement more clearly than anyone else. The clarity is of course not contained in the specific account of that architecture, in the written text or in the particular images selected. Rather, it is in their thorough understanding of the media: the exhibition and its accompanying catalogue and the subsequent book. In this particular sense, they were following Le Corbusier very closely.

Alfred Barr (founding director of the museum) begins his introduction to the catalogue with the sentence: "Expositions and exhibitions have perhaps changed the character of American architecture of the last forty years more than any other factor." That is, he proclaims from the start that exhibitions are more effective than schools, newspapers, magazines, and, of course, the actual practice of building in shaping American architecture. In other words, exhibitions are more "public" than buildings. This sensitivity to the media is also evident in his introduction to the book *The International Style* where he laments the chaos and confusion of contemporary American architecture, a confusion that significantly he reads not in the real city but as represented in two American magazine articles, "New Building for the New Age," which is "supposedly representative of what is happening in Europe," and "Poets in Steel," an article on modern American architecture.[6] Barr argues that the "confusion" in American architecture is first of all a confusion of

Front cover of the exhibition catalogue for "Modern Architecture: International Exhibition," Museum of Modern Art, New York, 9 February–23 March 1932.

public opinion. "Modern Architecture: International Exhibition" and the book *The International Style* were set up as a publicity campaign aimed at changing that opinion.

In fact, as Terence Riley has pointed out, the International Style was conceived first as a book and only later as an exhibition.[7] The initial plan was to rewrite Hitchcock's *Modern Architecture* (1929) in a more popular way and with more illustrations. Barr had reviewed the book before Hitchcock and Johnson sailed for Europe, and while praising it as a "scholarly achievement," he also found it "too erudite" for the general reader and "parsimonious" in its illustrations.[8] It was in great part due to publishing difficulties that the idea of the exhibition emerged. "No one wants another book on modern architecture here in Germany," wrote Johnson in a letter to his mother of July 1930. "In vain do we explain that there has been no book covering the whole style and nothing but the style."[9] In December 1930 the first proposal for an exhibition was presented.

From the beginning, the organizers proclaimed their commitment to publicity. In their proposal to the museum they wrote: "Publicity for the Show will be extensive. Besides announcements and comments in newspapers and magazines, the general appeal of the Show, it is safe to assume, will attract further attention from Architects, Engineers, Industrialists, Builders, as well as the general public. The experimental nature of the Show coupled with its timely appearance will undoubtedly provoke lively and fruitful controversy."[10] The importance of the catalogue was stressed as a "propagandistic" tool rather than merely a "documentary" source. In addition, the authors pointed to its permanent value (over the relatively ephemeral value of the exhibition).

But even the exhibition itself was to be multiplied by having it travel extensively throughout the United States. (In fact, after its closing at the

Museum of Modern Art it traveled for about seven years.) A further attempt was made to engage the general public with a series of lectures by Hitchcock and Johnson that were planned from the beginning and offered throughout the country, not only at museums and other art institutions but also, and more significantly, at department stores such as Sears, Roebuck & Co. in Chicago and Bullock's in Los Angeles, to which even the exhibition had traveled. Just as Le Corbusier had attempted through *L'Esprit nouveau* to engage French department stores in his battle for the modernization of the house, so were Johnson and Hitchcock trying to break into the highly conservative middle-class market of the home. Johnson was particularly vocal in this respect: "The most interesting exhibit [for the public] is still that of the private house." The private house was singled out as the vehicle for the popularization of "the style," and therefore made into a privileged item in the exhibition. Johnson went so far as to entice architects to present houses by offering more space in the exhibition to those who did: "I wish to have as many private houses as I can. Indeed I am thinking of suggesting to the architects that they may submit more than one model if one of them is a private house."[11] In the event, the exhibition was made up almost entirely of domestic architecture: Frank Lloyd Wright presented the model of his project for a house on the mesa and photographs of the Robie house, Roberts house, Millard house, and Jones house; Le Corbusier, the model of Villa Savoye and photographs of the Beistegui apartment, Villa Stein, and Double House in the Weissenhof Siedlung; Oud, the model of the project for a house at Pinehurst; Mies, the model of the Tugendhat house and photographs of Lange house, Johnson apartment, and the Barcelona Pavilion (arguably a domestic project if not a house).

If the International Style is to be thought of as a publicity campaign for modern architecture, this publicity was aimed at a public much larger than that which "can afford art": the department store public, middle-

Installation view of the "Modern Architecture" exhibition, Museum of Modern Art.

class and mainly women. It is not just the house that is for sale in these promotions. After all, the museum's department of architecture that emerged from the exhibition was the department of "architecture and design." The International Style publicized the private, not simply because it exhibited the private houses of some art collectors, but because it offered that image for mass consumption in the form of the multiple, relatively affordable, designer objects that were part of it: rugs, chairs, lamps, tables, appliances, and so on.

Le Corbusier had already argued in *L'Art décoratif d'aujourd'hui* that art was "everywhere"—in the street, in the city—but missing at home. His own campaign was precisely aimed at bringing the house up to speed for the twentieth century. The Museum of Modern Art effectively achieved some of that goal. Even Mumford, traditionally a spokesman for the city, was extremely articulate in his assessment of the relevance of the private house. In his chapter on housing in the original catalogue "Modern Architecture: International Exhibition" (a chapter not included in the *International Style* book), he writes:

> **The building of houses constitutes the major architectural work of any civilization. During the past hundred years the conditions of our life have been completely transformed; but it is only during the last generation that we have begun to conceive of a new domestic environment which will utilize our technical and scientific achievement for the benefit of human living. The laying down of a new basis for housing has been, since 1914, one of the chief triumphs of modern architecture. . . .**
>
> **With the return of entertainment to the home, through the mechanical invention of the phonograph, the radio, the motion picture, and the near prospect of television, the house has made up by gains in recreational facilities what it has lost through the disappearance of earlier household**

> **industries. Hence the proper design of the house has a new importance, in that, with greater leisure for the whole community, more time will probably be spent within its walls.**[12]

If for Johnson the modern house was to be publicized through the media apparatus put in motion by the museum, what Mumford identifies here is that the modern house has itself been transformed through its incorporation of the media. The house is now a media center, a reality that will forever transform our understanding of both public and private. Here Mumford is closer to Le Corbusier than he would ever want to imagine. Even his invocation of the year 1914 could not have been casual. It resonates with Le Corbusier's own identification of modern architecture with war, the modern house being constructed by recycled military technologies that include those of the media.

Furthermore, the main architects of the media event, Barr, Johnson, and Hitchcock, understood their publicity campaign as a military campaign. Throughout the book a military rhetoric is deployed: "American nationalists will oppose the Style as another European *invasion*. . . . Nevertheless, the International Style has already gained signal *victories* in America as is proven by a glance at the illustration of the skyscraper by Howe and Lescaze. . . . In Europe, too, . . . Peter Behrens . . . and Mendelsohn . . . have both *gone over* to the International Style."[13]

The book is conceived as a publicity weapon to disseminate modern architecture in America. Images are used as ammunition. The text is completely subordinated to the carefully chosen image. They write: "As in this book the text itself is intended as an introduction to the illustrations one need scarcely speak at length about them. The authors have spent nearly two years in assembling the photographic and documentary material from which the illustrations were chosen."[14] Complete projects are taken in one decisive shot, an advertising image that becomes as canonic as the building itself (if it does not in fact take over).

In these terms, the museum was particularly sensitive to Le Corbusier's engagement with the mass media: "The man who first made the world aware that a new style was being born was Le Corbusier. . . . The influence of Le Corbusier was the greater . . . because of the vehement propaganda which he contributed to the magazine *L'Esprit Nouveau*, 1920–1925. Since then, moreover, he has written a series of books effectively propagandizing his technical and aesthetic theories."[15] For that reason, the institution used Le Corbusier as a publicist. As he recounts in *My Work:* "1935; invitation from Rockefeller (Museum of Modern Art) for a programme of 23 lectures on architecture and town planning in New York, Boston, Philadelphia, Baltimore, Chicago and elsewhere. . . . 400 yards of architectural sketches, in charcoal and coloured chalk on six rolls of paper, were cut into 180 sheets approximately 6 ft. 6 in. by 4 ft. 6 in. in the course of this tour around America. Twelve years later in June 1947 . . . Mr. Nelson Rockefeller said to Le Corbusier at a private dinner at his home near Central Park: 'You were the man who changed the face of architecture in the United States in 1935.'"[16] But Le Corbusier did not change the face of architecture in the United States significantly. His influence was really in the techniques of representing and promoting architecture. The International Style was a myth sustained by the strategic deployment of mass culture advertising techniques. Le Corbusier's concern with these techniques was thus returned to the country from which they had originated (without being identified as such).

Thus, while the basic account of modern architecture provided by *The International Style* isolated it from everyday life and thereby suppressed its political agenda (as many critics have pointed out), in fact the publicity campaign launched by the Museum of Modern Art paradoxically returned modern architecture to everyday life by transforming it into a commodity, a fashion to be consumed by a worldwide and (to a large extent) middle-class market. After all, the fact that the International Style was not simply a representation of an already existing architecture but a production parallels Le Corbusier's own role as producer rather than interpreter of the existing industrial reality. Perhaps that is why, despite the clear mistranslation of his work, the vocal Le Corbusier never complained about it publicly (as Wright, for example, so famously did). Indeed, the very success of the exhibition in disseminating modern architecture throughout the world, to such an extent that it become anonymous, can be argued to be a realization of one of Le Corbusier's earliest dreams, as articulated in the years of *L'Esprit nouveau*.

Faut-il brûler le Louvre?

The key to Le Corbusier's position on universal culture is to be found in his very idea of the museum: "The true museum is the one that contains everything." Le Corbusier makes this comment in the context of his publication of the bidet. With this definition, however, the museum and the world become conflated with each other. Perhaps, then, Le Corbusier is not talking about museums after all, at least not in the literal sense of a bounded space, an enclosure containing objects, especially since, as we saw, he is not suggesting that the bidet is an art object: the bidet is an everyday object that will explain to future generations something about contemporary culture. Le Corbusier's concern with the museum is with the idea of a cultural record, but the contemporary transformations in culture cannot be registered by the traditional mechanism of the museum. Le Corbusier's displacement of the concept of the museum becomes evident later in *L'Art décoratif d'aujourd'hui* when he moves effortlessly from the idea of the museum into a discussion of popular literature (*Je sais tout, Sciences et vie, Sciences et voyages*), cinema, newspapers, photography, and everything from the new culture industry that brings, as it were, the world into our living rooms.[17]

What makes the museum obsolete as a nineteenth-century accumulative institution is the mass media. Thus when Le Corbusier says that the true museum should contain everything, he is talking about an imaginary museum, a museum that comes into being with the new means of communication, something close to what Malraux would later call the "museum without walls."[18] "For a long time," says Le Corbusier in a manuscript entitled "Lettre de Paris" kept in the Fondation Le Corbusier, "painting had as its main objective the creation of documents. Those documents were the first books. . . . But a hundred years ago photography arrived, and thirty years ago cinema. Documents are obtained today by an objective click, or by a film that rotates."[19]

Since everything is known to us through the media, the problem is no longer one of mere documentation but of the classification of information. The question of museums gives way, in Le Corbusier's argument, to that of classification. As he says of Ronéo file cabinets, "They will show that in the XXth [century] we have learned to classify."[20] But classification is not just recorded as a mark of culture by placing filing cabinets within the museum. Classification is the technology of recording, a displacement of the museum. The filing cabinet is a museum. (The Fondation Le Corbusier is, in this sense, a "true museum" of Le Corbusier.)

Malraux begins his "Museum without Walls" by reflecting on the transformation of the "work of art" in the context of the museum:

> **A Romanesque crucifix was not regarded by its contemporaries as a work of sculpture, nor Cimabue's *Madonna* as a picture. . . . Museums have imposed on the spectator a wholly new attitude towards the work of art.**

RÉPONSES A NOTRE ENQUÊTE (FIN)

FAUT-IL

BRULER LE LOUVRE?

C

Title block of an article in L'Esprit nouveau *6 (1921).*

Le Corbusier, Museum of Unlimited Growth, 1939.

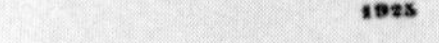

70 1925

des corniches et des baldaquins et se fait plus utilement coupeur chez un tailleur, un homme étant devant lui, et lui, un mètre à la main, prenant des mesures sur son homme. Nous revoici sur le plancher des vaches. Sérénité tonifiante des certitudes!

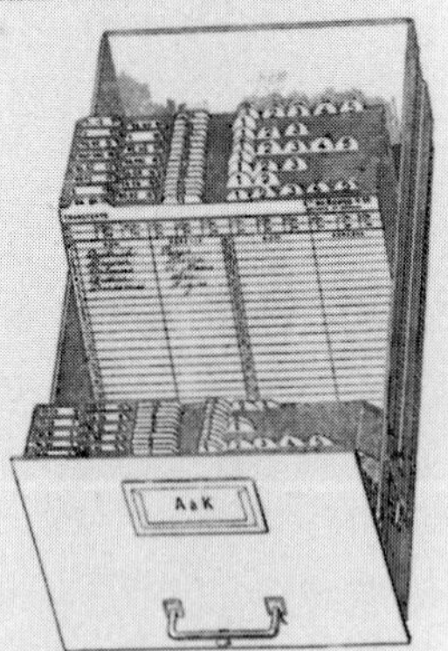

Les fiches « Ronéo ».

Lorsqu'un facteur de notre équation technico-cérébro-sentimentale a démesurément poussé, survient une crise, les rapports

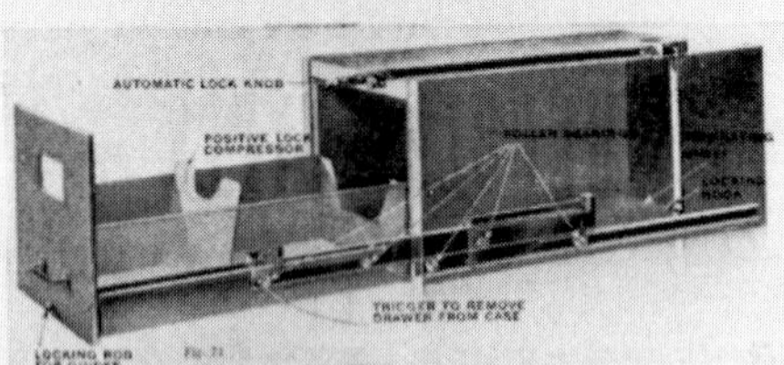

Les tiroirs roulent doucement sur des galets (Ronéo)

"*Besoins-Type*," L'Esprit nouveau 23 (1924), *reprinted in* L'Art décoratif d'aujourd'hui.

> **For they have tended to estrange the works they bring together from their original functions and to transform even portraits into pictures.**[21]

The museum, Malraux argues, is the place where the work of art is constituted as such. Walter Benjamin takes somehow the reverse route when he writes:

> **By the absolute emphasis on its cult value, it [the work of art in prehistoric times] was, first and foremost, an instrument of magic. Only later did it come to be recognized as a work of art. In the same way today, by the absolute emphasis on its exhibition value the work of art becomes a creation with entirely new functions, among which the one we are conscious of, the artistic function, later may be recognized as incidental.**[22]

Mechanical reproduction, suggests Benjamin, qualitatively modifies the nature of art in modifying the relation of the public with it. Something of this order was understood by Le Corbusier when he wrote (in response to Marcel Temporal, who was heading a group of painters attempting to recuperate the fresco as an artistic medium):

> **The fresco wrote history upon the walls of churches and palaces, told stories of virtue or of vanity. There were no books—one read the frescoes. (In passing, a quick homage to Victor Hugo: "This will kill that.") . . . The poster is the modern fresco, and its place is in the street. It lasts not five centuries but two weeks, and then it is replaced.**[23]

Not only has the modern poster successfully replaced the fresco and made it unnecessary as a medium but "art is everywhere in the street, which is the museum of the present and the past," Le Corbusier goes on to say in *L'Art décoratif d'aujourd'hui*.[24] The works in this imaginary "museum" are the poster, fashion, the industrial design object, adver-

"Fresque." Illustration in L'Esprit nouveau *19 (1923).*

tising; they are the equivalent in our time of the madonnas, crucifixes, and frescoes of medieval society. That is to say, we do not perform in front of them an intellectual operation. We perceive them in a mood of relaxation that, among other things, allows advertising to become effective. They constitute the objects of a cult, the cult of consumption, as necessary to the reproduction of the social system as religious images were in medieval times. They embody the values and myths of our society. As Adorno and Horkheimer noted, they are not only the vehicles of an ideology, they are ideology itself.

An ideological critique of contemporary architectural work must take into account the status of the media, a status that forces Le Corbusier to ask: if "the press and the book operate much more efficiently than Art relative to religious, moral, or political aims, what destiny is left to art in an industrial society?" For him the everyday object, the industrial product, the engineer's construction were not works of art in the traditional sense:

> **I discard, I discard. . . . My life isn't meant to preserve dead things. I discard Stevenson's locomotive. . . . I will discard everything, for my twenty-four hours must be productive, brilliantly productive. I will discard everything of the past, everything except that which still serves. Certain things serve forever: they are Art.**[25]

With such a statement Le Corbusier distinguishes himself from the avant-garde, understood as an attack on high art. For him, permanence still differentiates the artwork from the everyday object, architecture from engineering, painting from posters. The artist as maker is set apart from the rest of producers in industrial society. The institution of art, its autonomy from everyday life, remains intact. Nor is Le Corbusier the quintessentially modernist figure we are accustomed to see portrayed in conventional histories. Perhaps the best evaluation is still Manfredo

Tafuri's when, in his *Theories and History of Architecture*, he notes in passing that Le Corbusier did not accept the new industrial conditions as an external reality, did not relate to them as an "interpreter," but rather aspired to enter into them as a "producer."

Interpreters are those who "perpetuate the figure of the *artist-magician*," in the Benjaminian definition, those who, faced by the "new nature of artificial things" to be used as raw material in their artistic work, remain "anchored to the principle of *mimesis*." On the opposite side is the *artist-surgeon*, again in the Benjaminian sense, one who has understood that reproduction techniques create new conditions for the artist, the public, and the media of production. Instead of simply representing the "equipment," they "go behind it and use it."[26]

This difference turns on the status of representation, specifically the transformation of publicity. Le Corbusier is perhaps the first architect to fully engage the modern condition of the media (to put it bluntly, he published about fifty books and built some fifty or so buildings). In these terms, traditional modes of interpretation exclusively founded on the aesthetic object are insufficient. The dichotomy between high art and mass culture, construed as a relation of opposition and exclusion, which is fundamental to these conventional readings, is undermined by Le Corbusier's work. His use of publicity material and clippings from newspapers next to images extracted from art books represents the intrusion of the materials of "low culture" into the realm of "high art," an intrusion that, if it cannot be considered a direct, avant-garde attack on the institution of art, nevertheless undermines its ideology of autonomy from the realm of everyday life. Despite Le Corbusier's claims—in the best modernist fashion—of a higher status for the artwork than for the everyday object, for architecture than for engineering and building, for painting than for posters, his work is, in more than one way, fundamentally contaminated by the materials of low culture. Le Corbusier's work is unthinkable outside the structural role of this contamination.

An Exhibition in a Suitcase

The role of Le Corbusier as "producer" can be further elaborated by comparing his *Oeuvre complète* with Marcel Duchamp's *Boîte en valise*. The *Boîte en valise* is a cardboard box covered with cloth, sometimes placed inside a leather suitcase, containing miniature replicas and color reproductions of Duchamp's works. In 1955 Duchamp, who had been working on the *Boîte* since 1936, said in a television interview with James Johnson Sweeney:

> **Here again, a new form of expression was involved. Instead of painting my aim was to reproduce the paintings and objects that I liked and to collect them in a space as small as possible. I did not know how to go about it. I first thought of a book, but I did not like the idea. Then, it occurred to me that it could be a box in which all my works would be collected and mounted like in a small museum, a portable museum, so to speak.**[27]

There were several editions of this work. The first one, produced in New York in 1941, consisted of 20 numbered copies. On each the name of the owner was inscribed in golden capital letters on the side of the leather suitcase. The contents included an original of some kind: a drawing, a manuscript, or a proof.

Duchamp's work is an acute comment on the art market, on the condition of the artist as salesman, his work reduced to commercial samples. But that comment is somewhat undermined by another condition: the objects in the suitcase are reproductions that have been reinvested with "aura," the very thing that the reproduction process eliminates.

Categories such as original and authentic are irrelevant in relation to Le Corbusier's *Oeuvre complète*. Stanislaus von Moos has written of Le Corbusier as the "architect" of his *Complete Works*. Borrowing Malraux's

Mardi 17 Mai 1921

TROISIEME EDITION

42e Année. — N° 14895

Une exposition dans une malle

C'est au « Salon du goût français » que l'on peut voir cette trouvaille utile à la propagande française

Le 18 mai s'ouvrira, au Palais de Glace, avenue des Champs-Elysées, le Salon du « Goût français ». Les industries d'art y grouperont leurs meilleures productions : décoration, ferronnerie, reliure, verrerie, bronzes, ameublements, porcelaines, cristaux, céramiques, carrosserie, décoration intérieure de paquebots, tissus d'ameublement, antiquités, bijouterie-joaillerie-orfèvrerie, articles de voyage, passementerie pour modes, dentelles et broderies, mode, éventails, ombrelles, postiches, ivoire et écaille, bonneterie, lingerie, fourrures et couture.

On évoque, à lire une pareille énumération, la joie artistique que procurent ces mille accessoires de la vie civilisée, le bien-être sensuel de l'individu raffiné parmi le « confort moderne » : Bonheur intime du « home » agréablement installé, fête des yeux et du toucher parmi l'ordre et l'harmonie, triomphe, en un mot, *du goût français.*

Or, cette exposition est un merveilleux instrument de propagande : Elle offre ceci d'assez particulier, convenez-en, qu'elle peut être enfermée tout entière dans une malle de 60 kilos et promenée à travers le monde entier.

Et voici l'explication de cette gageure : M. Louis Lumière, de l'Académie des sciences, a découvert, comme l'on sait, en 1907, la photographie en couleurs. Jusqu'ici cette découverte n'avait pas reçu d'application pratique perfectionnée. Les photos prises à la lumière artificielle ne donnaient que des effets inexacts et décevants. Or, M. Lumière vient d'inventer un écran spécial, dont le principe est connu de lui seul, et qui contient de la gélatine colorée entre deux plaques de verre. Cet écran, placé entre l'appareil photographique et l'objet à photographier à la lumière électrique, restitue à celui-ci, sur le cliché, ses véritables teintes. Les clichés, vraiment merveilleux, éclairés par transparence, donnent absolument l'image fidèle de la réalité.

Tout par clichés

C'est en ceci que réside l'originalité de cette exposition du goût français : Elle sera constituée uniquement par des clichés de ce genre, 2.300 clichés dont quelques-uns ont 50 centim. sur 60 de dimension, représentant les productions les plus artistiques des 250 maisons exposantes, triées sur le volet.

M. Maurice Devriès, un des plus actifs organisateurs de ce salon me l'expliquait fort bien ce matin : ce procédé permettra aux visiteurs de contempler des « intérieurs » comme on n'a jamais l'occasion d'en voir. Les idées françaises, le génie de notre industrie pourront ainsi être présentés sous des aspects parfaitement suggestifs et fidèles et circuler à travers le monde entier.

M. Dior, ministre du commerce, qui inaugurera cette exposition le 18 mai prochain, à 9 h. du matin, disait ces jours-ci, avec M. Charmeil, conseiller d'Etat, directeur de *l'Expansion économique* : « Il faudra organiser une croisière sur les mers, et des trains dans les pays étrangers, et promener ainsi cette exposition ! »

Quelle propagande pour nous !

Car cette exposition, utilisant la découverte *française* du savant, M. Lumière, ne comprend que des exposants *français.* Ces exposants, qui ne sont pas seulement parisiens, mais de toute la France, ont une occasion unique de montrer, sans risque de vol ou d'accident, les trésors de leurs productions : ameublements, bijoux, fourrures, etc., d'inestimable valeur. — M. M.

"Une exposition dans une malle," newspaper clipping in L'Esprit nouveau *archives.*

Marcel Duchamp, Boîte en valise.

MALLETTE GARNIE POUR DAMES

Mesures extérieures 40 c/m × 30 c/m × 12 c/m.

CARACTÉRISTIQUES :

I. Maroquin du Cap premier choix. Entièrement cousu main. Doublure peau.

II. Garniture cristal et argent. Glace biseautée.

III Brosserie ivoire plein. Soies longues.

IV. Plateau manucure complet. Fer à friser. Coutellerie acier Sheffield.

V. Serrure américaine de sûreté. Poignée extra forte.

***Page from an Innovation catalogue in the archives of* L'Esprit nouveau.**

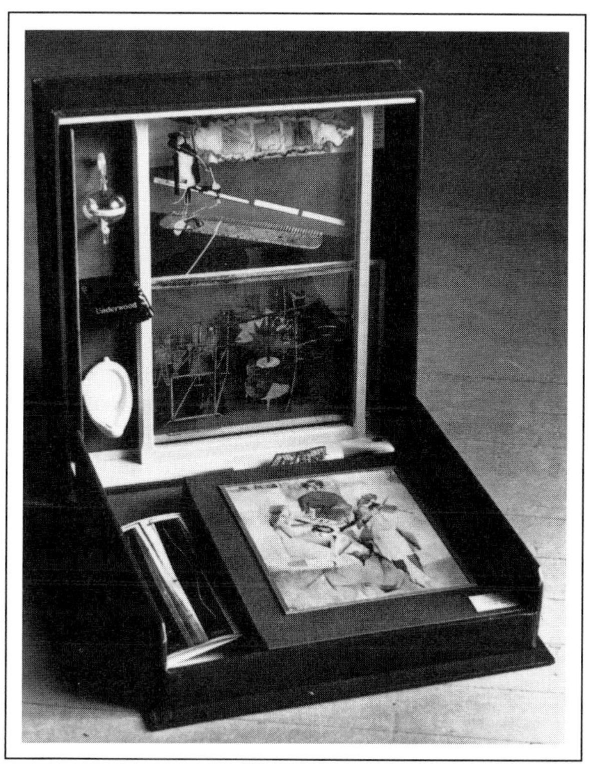

Marcel Duchamp, Boîte en valise.

comment on Picasso—"His final goal is not his paintings, but the albums of reproductions by Zervos in which the breathless succession of the works is far more significant than the best single one among them can be by itself"—von Moos suggests that the same applies to Le Corbusier, if we substitute buildings for paintings and the publisher Boesiger for Zervos.[28] But the volumes of the *Oeuvre complète* are not albums of reproductions as in a traditional art book. The images are not employed here to represent preexisting, authorized objects (the built works of Le Corbusier). The images construct another kind of object, they are used to produce a new kind of spectacle. Le Corbusier is using the means of reproduction for productive purposes. He is the author as producer.

The "soldier-architect's" advertising campaign is fought on two fronts, the *Oeuvre complète* and the Fondation Le Corbusier. Both problematize the distinction between high and low art. This problematization necessarily transforms the status of both the work of art and the everyday object. But Duchamp's criticism of the institution of art paradoxically restores the authority of both the creative artist and the art object. Everything turns on the privileged "signature" of the author-artist: *Fountain by R. Mutt* is an art object because "He CHOSE it." The *Boîte en valise* is a traditional space, a bounded enclosure, filled with auratic objects. Le Corbusier's *Oeuvre complète* cannot be thought of in terms of either space or object. It displaces architecture from an economy of objects and spaces into that of the media. Le Corbusier's displacement of the museum into the filing cabinet, and of the filing cabinet into the mass media, is not just a displacement of one architecture, one kind of object for another, but a displacement of the whole institution of architecture, a displacement of all objects.

What is at stake is a displacement of *interiority*. When Le Corbusier takes on the actual physical problem of the museum, he precisely undermines the traditional sense of enclosure, the boundary between inside and outside. For example, about his project *Musée d'art contemporain*, in Paris, he writes:

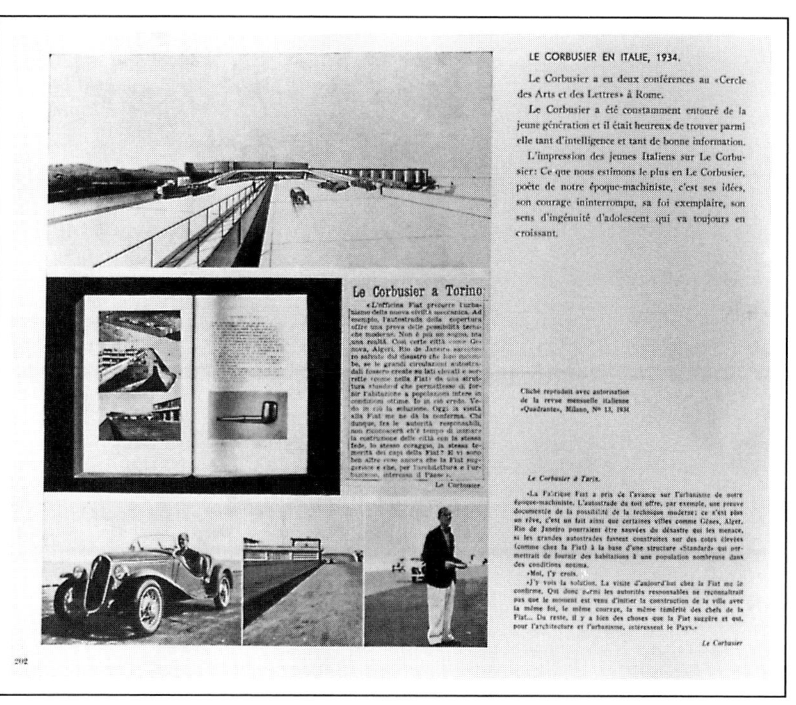

LE CORBUSIER EN ITALIE, 1934.

Le Corbusier a eu deux conférences au «Cercle des Arts et des Lettres» à Rome.

Le Corbusier a été constamment entouré de la jeune génération et il était heureux de trouver parmi elle tant d'intelligence et tant de bonne information.

L'impression des jeunes Italiens sur Le Corbusier: Ce que nous estimons le plus en Le Corbusier, poète de notre époque-machiniste, c'est ses idées, son courage ininterrompu, sa foi exemplaire, son sens d'ingénuité d'adolescent qui va toujours en croissant.

Cliché reproduit avec autorisation de la revue mensuelle italienne «Quadrante», Milano, Nº 13, 1934

Le Corbusier à Turin.

«La Fabrique Fiat a pris de l'avance sur l'urbanisme de notre époque-machiniste. L'autostrade du toit offre, par exemple, une preuve documentée de la possibilité de la technique moderne; ce n'est plus un rêve, c'est un fait ainsi que certaines villes comme Gênes, Alger, Rio de Janeiro pourraient être sauvées du désastre qui les menace, si les grandes autostrades fussent construites sur des cotes élevées (comme chez la Fiat) à la base d'une structure «Standard» qui permettrait de fournir des habitations à une population nombreuse dans des conditions optima.

»Moi, j'y crois.

»J'y vois la solution. La visite d'aujourd'hui chez la Fiat me le confirme. Qui donc parmi les autorités responsables ne reconnaîtrait pas que le moment est venu d'initier la construction de la ville avec la même foi, le même courage, la même témérité des chefs de la Fiat... Du reste, il y a bien des choses que la Fiat suggère et qui, pour l'architecture et l'urbanisme, intéressent le Pays.»

Le Corbusier

202

Page from Le Corbusier,* Oeuvre complète, *1929–34.

Marcel Duchamp, Boîte en valise.

> **The museum has no facade; the visitor will never see a facade; he will only see the interior of the museum. One enters the heart of the museum by means of an underground passage, and the wall opening for the entrance door would, once the museum has reached its full magnificent size, comprise the 9000th meter of the total developed length of the museum. . . . The museum is extensible at will: its plan is that of a spiral; a true form of harmonious and regular growth. The donor of a picture could also donate the wall (or partition) destined to receive his picture; two columns, plus two girders, plus five or six beams, plus several square meters of partition. And this small gift would permit him to attach his name to the room in which his pictures are displayed.**[29]

The space of the traditional museum has been transformed into a length, a wall continuously folding on itself. This wall does not define traditional space because it cannot be seen through or passed through. It has no openings. The project is entered from below. There is an interior, but no outside. This is the space of twentieth-century communication. The same condition is evident in Le Corbusier's earlier project of the Mundaneum and the World Museum (1929) and the later project of a *Musée à croissance illimitée* (Museum of Unlimited Extension), 1939. But nowhere is this displacement of *interiority* more evident than in domestic space.

With modernity the interior ceases to be simply bounded territory in opposition to the outside, whether physical or social. An analysis of the status of the house in Loos and Le Corbusier could be used to trace more precisely the transformations of the relationship between private and public space and the convolution of boundaries between inside and outside instigated by the emerging reality of the technologies of communication: newspaper, telephone, radio, film, and television.

MUSÉE D'ART CONTEMPORAIN, PARIS 1931

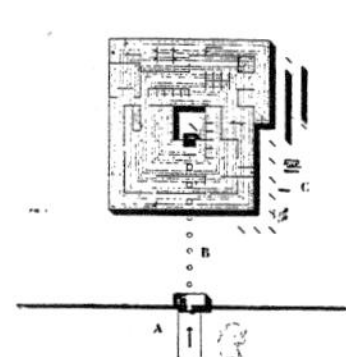

Ici, cent vingt poteaux et 2800 m de cimaise: des épines intermédiaires ont permis de composer des salles multiformes. La spire pointillée montre l'éclairage de jour et de nuit calculé suivant l'angle d'incidence pour éviter les reflets. Les rectangles ponctués représentent des resserres, bureaux d'administration, etc.

Le musée peut être commencé sans argent; à vrai dire avec 100.000 francs on fait la première salle.

Il peut se continuer par une, deux, quatre salles nouvelles, le mois suivant ou deux ou quatre années après, à volonté.

Le musée *n'a pas de façade;* le visiteur ne verra jamais de façade; *il ne verra que l'intérieur du musée.* Car il entre au cœur du musée par un souterrain dont la porte d'entrée est ouverte dans un mur qui, si le musée arrivait à une étape de croissance magnifique, offrirait à ce moment le neuf millième mètre de cimaise.

Poteaux standard, cloisons-membranes fixes ou amovibles, plafonds standard. Economie maximum.

Le musée est extensible à volonté: son plan est celui d'une spirale; véritable forme de croissance harmonieuse et régulière.

Le donateur d'un tableau pourra donner le mur (la cloison) destinée à recevoir son tableau; deux poteaux, plus deux sommiers, plus cinq à six poutrelles, plus quelques mètres carrés de cloison. Et ce don minuscule lui permettra d'attacher son nom à la salle qui abritera ses tableaux.

Le musée s'élève dans quelque banlieue ou grande banlieue de Paris. Il s'élève au milieu d'un champ de pommes de terre ou de betteraves. Si le site est magnifique, tant mieux. S'il est laid et attristé de pignons de lotissements ou de cheminées d'usines, ça ne fait rien: par la construction des murs de compartimentage, nous composerons avec... les cheminées d'usines. Etc., etc...

Mon cher Zervos, telle est l'idée de notre musée que je n'avais donnée jusqu'ici à personne. Je vous la donne. Maintenant, elle est dans le domaine public. Que la bonne chance vous accompagne!

Votre LE CORBUSIER, *8 décembre 1930.*

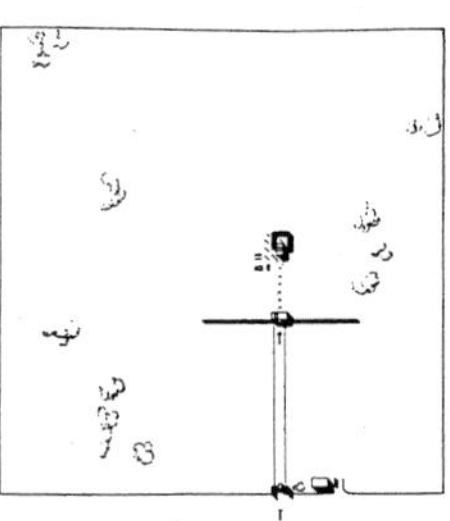

Début de l'entreprise: la première salle est construite 14 × 14 m: le souterrain qui vient du portique: le portique s'appuie sur un mur qui empêchera dorénavant de voir le chantier permanent du musée. En bas, l'entrée du domaine avec la loge du concierge. Du barbelé clôture le terrain

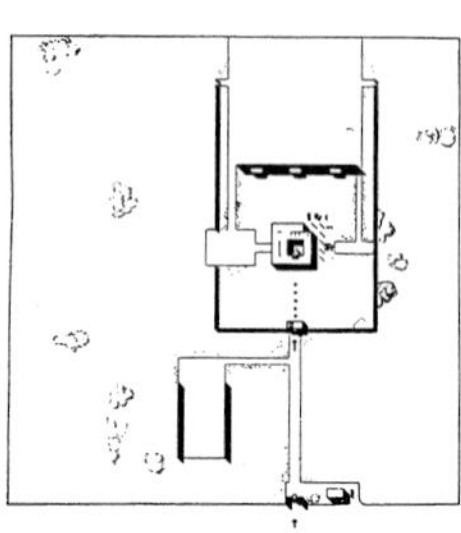

Les fonds parvenus ont permis d'entourer la première salle d'une nef en hélice comportant (ici déjà) vingt cellules de 7 × 7 m, soit 315 m de cimaise: il a fallu 26 poteaux. On voit le chantier qui continue. Déjà, on peut passer à l'extérieur, assister au montage d'une nouvelle cellule de 7 m. Les sculptures trouvent, en plein air, des murs formant fond utile

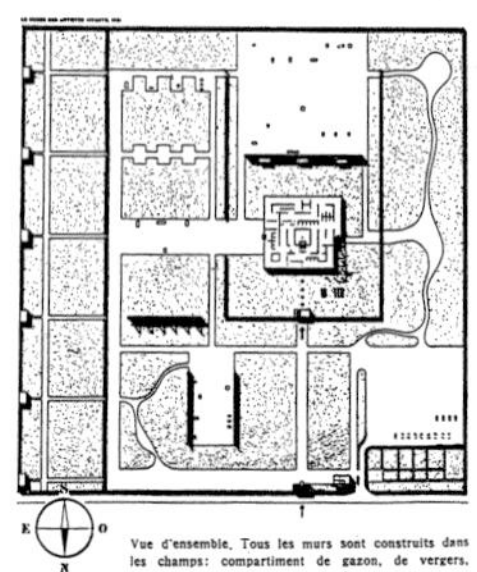

Vue d'ensemble. Tous les murs sont construits dans les champs: compartiment de gazon, de vergers, grands arbres isolés ou groupés. La statutaire trouve cent modes d'exposition. Mais la construction du musée continue. Ici on a figuré, à gauche, un enclos allongé qui abrite six ateliers, où un jour éventuel pourrait se constituer une fondation. Dans le coin à droite, en bas, la loge du jardin, le portail des autos, le parking des autos

Le Corbusier,* Musée d'art contemporain, *Paris, 1931.

Interior

"To live is to leave traces," writes Walter Benjamin, discussing the birth of the interior. "In the interior these are emphasized. An abundance of covers and protectors, liners and cases is devised, on which the traces of objects of everyday use are imprinted. The traces of the occupant also leave their impression on the interior. The detective story that follows these traces comes into being. . . . The criminals of the first detective novels are neither gentlemen nor apaches, but private members of the bourgeoisie."[1]

There is an interior in the detective novel. But can there be a detective story of the interior itself, of the hidden mechanisms by which space is constructed as interior? Which may be to say, a detective story of detection itself, of the controlling look, the look of control, the controlled look. But where would the traces of the look be imprinted? What do we have to go on? What clues?

There is an unknown passage of a well-known book, Le Corbusier's *Urbanisme* (1925), that reads: "Loos told me one day: 'A cultivated man does not look out of the window; his window is a ground glass; it is there only to let the light in, not to let the gaze pass through.'"[2] It points to a conspicuous yet conspicuously ignored feature of Loos's houses: not only are the windows either opaque or covered with sheer curtains, but the organization of the spaces and the disposition of the built-in furniture (the *immeuble*) seem to hinder access to them. A sofa is often placed at the foot of a window so as to position the occupants with their back to it, facing the room, as in the bedroom of the Hans Brummel apartment (Pilsen, 1929). This even happens with the windows that look into other interior spaces—as in the sitting area of the ladies' lounge of the Müller house (Prague, 1930). Or, more dramatically, in the houses for the Vienna Werkbundsiedlung (Vienna, 1930–1932), a late project where Loos has finally brought himself to make a thoroughly modern, double-height window; not only is this opening still veiled with a curtain, but a couch in the sitting nook of the upper-level gallery places the occupants with their back to the window, hovering dangerously over the space. (Symptomatically, and we must return to this point, when the sitting nook in an identical house is used as a man's study, the seat faces the window.) Moreover, upon entering a Loos interior one's body is continually turned around to face the space one has just moved through, rather than the upcoming space or the space outside. With each turn, each return look, the body is arrested. Looking at the photographs, it is easy to imagine oneself in these precise, static positions, usually indicated by the unoccupied furniture. The photographs suggest that it is intended that these spaces be comprehended by occupation, by using this furniture, by "entering" the photograph, by inhabiting it.[3]

In the Moller house (Vienna, 1928) there is a raised sitting area off the living room with a sofa set against the window. Although one cannot see out the window, its presence is strongly felt. The bookshelves surround-

Adolf Loos, flat for Hans Brummel, Pilsen, 1929. Bedroom with a sofa set against the window.

Adolf Loos, house for the Vienna Werkbundsiedlung, Vienna, 1930–1932. Living room on two levels with a sofa "against" the window and suspended in the space.

House for the Vienna Werkbundsiedlung. Corner study in the gallery, photo 1932.

ing the sofa and the light coming from behind it suggest a comfortable nook for reading. But comfort in this space is more than just sensual, for there is also a psychological dimension. A sense of security is produced by the position of the couch, the placement of its occupants against the light. Anyone who, ascending the stairs from the entrance (itself a rather dark passage), enters the living room, would take a few moments to recognize a person sitting on the couch. Conversely, any intrusion would soon be detected by a person occupying this area, just as an actor entering the stage is immediately seen by a spectator in a theater box.

Loos refers to this idea in noting that "the smallness of a theater box would be unbearable if one could not look out into the large space beyond."[4] While Kulka, and later Münz, read this comment in terms of the economy of space provided by the *Raumplan*, they overlook its psychological dimension. For Loos, the theater box exists at the intersection between claustrophobia and agoraphobia.[5] This spatial-psychological device could also be read in terms of power, regimes of control inside the house. The raised sitting area of the Moller house provides the occupant with a vantage point overlooking the interior. Comfort in this space is related to both intimacy and control.

This area is the most intimate of the sequence of living spaces, yet, paradoxically, rather than being at the heart of the house, it is placed at the periphery, pushing a volume out of the street facade, just above the front entrance. Moreover, it corresponds with the largest window on this elevation (almost a horizontal window). The occupant of this space can both detect anyone crossing-trespassing the threshold of the house (while screened by the curtain) and monitor any movement in the interior (while "screened" by the backlighting).

In this space, the window is only a source of light, not a frame for a view. The eye is turned toward the interior. The only exterior view that

Adolf Loos, Moller house, Vienna, 1928. The raised sitting area off the living room.

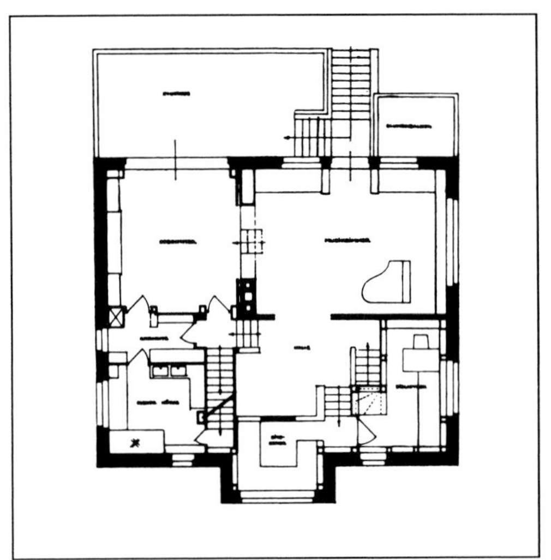

Moller house. Plan of the elevated ground floor, with the alcove drawn narrower than it was built.

Moller house. The staircase leading from the entrance hall into the living room.

Moller house. View from the street.

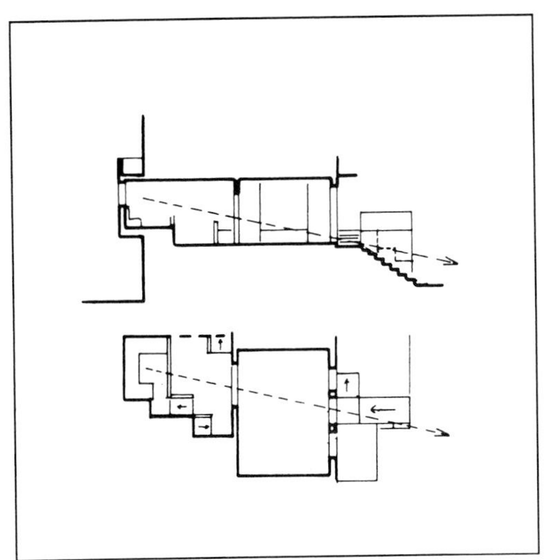

Moller house. Plan and section tracing the journey of the gaze from the raised sitting area to the back garden. Drawing by Johan van de Beek.

would be possible from this position requires that the gaze travel the whole depth of the house, from the alcove to the living room to the music room, which opens onto the back garden. Thus, the exterior view depends upon a view of the interior.

The look folded inward upon itself can be traced in other Loos interiors. In the Müller house, for instance, the sequence of spaces, articulated around the staircase, follows an increasing sense of privacy from the drawing room to the dining room and study to the "lady's room" (*Zimmer der Dame*) with its raised sitting area, which occupies the center or "heart" of the house.[6] But the window of this space looks onto the living space. Here, too, the most intimate room is like a theater box, placed just over the entrance to the social spaces in this house, so that any intruder could easily be seen. Likewise, the view of the exterior, toward the city, from this "theater box" is contained within a view of the interior. Suspended in the middle of the house, this space assumes the character both of a "sacred" space and of a point of control. Comfort is produced by two seemingly opposing conditions, intimacy and control.

This is hardly the idea of comfort that is associated with the nineteenth-century interior as described by Walter Benjamin in "Louis-Phillippe, or the Interior."[7] In Loos's interiors the sense of security is not achieved by simply turning one's back on the exterior and immersing oneself in a private universe—"a box in the world theater," to use Benjamin's metaphor. It is no longer the house that is a theater box; there is a theater box inside the house, overlooking the internal social spaces. The inhabitants of Loos's houses are both actors in and spectators of the family scene—involved in, yet detached from, their own space.[8] The classical distinction between inside and outside, private and public, object and subject, becomes convoluted.

Traditionally, the theater box provided for the privileged a private space within the dangerous public realm, by reestablishing the boundaries

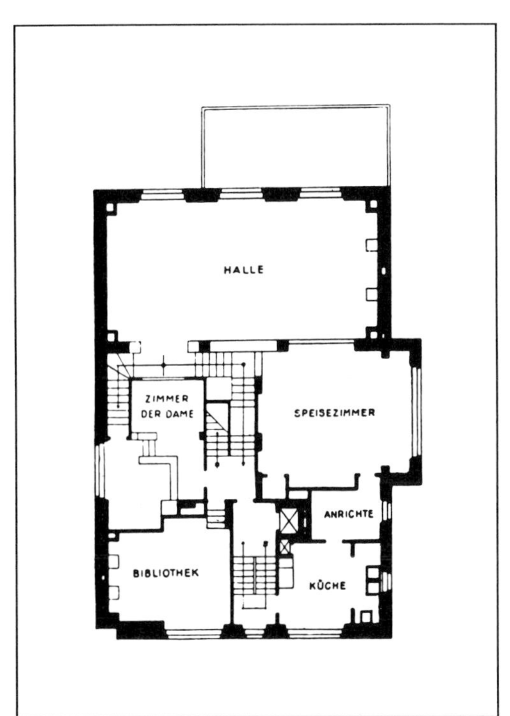

Adolf Loos, Müller house, Prague, 1930. Plan of the main floor.

Müller house. The raised sitting area in the Zimmer der Dame *with the window looking onto the living room.*

Müller house. Zimmer der Dame.

between inside and outside. It is significant that when Loos designed a theater in 1898 (an unrealized project), he omitted the boxes, arguing they "didn't suit a modern auditorium."[9] Thus he removes the box from the public theater, only to insert it into the "private theater" of the house. The public has entered the private house by way of the social spaces,[10] but there is a last site of resistance to this intrusion in the domestic "theater box."

The theater boxes in the Moller and Müller houses are spaces marked as "female," the domestic character of the furniture contrasting with that of the adjacent "male" space, the library. In these, the leather sofas, the desks, the chimney, the mirrors represent a "public space" within the house—the office and the club invading the interior. But it is an invasion that is confined to an enclosed room—a space that belongs to the sequence of social spaces within the house, yet does not engage with them. As Münz notes, the library is a "reservoir of quietness," "set apart from the household traffic." The raised alcove of the Moller house and the *Zimmer der Dame* of the Müller house, on the other hand, not only overlook the social spaces but are exactly positioned at the end of the sequence, on the threshold of the private, the secret, the upper rooms where sexuality is hidden away. At the intersection of the visible and the invisible, women are placed as the guardians of the unspeakable.[11]

But the theater box is a device that both provides protection and draws attention to itself. Thus, when Münz describes the entrance to the social spaces of the Moller house, he writes: "Within, entering from one side, one's gaze travels in the opposite direction till it rests in the light, pleasant alcove, raised above the living room floor. *Now we are really inside the house*."[12] So, where were we before? we may ask, when we crossed the threshold of the house and occupied the entrance hall and the cloakroom in the ground floor or while we ascended the stairs to the reception rooms on the second or elevated ground floor. The intruder is

Müller house. The library.

"inside," has penetrated the house, only when his/her gaze strikes this most intimate space, turning the occupant into a sihouette against the light. The "voyeur" in the "theater box" has become the object of another's gaze; she is caught in the act of seeing, entrapped in the very moment of control. In framing a view, the theater box also frames the viewer. It is impossible to abandon the space, let alone leave the house, without being seen by those over whom control is being exerted. Object and subject exchange places. Whether there is actually a person behind either gaze is irrelevant:

> **I can feel myself under the gaze of someone whose eyes I do not even see, not even discern. All that is necessary is for something to signify to me that there may be others there. The window if it gets a bit dark and if I have reasons for thinking that there is someone behind it, is straightway a gaze. From the moment this gaze exists, I am already something other, in that I feel myself becoming an object for the gaze of others. But in this position, which is a reciprocal one, others also know that I am an object who knows himself to be seen.**[13]

Architecture is not simply a platform that accommodates the viewing subject. It is a viewing mechanism that produces the subject. It precedes and frames its occupant.

The theatricality of Loos's interiors is constructed by many forms of representation (of which built space is not necessarily the most important). Many of the photographs, for instance, tend to give the impression that someone is just about to enter the room, that a piece of domestic drama is about to be enacted. The characters absent from the stage, from the scenery and from its props—the conspicuously placed pieces of furniture—are conjured up.[14] The only published photograph of a Loos domestic interior that includes a human figure is a view of the entrance to the drawing room of the Rufer house (Vienna, 1922). A

Adolf Loos's flat, Vienna, 1903. View from the living room into the fireplace nook.

male figure, barely visible, is about to cross the threshold through a peculiar opening in the wall.[15] But it is precisely at this threshold, slightly off stage, that the actor/intruder is most vulnerable, for a small window in the reading room looks down onto the back of his or her neck. This house, traditionally considered to be the prototype of the *Raumplan,* also contains the prototype of the theater box.

In his writings on the question of the house, Loos describes a number of domestic melodramas. In *Das Andere,* for example, he writes:

> **Try to describe how birth and death, the screams of pain for an aborted son, the death rattle of a dying mother, the last thoughts of a young woman who wishes to die . . . unfold and unravel in a room by Olbrich! Just an image: the young woman who has put herself to death. She is lying on the wooden floor. One of her hands still holds the smoking revolver. On the table a letter, the farewell letter. Is the room in which this is happening of good taste? Who will ask that? It is just a room![16]**

One could as well ask why it is only the women who die and cry and commit suicide. But leaving aside this question for the moment, Loos is saying that the house must not be conceived of as a work of art, that there is a difference between a house and a "series of decorated rooms." The house is the stage for the theater of the family, a place where people are born and live and die. Whereas a work of art, a painting, presents itself to a detached viewer as an object, the house is received as an environment, as a stage, in which the viewer is involved.

To set the scene, Loos breaks down the condition of the house as an object by radically convoluting the relation between inside and outside. One of the strategies he uses is mirrors that, as Kenneth Frampton has pointed out, appear to be openings, and openings that can be mistaken for mirrors.[17] Even more enigmatic is the placement, in the dining room

Adolf Loos, Rufer house, Vienna, 1922. Entrance to the living room.

Adolf Loos, Tristan Tzara house, Paris, 1926–1927. Entrance hall.

of the Steiner house (Vienna, 1910), of a mirror just beneath an opaque window.[18] Here again the window is only a source of light. The mirror, placed at eye level, returns the gaze to the interior, to the lamp above the dining table and the objects on the sideboard, recalling Freud's studio in Berggasse 19, where a small framed mirror hanging against the window reflects the lamp on his work table. In Freudian theory the mirror represents the psyche. The reflection in the mirror is also a self-portrait projected onto the outside world. The placement of Freud's mirror on the boundary between interior and exterior undermines the status of the boundary as a fixed limit. Inside and outside cannot simply be separated. Similarly, Loos's mirrors promote the interplay between reality and illusion, between the actual and virtual, undermining the status of the boundary between inside and outside.

This ambiguity between inside and outside is intensified by the separation of sight from the other senses. Physical and visual connections between the spaces in Loos's houses are often separated. In the Rufer house, a wide opening establishes a visual connection between the raised dining room and the music room that does not correspond to the physical connection. Similarly, in the Moller house there appears to be no way of entering the dining room from the music room, which is 70 centimeters below; the only means of access is by unfolding steps that are hidden in the timber base of the dining room.[19] This strategy of physical separation and visual connection, of "framing," is repeated in many other Loos interiors. Openings are often screened by curtains, enhancing the stagelike effect. It should also be noted that it is usually the dining room that acts as the stage, and the music room as the space for the spectators. What is being framed is the traditional scene of everyday domestic life.

But the breakdown between inside and outside, and the split between sight and touch, is not located exclusively in the domestic scene. It also

Adolf Loos, Steiner house, Vienna, 1910. View of the dining room showing the mirror beneath the window.

Sigmund Freud's study, Berggasse 19, Vienna. Detail of the mirror in the window near his worktable.

Moller house. View from the music room into the dining room. In the center of the threshold are steps that can be let down.

Moller house. View from the dining room into the music room.

occurs in Loos's project for a house for Josephine Baker (Paris, 1928)—a house that excludes family life. However, in this instance the "split" acquires a different meaning. The house was designed to contain a large top-lit, double-height swimming pool, with entry at the second-floor level. Kurt Ungers, a close collaborator of Loos in this project, wrote:

> **The reception rooms on the first floor arranged round the pool—a large salon with an extensive top-lit vestibule, a small lounge and the circular café—indicate that this was intended not for private use but as a *miniature entertainment centre.* On the first floor, low passages surround the pool. They are lit by the wide windows visible on the outside, and from them, thick, transparent windows are let into the side of the pool, so that it was possible to watch swimming and diving in its crystal-clear water, flooded with light from above: an *underwater revue,* so to speak.**[20]

As in Loos's earlier houses, the eye is directed toward the interior, which turns its back on the outside world; but the subject and object of the gaze have been reversed. The inhabitant, Josephine Baker, is now the primary object, and the visitor, the guest, is the looking subject. The most intimate space—the swimming pool, paradigm of a sensual space—occupies the center of the house, and is also the focus of the visitor's gaze. As Ungers writes, entertainment in this house consists in looking. But between this gaze and its object—the body—is a screen of glass and water, which renders the body inaccessible. The swimming pool is lit from above, by a skylight, so that inside it the windows would appear as reflective surfaces, impeding the swimmer's view of the visitors standing in the passages. This view is the opposite of the panoptic view of a theater box, corresponding, instead, to that of a peephole, where subject and object cannot simply exchange places.

The *mise en-scène* in the Josephine Baker house recalls Christian Metz's description of the mechanism of voyeurism in cinema:

Adolf Loos, project for a house for Josephine Baker in Paris, 1928. Model.

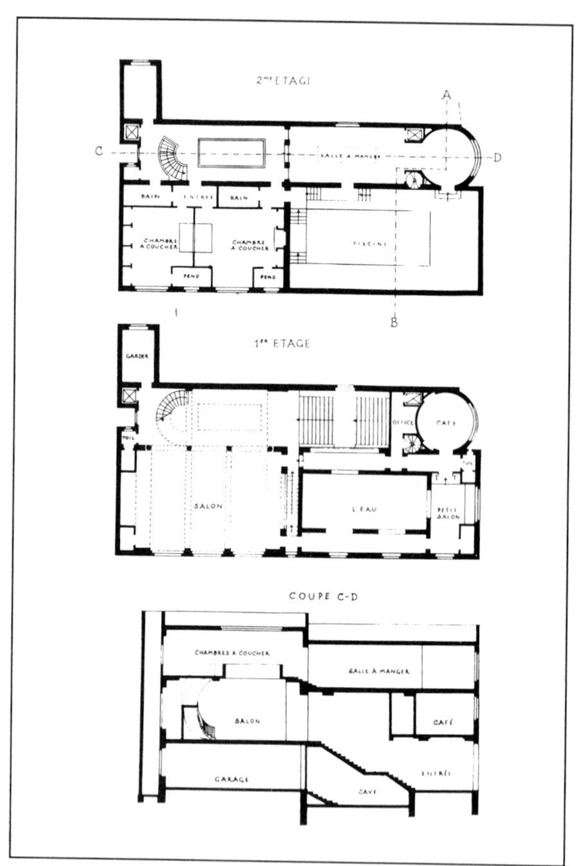

Josephine Baker house. Plans of first and second floors.

Josephine Baker.

> **It is even essential . . . that the actor should behave as though he were not seen (and therefore as though he did not see his voyeur), that he should go about his ordinary business and pursue his existence as foreseen by the fiction of the film, that he should carry on with his antics in a closed room, taking the utmost care not to notice that a glass rectangle has been set into one of the walls, and that he lives in a kind of aquarium.[21]**

But the architecture of this house is more complicated. The swimmer might also see the reflection, framed by the window, of her own slippery body superimposed on the disembodied eyes of the shadowy figure of the spectator, whose lower body is cut out by the frame. Thus she sees herself being looked at by another: a narcissistic gaze superimposed on a voyeuristic gaze. This erotic complex of looks in which she is suspended is inscribed in each of the four windows opening onto the swimming pool. Each, even if there is no one looking through it, constitutes, from both sides, a gaze.

The split between sight and the other physical senses that is found in Loos interiors is explicit in his definition of architecture. In "The Principle of Cladding," Loos's most Semperian text, he writes: "The artist, the architect, first senses the *effect* that he intends to realize and [then] sees the rooms he wants to create in his mind's eye. He senses the effect that he wishes to exert upon the *spectator* . . . homeyness if a residence."[22] For Loos, the interior is pre-Oedipal space, space before the analytical distancing that language entails, space as we feel it, as clothing; that is, as clothing before the existence of readymade clothes, when one had first to choose the fabric (and this act required, or I seem to remember as much, a distinct gesture of looking away from the cloth while feeling its texture, as if the sight of it would be an obstacle to the sensation).

Loos seems to have reversed the Cartesian schism between the perceptual and conceptual. Whereas Descartes, as Franco Rella has written, deprived the body of its status as "the seat of valid and transmissible knowledge" ("In sensation, in the experience that derives from it, harbors error"),[23] Loos privileges the bodily experience of space over its mental construction: the architect first senses the space, then he visualizes it.

For Loos, architecture is a form of covering. But it is not simply the walls that are covered. Structure plays a secondary role, and its primary function is to hold the covering in place. Following Semper almost literally, Loos writes:

> **The architect's general task is to provide a warm and livable space. Carpets are warm and livable. He decides for this reason to spread one carpet on the floor and to hang up four to form the four walls. But you cannot build a house out of carpets. Both the carpet on the floor and the tapestry on the wall require a structural frame to hold them in the correct place. To invent this frame is the architect's second task.**[24]

The spaces of Loos's interiors cover the occupants as clothes cover the body (each occasion has its appropriate "fit"). José Quetglas has written: "Would the same pressure on the body be acceptable in a raincoat as in a gown, in jodhpurs or in pyjama pants? . . . All the architecture of Loos can be explained as the envelope of a body." From Lina Loos's bedroom (this "bag of fur and cloth") to Josephine Baker's swimming pool ("this transparent bowl of water"), the interiors always contain a "warm bag in which to wrap oneself." It is an "architecture of pleasure," an "architecture of the womb."[25]

But space in Loos's architecture is not just felt. It is significant, in the quotation above, that Loos refers to the inhabitant as a "spectator," for

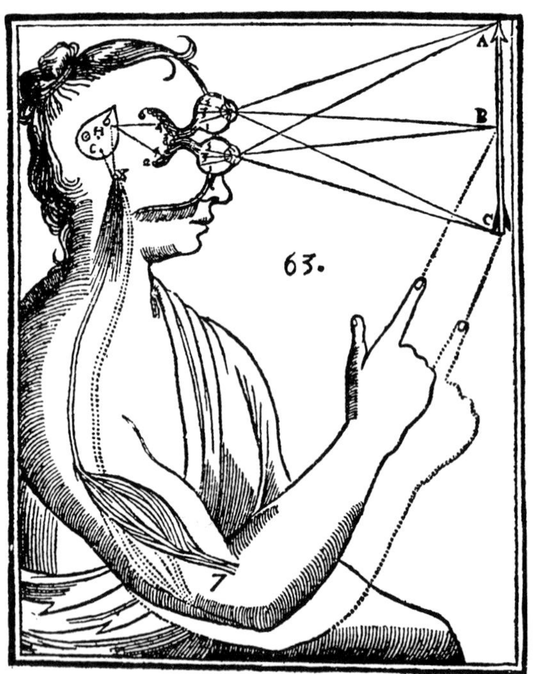

Diagram from the Traité des passions *of René Descartes.*

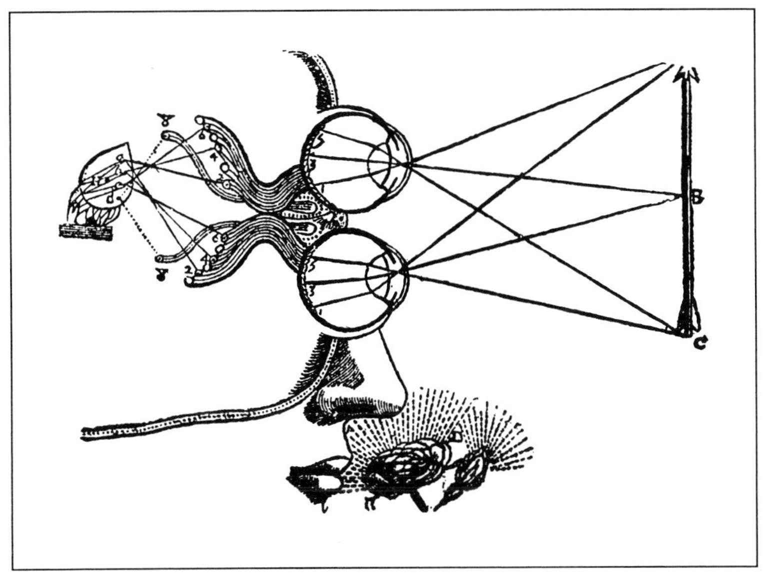

From the Traité des passions.

Adolf Loos's flat. Lina Loos's bedroom.

his definition of architecture is really a definition of theatrical architecture. The "clothes" have become so removed from the body that they require structural support independent of it. They become a "stage set." The inhabitant is both "covered" by the space and "detached" from it. The tension between sensation of comfort and comfort as control disrupts the role of the house as a traditional form of representation.

It also disrupts any representation of the house. The status of the architectural drawing, for example, is radically transformed. In "Architecture" Loos writes: "The mark of a building which is truly established is that it remains *ineffective* in two dimensions."[26] By "ineffective" he means that the drawing cannot convey the "sensation" of space, as this involves not only sight but also the other physical senses.[27] Loos devised the *Raumplan* as a means of conceptualizing space as it is felt, but, revealingly, he left no theoretical definition of it. As Kulka has noted, he "will make many changes during construction. He will walk through the space and say: 'I do not like the height of this ceiling, change it!' The idea of the *Raumplan* made it difficult to finish a scheme before construction allowed the visualization of the space as it was." Or as Neutra recalls, Loos "prided himself on being an architect without a pencil":

> In the year 1900, Adolf Loos started a revolt against the practice of indicating dimensions in figures or measured drawings. He felt, as he often told me, that such a procedure dehumanizes design. "If I want a wood paneling or wainscot to be of a certain height, I stand there, hold my hand at that certain height, and the carpenter makes his pencil mark. Then I step back and look at it from one point and from another, visualizing the finished result with all my powers. This is the only human way to decide on the height of a wainscot, or on the width of a window." Loos was inclined to use a minimum of paper plans; he carried in his head all the details of even his most complex designs.[28]

But Loos was not simply opposing sensual experience to abstraction. Rather, he was dealing with the intranslatability of languages. Because a drawing cannot convey the tension between the other senses and sight it cannot adequately translate a building. For Loos, the architect's drawing was a consequence of the division of labor, it could never be more than a mere technical statement, "the attempt [by the architect] to make himself understood by the craftsman carrying out the work."[29]

Loos's critique of the photography of architecture and its dissemination through architectural journals was based on the same principle, that it is impossible to represent a spatial effect or a sensation. When he writes: "It is my greatest pride that the interiors which I have created are totally *ineffective* in photographs. I am proud of the fact that the inhabitants of my spaces do not recognise their own apartments in the photographs, just as the owner of a Monet painting would not recognise it at Kastan's,"[30] his point is that photographs and drawings could not adequately reproduce his interiors because these possess tactile as well as optical qualities.

But also, inhabitants fail to recognize their own houses in the photographs because of the transformation that occurs in the process of reproduction. The inhabited house is perceived as an environment, not as an object, and therefore its reception occurs in a state of distraction. The photographs of a house in an architectural journal require a different kind of attention, an attention that presupposes distance. This distance is closer to that required of a spectator in the contemplation of a work of art in a museum: Loos's Monet example. Loos interiors are experienced as a frame for action rather than as an object in a frame.

However, there is something systematic about the photographs of Loos's interiors that seems to suggest his involvement in their production. The repeated presence of certain objects, such as the Egyptian stool, in nearly every interior view has been noted by Kenneth Frampton. Loos also seems to have adjusted the photographs to better represent his own idea of the house. The archives containing the photographs used to illustrate Kulka's book reveal a few of these tricks: the view through the "horizontal window" in the photograph of the Khuner villa (near Payerbach, 1930) is a photomontage,[31] as is the cello in the cabinet of the music room of the Moller house. A story was added to the photograph of the street facade of the Tristan Tzara house (Paris, 1926–1927) so as to make it more like the original project, and numerous "distracting" domestic objects (lamps, rugs, plants) were erased throughout. These interventions suggest that images were carefully controlled, that the photographs of Loos's buildings cannot simply be considered as a form of representation subordinate to the building itself.

For example, Loos often frames a spatial volume, as in the bedroom of the Khuner villa or the fireplace nook of his own apartment. This has the effect of flattening the space seen through the frame, making it seem more like a photograph. As with the device of obscuring the differences between openings and mirrors, this optical effect is enhanced, if not produced, by the photographs themselves, which are taken only from the precise point where the effect occurs.[32] Loos's critique of the photographic representation of architecture should not be mistaken for a nostalgia for the "real" object. What he achieves in this play with reflective surfaces and framing devices is a critique of photography as a transparent medium, and by extension a critique of classical representation. Such framing devices undermine the referential status of the photographic image and its claim to represent reality "as it is." The photographs draw the viewer's attention to the artifice involved in the photographic process. Like drawings, they are not representations in the traditional sense; they do not simply refer to a preexisting object, they produce the object; they literally construct their object.

Loos's critique of traditional notions of architectural representation is bound up with the phenomenon of an emergent metropolitan culture.

Adolf Loos, Khuner villa, near Payerbach, Austria, 1930. The "view" through the window is a photomontage.

He recognized social institutions as systems of representation, and his attacks on the family, Viennese society, professional organizations, and the state, launched in *Das Andere,* were implicit in his buildings. Architecture in all its possible manifestations—drawing, photograph, text, or building—is, after all, only a practice of representation. The subject of Loos's architecture is the citizen of the metropolis, immersed in its abstract relationships and striving to assert the independence and individuality of its existence in the face of the leveling power of society. This battle, according to George Simmel, is the modern equivalent of primitive man's struggle with nature; clothing is one of the battlefields, and fashion is one of its strategies.[33] He writes: "The commonplace is good form in society. . . . It is bad taste to make oneself conspicuous through some individual, singular expression. . . . Obedience to the standards of the general public in all externals [is] the conscious and desired means of reserving their personal feelings and their taste."[34] In other words, fashion is a mask that protects the intimacy of the metropolitan being.

Loos writes about fashion in precisely such terms: "We have become more refined, more subtle. Primitive men had to differentiate themselves by various colors, modern man needs his clothes as a mask. His individuality is so strong that it can no longer be expressed in terms of items of clothing. . . . His own inventions are concentrated on other things."[35] Fashion and etiquette, in Western culture, constitute the language of behavior, a language that does not convey feelings but acts as a form of protection—a mask. As Loos writes, "How should one dress? Modern. One is modernly dressed when one stands out the least."

Significantly, Loos writes about the exterior of the house in the same terms as he writes about fashion:

> **When I was finally given the task of building a house, I said to myself: in its external appearance, a house can only have changed as much as a**

dinner jacket. Not a lot therefore. . . . I had to become significantly simpler. I had to substitute the golden buttons with black ones. The house has to look inconspicuous.[36]

The house does not have to tell anything to the exterior; instead, all its richness must be manifest in the interior.[37]

Loos seems to establish a radical difference between interior and exterior, which reflects the split between the intimate and the social life of the metropolitan being: "outside," the realm of exchange, money, and masks; "inside," the realm of the inalienable, the nonexchangeable, and the unspeakable. Moreover, this split between inside and outside, between the other senses and sight, is gender-loaded. The exterior of the house, Loos writes, should resemble a dinner jacket, a male mask, as the unified self, protected by a seamless facade, is masculine. The interior is the scene of sexuality and of reproduction, all the things that would divide the subject in the outside world. However, this dogmatic division in Loos's writings between inside and outside is undermined by his architecture.

The suggestion that the exterior is merely a mask that clads some preexisting interior is misleading, for the interior and exterior are constructed simultaneously. When he was designing the Rufer house, for example, Loos used a dismountable model that would allow the internal and external distributions to be worked out simultaneously. The interior is not simply the space that is enclosed by the facades. A multiplicity of boundaries is established, and the tension between inside and outside resides in the walls that divide them, its status disturbed by Loos's displacement of traditional forms of representation. To address the interior of Loos is to address the splitting of the wall.

Take, for instance, the shift of drawing conventions in Loos's four pencil drawings of the elevation of the Rufer house. Each one shows not only

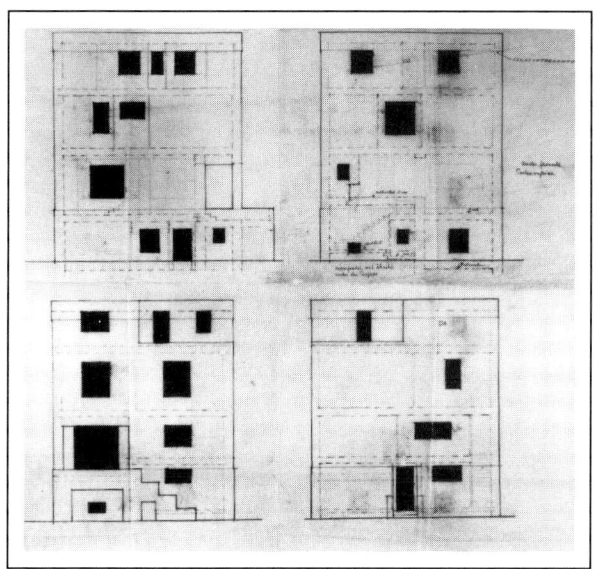

Rufer house. Elevations.

the outlines of the facade but also, in dotted lines, the horizontal and vertical divisions of the interior, the position of the rooms, and the thickness of the floors and the walls, while the windows are represented as black squares, with no frame. These are drawings of neither the inside nor the outside but the membrane between them: between the representation of habitation and the mask is the wall. Loos's subject inhabits this wall. This inhabitation creates a tension on that limit, tampers with it.

This is not simply a metaphor. In every Loos house there is a point of maximum tension, and it always coincides with a threshold or boundary. In the Moller house it is the raised alcove protruding from the street facade, where the occupant is ensconced in the security of the interior yet detached from it. The subject of Loos's houses is a stranger, an intruder in its own space. In Josephine Baker's house, the wall of the swimming pool is punctured by windows. It has been pulled apart, leaving a narrow passage surrounding the pool, and splitting each of the windows into an internal window and an external window. The visitor literally inhabits this wall, which enables him to look both inside, at the pool, and outside, at the city, but he is neither inside nor outside the house. In the dining room of the Steiner house, the gaze directed toward the window is folded back by the mirror beneath it, transforming the interior into an exterior view, a scene. The subject has been dislocated: unable to occupy the inside of the house securely, it can only occupy the insecure margin between window and mirror.

This tampering with the limits is intensified in Loos's Goldman & Salatsch men's wear store in Vienna of 1898. The space of this shop is halfway between the private universe of the interior and the outside world. It occupies the intersection between body and language, between the space of domesticity and that of social exchange, of economy. Goldman & Salatsch provided its clients with underwear and external accessories such as ties, hats, and walking sticks—that is, with the most intimate garments, the clothes most closely held to the body, as well as the objects that support (literally and symbolically) the body as a figure (the body's props, its prostheses). In this store, the "invisible," the most intimate garments, are exhibited and sold: they have abandoned the sphere of domesticity for the sphere of exchange. Conversely, the "visible," the objects that most obviously represent the site of exchange, the mask that safeguards the coherence of the human figure in the public realm, have entered the interior.

A photograph published in *Das Interieur* in 1901 shows a space clad with tall rectangular mirrors set in dark frames. Some of the mirrors are fixed, others are cabinet doors, yet others coincide with openings into other spaces. There are two male figures, one presumably a client emerging from the intimate atmosphere of the fitting room, the other an accountant who has entered from the exterior world of finance. They are both occupying the same wall, but the nature of that occupation is unclear. One of them seems to be standing at the threshold of an opening, his image reflected on the mirror-door, perhaps again in the cupboard door to the right. Even more enigmatic is the other figure, for only the upper part of the body is visible, behind bars, as if confined within a cage. Even with the recently reconstructed plan of the shop (which no longer exists), the actual position of the figures within the space cannot be established. One of them seems to be standing beside the image of his back—or is it the other way around? The depth of his body, its material presence, has been erased. Other reflections appear throughout the space, without any body to ground them.

In the midst of the intricate space of this photograph, only the figure of a woman is "complete" and clearly there, *in* the space. As if to indicate, once more, that in modernity it is the male subject, or rather the construct of masculinity itself, that no longer knows where to stand. The threat of modernity, how to master the uncontrollability of the metropolis, is that of castration. In this sense, perhaps one should pay closer

Adolf Loos, showroom, Goldman & Salatsch men's wear shop, Vienna, 1898.

attention to the repeated association of the metropolis and its undefined boundaries with femininity.

Furthermore, the subject that is split and its fragments multiplied in the photograph of Goldman & Salatsch is not the only "inhabitant" of the space. The dissolution of the figures into the wall surfaces questions not only their position but also that of the person viewing the photograph. The spectator of the photograph, attempting to master the image, no longer knows where he or she stands in relationship to the picture.

Even Loos, supposedly the very figure of mastery as the architect of the space, is also a troubled spectator of his own work. The illusion of Loos as an authority, a man in control, in charge of his own work, an undivided subject, is suspect. In fact, he is constructed, controlled, and fractured by the work. The idea of the *Raumplan*, for example: Loos constructs a space (without having completed the working drawings), then allows himself to be manipulated by this construction. Like the occupants of his houses, he is both inside and outside the object. The object has as much authority over him as he over it. He is not simply an author.[38]

The critic is no exception to this phenomenon. Incapable of detachment from the object, the critic simultaneously produces a new object and is produced by it. Criticism that presents itself as a new interpretation of an existing object is in fact constructing a completely new object. The Loos of the 1960s, the austere pioneer of the modern movement, was replaced in the 1970s by another Loos, all sensuality, and in the 1980s by Loos the classicist. On the other hand, readings that claim to be noninterpretive, purely objective inventories, the standard monographs on Loos—Münz and Künstler in the 1960s and Gravagnuolo in the 1980s—are thrown off balance by the very object of their control. Nowhere is this alienation more evident than in their interpretations of the house for Josephine Baker.

Münz, otherwise a wholly circumspect writer, begins his appraisal of this house with the exclamation: "Africa: that is the image conjured up more or less firmly by a contemplation of the model," but he then confesses not to know why he invoked this image.[39] He attempts to analyze the formal characteristics of the project, but all he can conclude is that "they look strange and exotic." What is most striking in this passage is the momentary uncertainty as to whether Münz is referring to the model of the house or to Josephine Baker herself. He seems unable either to detach himself from this project or to enter into it.

Like Münz, Gravagnuolo finds himself writing things without knowing why, reprimands himself, then tries to regain control:

> **First there is the charm of this gay architecture. It is not just the dichromatism of the façades but—as we shall see—the spectacular nature of the internal articulation that determines its refined and seductive character. Rather than abandon oneself to the pleasure of suggestions, it is necessary to take this "toy" to pieces with *analytical detachment* if one wishes to understand the mechanism of composition.**[40]

He then institutes a regime of analytical categories ("the architectural introversion," "the revival of dichromatism," "the plastic arrangement") that he uses nowhere else in the book. And he concludes:

> **The water flooded with light, the refreshing swim, the voyeuristic pleasure of underwater exploration—these are the carefully balanced ingredients of this gay architecture. But what matters more is that the invitation to the spectacular suggested by the theme of the house for a cabaret star is handled by Loos with discretion and *intellectual detachment*, more as a poetic game, involving the mnemonic pursuit of quotations and allusions to the Roman spirit, than as a vulgar surrender to the taste of Hollywood.**[41]

Gravagnuolo ends up crediting Loos with the "detachment" (from Hollywood, vulgar taste, feminized culture) in "handling" the project that the critic himself was attempting to regain in its analysis. The insistence on detachment, on reestablishing the distance between critic and object of criticism, architect and building, subject and object, is of course indicative of the obvious fact that Münz and Gravagnuolo have failed to separate themselves from the object. The image of Josephine Baker offers pleasure but also represents the threat of castration posed by the "other": the image of woman in water—liquid, elusive, unable to be controlled, pinned down. One way of dealing with this threat is fetishization.

The Josephine Baker house represents a shift in the status of the body. This shift involves determinations not only of gender but also of race and class. The theater box of the domestic interiors places the occupant against the light. The body appears as a silhouette, mysterious and desirable, but the backlighting also draws attention to it as a physical volume, a bodily presence within the house with its own interior. The occupant controls the interior, yet it is trapped within it. In the Baker house, the body is produced as spectacle, the object of an erotic gaze, an erotic system of looks. The exterior of the house cannot be read as a silent mask designed to conceal its interior; it is a tattooed surface that does not refer to the interior, it neither conceals nor reveals it. This fetishization of the surface is repeated in the "interior." In the passages, the visitors consume Baker's body as a surface adhering to the windows. Like the body, the house is all surface; it does not simply have an interior.

Window

In the houses of Le Corbusier the reverse condition of Loos's interiors may be observed. In photographs windows are never covered with curtains, neither is access to them prevented by means of hampering objects. On the contrary, everything in these houses seems to be disposed in a way that continuously throws the subject toward the periphery of the house. The look is directed to the exterior in such a deliberate manner as to suggest the reading of these houses as frames for a view. Even when actually in an "exterior," in a terrace or in a "roof garden," walls are constructed to frame the landscape, and a view from there to the interior, as in a canonic photograph of Villa Savoye, passes right through it to the framed landscape (so that in fact one can speak about a series of overlapping frames). These frames are given temporality through the *promenade*. Unlike in Adolf Loos's houses, perception here occurs in motion. It is hard to think of oneself in static positions. If the photographs of Loos's interiors give the impression that somebody is about to enter the room, in Le Corbusier's the impression is that somebody was just there, leaving as traces a coat and a hat lying on the table

Le Corbusier, Villa Savoye, Poissy, 1929. **Jardin suspendu.**

Villa Savoye. The entrance hall.

Villa Savoye. The kitchen.

Le Corbusier, Villa à Garches, 1927. The kitchen.

Villa Savoye. The roof garden.

by the entrance of Villa Savoye or some bread and a jug on the kitchen table (note also that the door here has been left open, further suggesting the idea that we have just missed somebody), or a raw fish in the kitchen of Garches (whatever one can make of it). And even once we have reached the highest point of the house, as in the terrace of Villa Savoye on the sill of the window that frames the landscape, the culminating point of the promenade, here also we find a hat, a pair of sunglasses, a little package (cigarettes?) and a lighter, and now, where did the *gentleman* go? Because of course, as you would have noticed already, the personal objects are all male objects (never a handbag, a lipstick, or some piece of women's clothing). But before that. We are following somebody, the traces of his existence presented to us in the form of a series of photographs of the interior. The look into these photographs is a forbidden look. The look of a detective. A voyeuristic look.[1]

In the movie *L'Architecture d'aujourd'hui* (1929), directed by Pierre Chenal with Le Corbusier,[2] the latter as the main actor drives his own car to the entrance of the Villa à Garches, descends and enters the house in an energetic manner. He is wearing a dark suit with bow tie, his hair is glued with brilliantine, every hair in place, he is holding a cigarette in his mouth. The camera pans through the exterior of the house and arrives at the "roof garden," where there are women sitting down and children playing. A little boy is driving his toy car. At this point Le Corbusier appears again but on the other side of the terrace (he never comes in contact with the women and children). He is puffing his cigarette. He then very athletically climbs up the spiral staircase that leads to the highest point of this house, a lookout point. Still wearing his formal attire, the cigarette still sticking out of his mouth, he pauses to contemplate the view from that point. He looks out.

There is also a figure of a woman going through a house in this movie. The house that frames her is Villa Savoye. Here there is no car arriving. The camera shows the house from the distance, an object sitting in the

Villa à Garches. Still from
L'Architecture d'aujourd'hui, *1929.*

Villa à Garches. Still from
L'Architecture d'aujourd'hui.

Villa Savoye. Still from
L'Architecture d'aujourd'hui: *"Une maison ce n'est pas une prison: l'aspect change à chaque pas."*

landscape, and then pans the outside and the inside of the house. And it is there, halfway through the interior, that the woman appears on the screen. She is already inside, already contained by the house, bounded. She opens the door that leads to the terrace and goes up the ramp toward the roof garden, her back to the camera. She is wearing "inside" (informal) clothes and high heels and she holds to the handrail as she goes up, her skirt and hair blowing in the wind. She appears vulnerable. Her body is fragmented, framed not only by the camera but by the house itself, behind bars. She appears to be moving from the inside of the house to the outside, to the roof garden. But this outside is again constructed as an inside, with a wall wrapping the space in which an opening with the proportions of a window frames the landscape. The woman continues walking along the wall, as if protected by it, and as the wall makes a curve to form the solarium, the woman turns too, picks up a chair, and sits down. She would be facing the "interior," the space she has just moved through. But for the camera, which now shows us a general view of the terrace, she has disappeared behind the bushes. That is, just at the moment when she has turned and could face the camera (there is nowhere else to go), she vanishes. She never catches our eye. Here we are literally following somebody, the point of view is that of a voyeur.

We could accumulate more evidence. Few photographs of Le Corbusier's buildings show people in them. But in those few, women always look away from the camera: most of the time they are shot from the back and they almost never occupy the same space as men. Take the photographs of Immeuble Clarté in the *Oeuvre complète*, for example. In one of them, the woman and the child are in the interior, they are shot from the back, facing the wall; the men are on the balcony, looking out, toward the city. In the next shot, the woman, again shot from the back, is leaning against the window to the balcony and looking at the man and the child who are on the balcony. This spatial structure is repeated very often,

Le Corbusier, Immeuble Clarté, Geneva, 1930–1932. View of the interior.

Immeuble Clarté. The terrace.

not only in the photographs but also in the drawings of Le Corbusier's projects. In a drawing of the Wanner project, for example, the woman in the upper floor is leaning against the veranda, looking down to her hero, the boxer, who is occupying the *jardin suspendu*. He looks at his punching bag. And in the drawing "Ferme radieuse," the woman in the kitchen looks over the counter toward the man sitting at the dining room table. He is reading the newspaper. Here again the woman is placed "inside," the man "outside"; the woman looks at the man, the man looks at the "world."

But perhaps no example is more telling than the photocollage of the exhibit of a living room in the Salon d'Automne 1929, including all the "equipment of a dwelling," a project that Le Corbusier realized in collaboration with Charlotte Perriand, whose credit for it has been practically erased. In fact, today we know this furniture as "Le Corbusier's" when some of the pieces, the *siège tournant*, for example, were designed, exhibited, and published by Perriand before she met Le Corbusier.[3] In this image, which Le Corbusier published in the *Oeuvre complète*, Perriand herself is lying on the *chaise-longue*, her head turned away from the camera. More significant, in the original photograph employed in this photocollage (as well as in another photograph in the *Oeuvre complète* that shows the *chaise-longue* in the horizontal position), one can see that the chair has been placed right against the wall. Remarkably, she is facing the wall. She is almost an attachment to the wall. She sees nothing.

And of course for Le Corbusier, who writes things such as "I exist in life only on condition that I see" (*Précisions*, 1930) or "This is the key: to look . . . to look/observe/see/imagine/invent, create" (1963), and in the last weeks of his life, "I am and I remain an impenitent visual" (*Mise au point*), everything is in the visual.[4] But what does *vision* mean here?

If we now return to the passage in *Urbanisme* where Le Corbusier refers to Loos's window ("Loos told me one day: 'A cultivated man does not look out of the window; his window is a ground glass; it is there only to let the light in, not to let the gaze pass through'"),[5] we find that he has left us a clue to the enigma in that very passage, when he goes on to say: "Such sentiment [that of Loos with regard to the window] can have an explanation in the congested, disordered city where disorder appears in distressing images; one could even admit the paradox [of a Loosian window] before a sublime natural spectacle, too sublime."[6]

For Le Corbusier the metropolis itself was "too sublime." The look in Le Corbusier's architecture is not that look which would still pretend to contemplate the metropolitan spectacle with the detachment of a nineteenth-century observer before a sublime natural landscape (as in the paintings of Caspar David Friedrich). It is not the look in Hugh Ferriss's drawings of *The Metropolis of Tomorrow*, for example, where a small figure perched on the top of a skyscraper looks down into the bottomless abyss of the canyons of an imaginary city, in the same way that Friedrich's small figures dressed in city clothes look into the unframable spectacle of nature.[7]

In this sense, the penthouse that Le Corbusier did for Charles de Beistegui in an existing building on the Champs-Elysées, Paris (1929–1931), becomes symptomatic. In this house, originally intended not to be inhabited but to receive visitors and to act as a frame for parties ("day parties, night parties," says Le Corbusier), there was no electric lighting. Beistegui wrote: "The candle has recovered all its rights because it is the only one which gives a *living* light."[8] Instead, "electricity, modern power, is invisible, it does not illuminate the dwelling, but activates the doors and moves the walls."[9] Invisible like the "docile servant" that Le Corbusier identifies in *L'Art décoratif d'aujourd'hui* with the "human limb objects" (those "extensions of our limbs" that respond

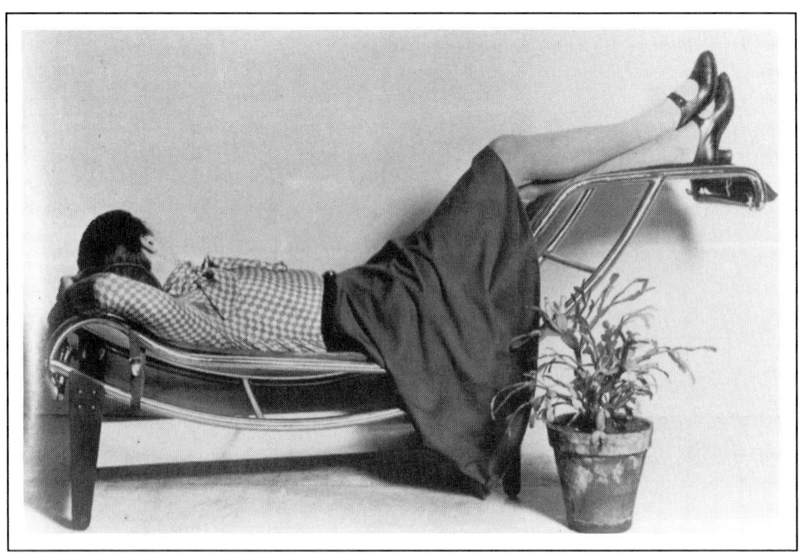

Charlotte Perriand in the chaise-longue *against the wall. Salon d'Automne 1929.*

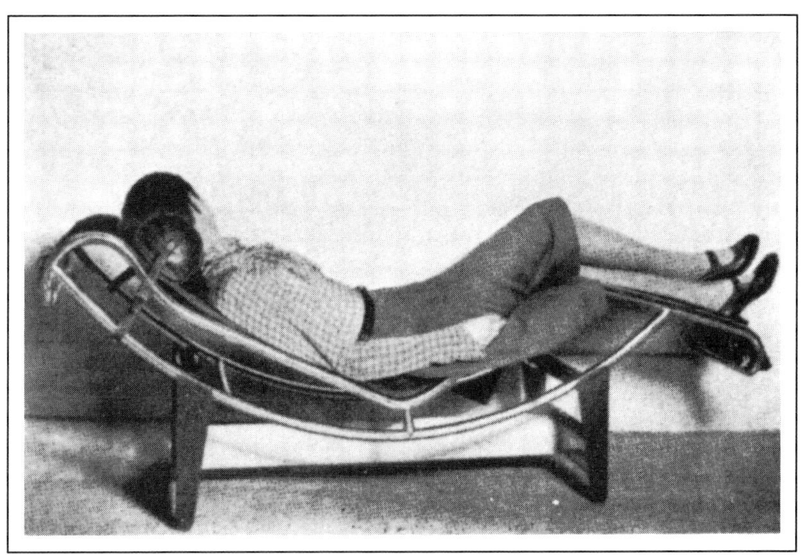

Chaise-longue *in the horizontal position.*

Le Corbusier, Charles de Beistegui apartment, Paris, 1929–1931.

to our "type-needs" [*besoins-types*]), "discreet and self-effacing, in order to leave his master free,"[10] electricity is used *inside* this apartment to slide away partition walls, operate doors, and allow cinematographic projections on the metal screen (which unfolds automatically as the chandelier rises up on pulleys), and *outside*, on the roof terrace, to slide the banks of hedges to frame the view of Paris: "En pressant un bouton électrique, la palissade de verdure s'écarte et Paris apparaît."[11] Electricity is not used here to illuminate, to make *visible*, but as a technology of framing. Doors, walls, hedges, that is to say traditional architectural framing devices, are activated with electric power, but so also are the built-in cinema camera and its projection screen, and when these modern frames are *lit*, the "living" light of the chandelier gives way to another living light, the flickering light of the movie, the "flick."

This new "lighting" of the movies displaces traditional forms of enclosure, as electricity had done before it. Around the time that the Beistegui apartment was built, La Compagnie parisienne de distribution d'électricité put out a publicity book, *L'Electricité à la maison*, attempting to gain clients. In this book, electricity is made *visible* through architecture. A series of photographs by André Kertész present views of interiors by contemporary architects, including A. Perret, Chausat, Laprade, and M. Perret. One of them, perhaps the most extraordinary, is a closeup of a "horizontal window" in the terrace (enclosed with glass) of an apartment by Chausat, with a view of Paris outside it and a fan sitting on the sill of the window. The image marks the split between two traditional functions of the window, ventilation and light, now displaced into powered machines, and the modern function of a window, to frame a view. The Beistegui apartment, on the other hand, is a commentary on the new conditions presented by the media. Not only is electricity used here to operate the new media apparatus ("*la T.S.F., le théâtrophone et le pick-up*, which are installed on multiple settings, on the roof garden, the drawing room, the bedroom . . .")[12] but the views from the inside and

L'Electricité à la maison. *Chaussat, architect. A. Kertész, photographer.*

outside spaces of the apartment are also technologically controlled: "From this belvedere Paris is visible in all its horizons . . . but the *parti* was to suppress this panoramic view of Paris . . . offering [instead], at precise places, moving views [*perspectives émouvantes*] of four of the things, visible from there, that establish the prestige of Paris: the Arc de Triomphe, the Eiffel Tower, Sacré-Coeur, Notre-Dame." Of the outside spaces, for example, the first landing of the terraces (which are organized in four levels) is enclosed by walls of hedges. From there one discovers, above the stone steps, a view of Notre-Dame isolated from the rest of the city. And on pressing an electrical button, the fence of greenery slowly slips away, revealing Paris. Of the inside spaces, the *salon* has two picture windows (one to the south, on the Eiffel Tower, the other to the east, on Notre-Dame); half of the window to the south moves electrically, opening the view on the big terrace where the Arc de Triomphe appears among trimmed box trees. These are but two of the multiple reframing devices employed in this project. Le Corbusier claimed that the complex mechanical and electrical installations in this apartment had absorbed 4,000 meters of cable, to which Peter Blake could not help commenting that only "a Frenchman in love with modern machinery would ever describe a landscaping project in terms of the length of electric cable required to make it function."[13]

These multiple technologies conspire with traditional architectural elements to problematize the distinctions between *inside* and *outside*. In this penthouse, once the upper level of the terrace is reached, the high walls of the *chambre à ciel ouvert* allow only fragments of the urban skyline to emerge: the tops of the Arc de Triomphe, the Eiffel Tower, Sacré-Coeur. And it is only by remaining inside and making use of the (submarine) periscope camera obscura that it becomes possible to enjoy the metropolitan spectacle. Tafuri has written: "The distance interposed between the penthouse and the Parisian panorama is secured by a technological device, the periscope. An 'innocent' reunification between

Beistegui apartment. Second and third levels of the terrace. The fence of greenery is slipping away, clearing the view of Notre-Dame.

Beistegui apartment. The wall that separates the salon from the dining room slips away electrically.

the fragment and the whole is no longer possible; the intervention of artifice is a necessity."[14]

But if this periscope, this primitive form of prosthesis, this "artificial limb," to return to Le Corbusier's concept in *L'Art décoratif d'aujourd'hui,* is *necessary* in the Beistegui apartment (as was also the rest of the *artifice* in this house, the electrically driven framing devices, the other prostheses), it is only because the apartment is *still* located in a nineteenth-century city: it is a penthouse in the Champs-Elysées. In "ideal" urban conditions, the house itself becomes the artifice.

For Le Corbusier the *new* urban conditions are a consequence of the media, which institute a relationship between artifact and nature that makes the "defensiveness" of a Loosian window, of a Loosian system, unnecessary. In *Urbanisme,* in the same passage where he makes reference to Loos's window, Le Corbusier goes on to write: "The horizontal gaze leads far away. . . . From our offices we will get the feeling of being lookouts dominating a world in order. . . . The skyscrapers concentrate everything in themselves: machines for abolishing time and space, telephones, cables, radios."[15] The inward gaze, the gaze turned upon itself, of Loos's interiors becomes with Le Corbusier a gaze of dominion over the exterior world. But why is this gaze horizontal?

The question returns us to the debate between Le Corbusier and Perret over the horizontal window.[16] At one point, Le Corbusier attempts to demonstrate in a quasi-scientific manner that the horizontal window illuminates better. Symptomatically, he relies on a photographer's chart giving times of exposure:

> **I have stated that the horizontal window illuminates better than the vertical window. Those are my observations of the reality. Nevertheless, I have passionate opponents. For example, the following sentence has been**

Beistegui apartment. "La chambre à ciel ouvert."

"Pélouse et murs au neuvième étage aux Champs-Elysées."

Beistegui apartment. Terrace with the periscope. "Paris est caché: on ne voit apparaître que quelques-uns des lieux sacrés de Paris: L'Arc de Triomphe, la Tour Eiffel, la perspective des Tuileries et de Notre-Dame, le Sacré-Coeur."

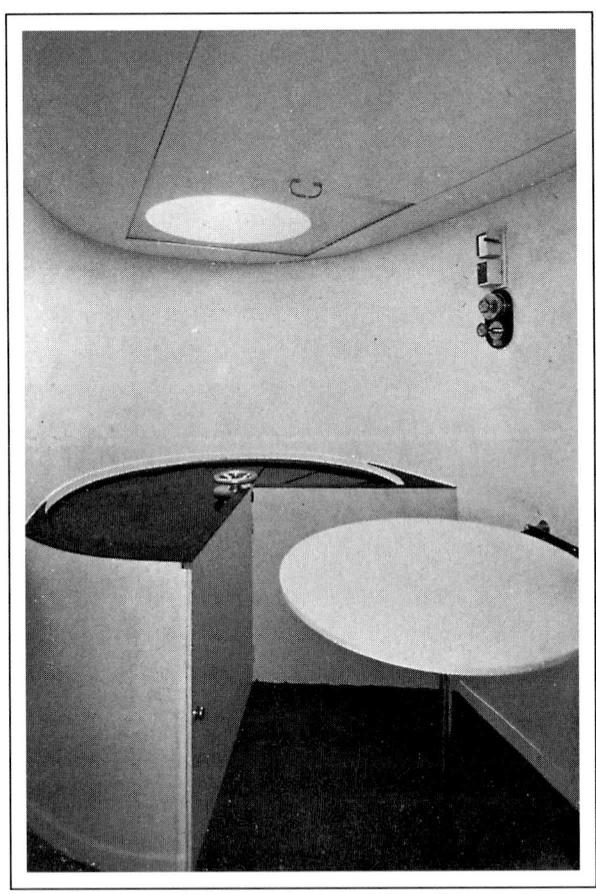

Beistegui apartment. Periscope—camera obscura. Arrival of the stairs that lead from the salon into the third level of the garden, and glass table where the periscope projects the views of Paris. The stairs are covered to remove the light. The table can be lowered to allow the trap door to be opened.

> **thrown at me: *"A window is a man, it stands upright!"* This is fine if what you want are "words." But I have discovered recently in a photographer's chart these explicit graphics; I am no longer swimming in the approximations of personal observations. I am facing sensitive photographic film that reacts to light. The table says this: . . . *The photographic plate in a room illuminated with a horizontal window needs to be exposed four times less than in a room illuminated with two vertical windows.* . . . Ladies and gentlemen . . . we have left the Vignolized shores of the Institutes. We are at sea; let us not separate this evening without having taken our bearings. First, architecture: the pilotis carry the weight of the house above the ground, up in the air. *The view of the house is a categorical view, without connection with the ground.*[17]**

If for Perret "a window is a man, it stands upright," with Le Corbusier the erected man behind Perret's *porte-fenêtre* has been replaced by a photographic camera. The view is free-floating, "without connection with the ground," or with the man behind the camera (a photographer's analytical chart has replaced "personal observations"). "The view from the house is a *categorical* view." In framing the landscape the house places the landscape into a system of categories. The house is a mechanism for classification. It collects views and, in doing so, classifies them. The house is a system for taking pictures. What determines the nature of the picture is the window. In another passage from the same book the window itself is seen as a camera lens: "When you buy a camera, you are determined to take photographs in the crepuscular winter of Paris, or in the brilliant sands of an oasis; how do you do it? *You use a diaphragm*. Your glass panes, your horizontal windows are all ready to be diaphragmed at will. You will let light in wherever you like."[18]

If the window is a lens, the house itself is a camera pointed at nature. Detached from nature, it is mobile. Just as the camera can be taken from Paris to the desert, the house can be taken from Poissy to Biarritz to Argentina. Again in *Précisions*, Le Corbusier describes Villa Savoye as follows:

> **The house is a box in the air, pierced all around, without interruption, by a *fenêtre en longueur*. . . . The box is in the middle of meadows, dominating the orchard. . . . The simple posts of the ground floor, through a precise disposition, cut up the landscape with a regularity that has the effect of *suppressing any notion of "front" or "back" of the house, of "side" of the house*. . . . The plan is pure, made for the most exact of needs. It is in its right place in the rural landscape of Poissy. But in Biarritz, it would be magnificent. . . . I am going to implant this very house in the beautiful Argentine countryside: we will have twenty houses rising from the high grass of an orchard where cows continue to graze.**[19]

The house is being described in terms of the way it frames the landscape and the effect this framing has on the perception of the house itself by the moving visitor. The house is in the air. It has no front, no back, no side.[20] The house can be in any place. It is *immaterial*. That is, the house is not simply constructed as a material object from which certain views then become possible. The house is no more than a series of views choreographed by the visitor, the way a filmmaker effects the montage of a film. Significantly, Le Corbusier has represented some of his projects, like Villa Meyer and the Guiette house, in the form of a series of sketches grouped together and representing the perception of the house by a moving eye.[21] As has been noted, these drawings suggest film storyboards, each of the images a still.[22]

Le Corbusier, Villa Meyer, Paris, 1925 (second project).

The description of Villa Savoye in *Précisions* recalls Le Corbusier's account, in the same book, of the process followed in the construction of the *petite maison* on the shores of Lake Geneva:

> **I knew that the region where we wanted to build consisted of 10 to 15 kilometers of hills along the lake. A fixed point: the lake; another, the magnificent view, frontal; another, the south, equally frontal.**
>
> **Should one first have searched for the site and made the plan in accordance with it? That is the usual practice. I thought it was better to make an exact plan, corresponding ideally to the use one hoped from it and determined by the three factors above. This done, to go out with the plan in hand to look for a suitable site.**[23]

"The key to the problem of modern habitation," continues Le Corbusier, is "to inhabit first . . . placing oneself afterward [*Habiter d'abord. . . . Venir se placer ensuite*]." But what is meant here by "inhabitation" and by "placement"? The "three factors" that "determine the plan" of the house—the lake, the magnificent frontal view, the south, equally frontal—are precisely the factors that determine a photograph of the site, or rather, a photograph taken from the site. "To inhabit" here means to inhabit that picture. Le Corbusier writes: "Architecture *is made in the head,*" then drawn.[24] Only then does one look for the site. But the site is only where the landscape is "taken," framed by a mobile lens. This photo opportunity is at the intersection of the systems of communication that establish that mobility: the railway and the landscape. But even the landscape is here understood as a 10- to 15-kilometer strip, rather than a *place* in the traditional sense. The camera can be set up anywhere along that strip. Geography is now defined by the network of the railway: "The geographical situation confirmed our choice, for at the railway station twenty minutes away trains stop that link up Milan, Zurich,

Amsterdam, Paris, London, Geneva, and Marseilles." Place is now defined by the communication system. It is precisely within this system that the house moves: "1922, 1923 I boarded the Paris-Milan express several times, or the Orient Express (Paris-Ankara). In my pocket was the plan of a house. A plan without a site? The plan of a house in search of a plot of ground? Yes!"[25]

The house is drawn with a picture already in mind. The house is drawn as a frame for that picture. The frame establishes the difference between "seeing" and merely looking. It produces the picture by domesticating the "overpowering" landscape. Le Corbusier writes:

> **The object of the wall seen here is to block off the view to the north and east, partly to the south, and to the west; for the ever-present and overpowering scenery on all sides has a tiring effect in the long run. Have you noticed that *under such conditions one no longer "sees"*? To lend significance to the scenery one has to restrict and give it proportion; the view must be blocked by walls that are only pierced at certain strategic points and there permit an unhindered view.**[26]

It is this domestication of the view that makes the house a house, rather than the provision of a domestic space, a place in the traditional sense. Two drawings published in *Une petite maison* speak about what Le Corbusier means by "placing oneself." In one of them, "On a découvert le terrain," a small human figure appears standing and next to it a big eye, independent of the figure, oriented toward the lake. The plan of the house lies between the eye and the lake: the house is represented as that which lies between the eye and the view. The small figure is almost an accessory. The other drawing, "Le plan est installé," does not show, as the title would indicate, the encounter of the plan with the site, as we traditionally understand it. The site is not in the drawing.

"On a découvert le terrain."
Une petite maison, *1954*.

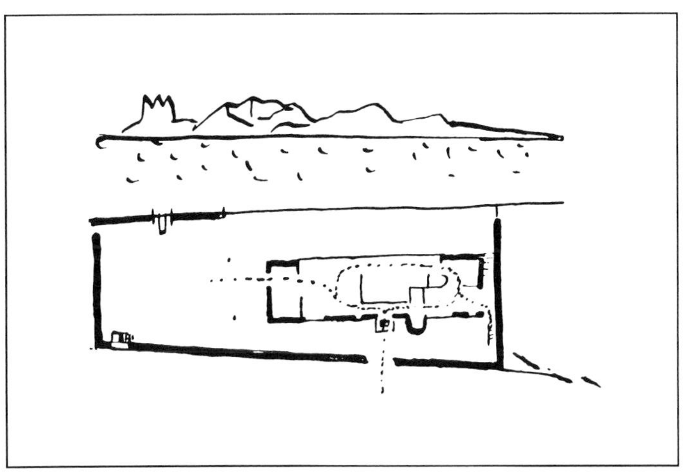

"Le plan est installé. . . ."
Une petite maison, ***1954.***

Even the curve of the shore of the lake in the other drawing has been erased. The drawing shows the plan of the house, a strip of lake, and a strip of mountains. That is, it shows the plan and above it the view. The "site" is a vertical plane, that of vision. The site is first and foremost a sight.

Of course, there is no "original" object in the new architecture, because the design is not dependent on any specific place. Throughout his writings, Le Corbusier insists on the relative autonomy of architecture and site. Referring again to the *petite maison,* he writes: "Today, the agreement of the ground with the house is no longer a question of site or of immediate context."[27] And in the face of a traditional site in Rio de Janeiro he constructs an "artificial site": "Here you have the idea: here you have *artificial sites,* countless new homes, and as for traffic— the Gordian knot has been severed."[28] All of this, however, does not mean that Le Corbusier's architecture is independent of place. It is the concept of place that has changed. We are talking here about a site that is defined by a sight. A sight can be accommodated in several sites.

"Property" has moved from the horizontal to the vertical plane, the space of vision. Even in the Beistegui apartment, the primary location (from a traditional point of view), the famous *address*—Champs-Elysées— is completely subordinated by the *view.*[29] In fact, the street cannot even be seen from the apartment. The eye is lifted up but not simply to attain a panorama. If Le Corbusier declines the panoramic view of Paris that the place made possible, "represses" that view, it is only to replace it with a series of precisely constructed and technologically controlled vistas of the city. Moreover these vistas, of the Arc de Triomphe, the Eiffel Tower, Notre-Dame, Sacré-Coeur, etc., coincide precisely with Paris's most touristic sites, with the "icons" of Paris, what Le Corbusier would call the *lieux sacrés de Paris*. The vistas reproduce, in fact, the "reality" of Paris as depicted by contemporary postcards. Indeed Le

Corbusier not only collected postcards but incorporated them into his architectural projects. It is not surprising in that respect to find Le Corbusier producing a drawing of his project for an apartment building in rue Fabert (1935) by pasting a postcard of Paris onto the paper and drawing his proposal on and around it. The city for Le Corbusier is not so much a material reality as a representation, a collage of images. The urban fabric, the public space of the street, has been replaced by a limited set of images (much like a standard set of postcards), which however do not add up to any simple unified whole.

If for Le Corbusier cities are collections of postcards, the window is first and foremost a problem of urbanism. That is why it becomes a central point in every urban proposal of Le Corbusier. In Rio de Janeiro, for example, he developed a series of drawings in vignette that represent the relation between domestic space and spectacle:[30]

> **This rock at Rio de Janeiro is celebrated.**
>
> **Around it range the tangled mountains, bathed by the sea.**
>
> **Palms, banana trees; tropical splendor animates the site.**
>
> **One stops, one installs one's armchair.**
>
> **Crack! a frame all around. Crack! the four obliques of a perspective. Your room is installed before the site. The whole sea-landscape enters your room.**[31]

First a famous sight, a postcard, a picture. (And it is not by chance that Le Corbusier has not only drawn this landscape from an actual postcard but has published the postcard alongside the drawings in *La Ville radieuse*.)[32] Then, one inhabits the space in front of that picture, installs an armchair. But this view, this picture, is only constructed at the same time as the house.[33] "Crack! a frame all around. Crack! the four obliques of a perspective." The house is installed *in front of* the site, not *in* the

Le Corbusier, photomontage for the apartment building in rue Fabert.

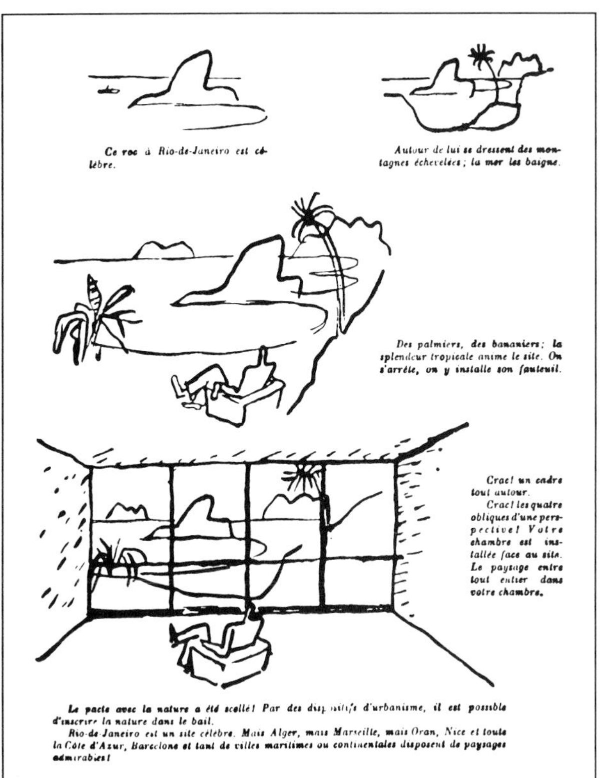

Rio de Janeiro. The view is constructed at the same time as the house. La Maison des hommes, *1942.*

Rio de Janeiro. Postcard view of the famous rock.

site. The house is a frame for a view. The window is a gigantic screen. But then the view *enters* the house, it is literally "inscribed" in the lease: "The pact with nature has been sealed! By means available to town planning it is possible *to enter nature in the lease*. Rio de Janeiro is a celebrated site. But Algiers, Marseilles, Oran, Nice and all the Côte d'Azur, Barcelona, and many maritime and inland towns can boast of admirable landscapes."[34]

Again, several sites can accommodate this project: different locations, different pictures (like the world of tourism). But also different pictures of the same location. The repetition of units with windows at slightly different angles, different framings, as happens when this cell becomes a unit in the urban project for Rio de Janeiro, a project that consists of a six-kilometer strip of housing units under a highway on pilotis, suggests again the idea of the movie strip, each apartment's window a still. This sense of the movie strip is felt both in the inside and the outside: "Architecture? Nature? Liners enter and see the new and *horizontal city:* it makes the site still more sublime. Just think of this broad *ribbon of light,* at night."[35] The strip of housing is a movie strip, on both sides.

For Le Corbusier, "to inhabit" means to inhabit the camera. But the camera is not a traditional place, it is a system of classification, a kind of filing cabinet. "To inhabit" means to employ that system. Only after this do we have "placing," which is to place the view in the house, to take a picture, to place the view in the filing cabinet, to classify the landscape.

This critical transformation of traditional architectural thinking about place can also be seen in *La Ville radieuse* where a sketch represents the house as a cell with a view. Here an apartment, high up in the air, is presented as a terminal for telephone, gas, electricity, and water. The apartment is also provided with "exact air" (heating and ventilation): "A

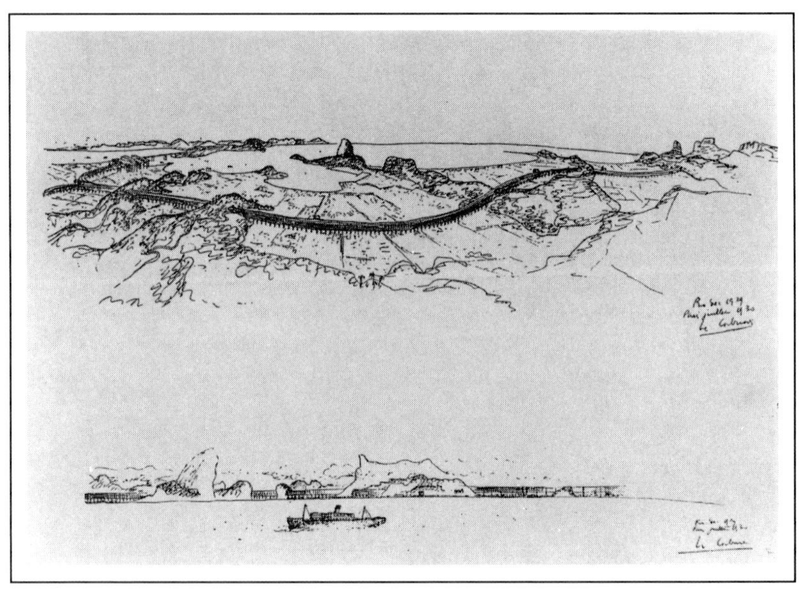

Rio de Janeiro. The highway, elevated 100 meters and "launched" from hill to hill above the city. La Ville radieuse, *1933.*

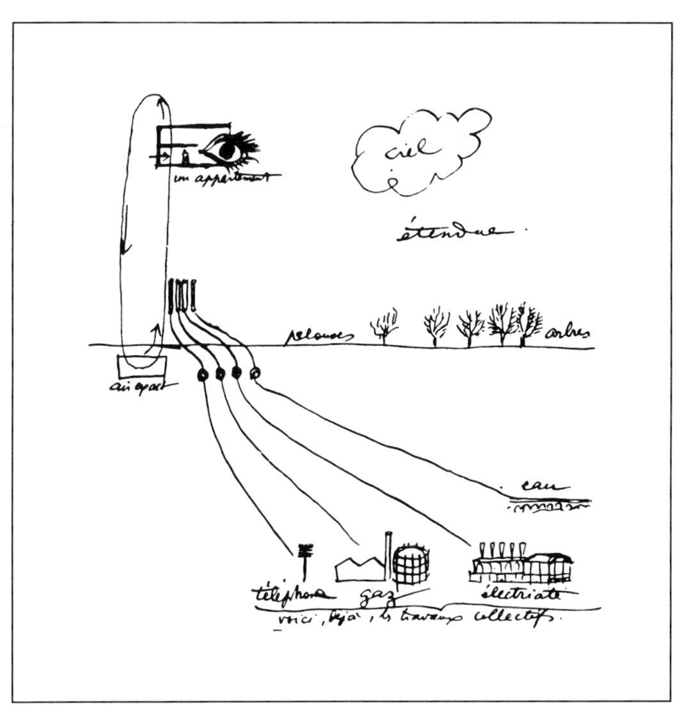

Sketch in La Ville radieuse, *1933.*

window is to give light, not to ventilate! To ventilate we use machines; it is mechanics, it is physics."[36] Whereas Loos's window had split sight from illumination, Le Corbusier's splits ventilation (in his words, *breathing*) from these two forms of "light."[37] Inside the apartment there is a small human figure, and at the window a huge eye looking outside. They do not coincide. The apartment itself is here the artifice between the occupant and the exterior world, a camera (and a breathing machine). The exterior world also becomes artifice; like the air, it has been conditioned, landscaped—it becomes landscape. The apartment defines modern subjectivity with its own eye. The traditional subject can only be the *visitor,* and as such a temporary part of the viewing mechanism. The humanist subject has been displaced.

It is precisely in terms of the *visitor* that Le Corbusier has written about the inhabitant of his houses. For example, about Villa Savoye he writes in *Précisions:*

> **The visitors, till now, turn round and round inside, asking themselves what is happening, understanding with difficulty the reasons for what they see and feel; they don't find anything of what is called a "house." They feel themselves within something entirely new. And . . . they are not bored, I believe![38]**

The inhabitants of Le Corbusier's house are displaced, first because they are disoriented. They do not know how to place themselves in relation to this house. It does not look like a "house." Then because the inhabitant is only a "visitor." Unlike the subject of Loos's houses who is both actor and spectator, both involved and detached from the domestic stage, Le Corbusier's subject is detached from the house with the distance of a visitor, a viewer, a photographer, a tourist.

The objects left as "traces" in the photographs of Le Corbusier's houses confirm this. They tend to be, again, the objects of a visitor (hat, coat, etc.). Never do we find any trace of "domesticity," as traditionally understood.[39] These objects could also be understood as standing for the architect. The hat, coat, glasses are definitely those of Le Corbusier. They play the same role that Le Corbusier plays as an actor in the movie *L'Architecture d'aujourd'hui*, where he passes through the house rather than inhabits it. Even the architect is *estranged* from his work with the distance of a visitor or a movie actor.

In a photograph of the interior of Villa Church, a casually placed hat and two open books on the table announce that somebody has just been there. A window with the traditional proportions of a painting is framed in a way that makes it read also as a screen. In the corner of the room a camera set on a tripod appears. It is the reflection on the mirror of the camera taking the photograph. As viewers of this photograph we are in the position of the photographer, that is, in the position of the camera, because the photographer, like the visitor, has already abandoned the room. (We have been advised to leave.) The subject (the visitor of the house, the photographer, the architect, and even the viewer of this photograph) has already left. The subject in Le Corbusier's house is estranged and displaced from his/her own home.

This estrangement is perhaps not dissimilar to that experienced by the movie actor before the mechanism of the cinematographic camera. In a passage cited by Benjamin, Pirandello has described it as follows:

> **The film actor feels as if in exile—exiled not only from the stage but also from himself. With a vague sense of discomfort he feels inexplicable emptiness: his body loses corporeality, it evaporates, it is deprived of reality, life, voice and the noises caused by its moving about, in order to**

Le Corbusier, Villa Church, Ville d'Avray, 1928–1929.

be changed into a mute image, flickering an instant on the screen, then vanishing into silence.[40]

Theater knows necessarily about emplacement, in the traditional sense. It is always about presence. Both the actor and the spectator are fixed in a continuous space and time, those of the performance. In the shooting of a movie there is no such continuity. The actor's work is split into a series of discontinuous, mountable episodes. The nature of the illusion for the spectator is a result of the montage. As Benjamin puts it: "The stage actor identifies himself with the character of his role. The film actor very often is denied this opportunity. His creation is by no means all of a piece; it is composed of many separate performances."[41]

The subject of Loos's architecture is the stage actor. But while the center of the house is left empty for the performance, we find the subject occupying the threshold of this space. Undermining its boundaries. The subject is split between actor and spectator of its own play. The completeness of the subject dissolves as also does the wall that s/he is occupying.

The subject of Le Corbusier's work is the movie actor, "estranged not only from the scene but from his own person." This moment of estrangement is clearly marked in the drawing of *La Ville radieuse* where the traditional humanist figure, the inhabitant of the house, is made incidental to the camera eye; it comes and goes, it is merely a visitor.

The split between the traditional humanist subject (the inhabitant or the architect) and the eye is the split between looking and seeing, between outside and inside, between landscape and site. In Le Corbusier's drawings, the inhabitant and the person in search of a site are represented as diminutive figures. Suddenly that figure *sees*. A picture is taken, a large eye, autonomous from the figure, represents that moment. This is precisely the moment of *inhabitation*. This inhabitation is independent from *place* (understood in a traditional sense); it turns the outside into an inside:

> **I perceive that the work we raise is not unique, nor isolated; that the air around it constitutes other surfaces, other grounds, other ceilings, that the harmony that has suddenly stopped me before the rock of Brittany exists, can exist, everywhere else, always. The work is not made only of itself: the outside exists. The outside shuts me in its whole which is like a room.**[42]

"Le dehors est toujours un dedans" (the outside is always an inside) means, among other things, that the "outside" is a picture. And that to inhabit means *to see*. In *La Maison des hommes* there is a drawing of a figure standing and (again), side by side, an independent eye: "Let us not forget that our eye is 5 feet 6 inches above the ground; our eye, this entry door of our architectural perceptions."[43] The eye is a "door" to architecture, and the "door" is, of course, an architectural element, the first form of a "window."[44] Later in the book, "the door" is replaced by media equipment, "the eye is the tool of recording":

> **The eye is a tool of registration. It is placed 5 feet 6 inches above the ground.**
> **Walking creates diversity in the spectacle before our eyes.**
> **But we have left the ground in an airplane and acquired the eyes of a bird. We see, in actuality, that which hitherto was only seen by the spirit.**[45]

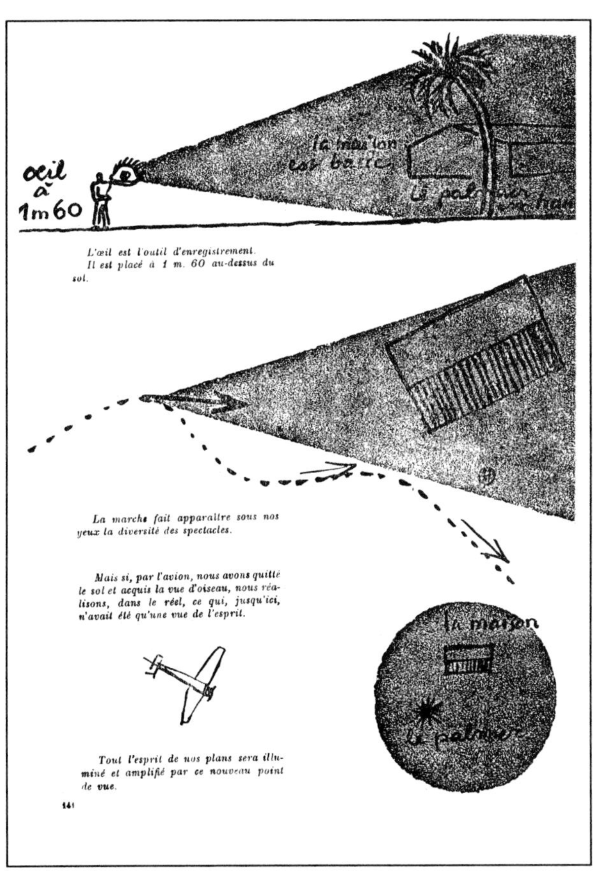

L'œil est l'outil d'enregistrement.

Il est placé à 1 m. 60 au-dessus du sol.

La marche fait apparaître sous nos yeux la diversité des spectacles.

Mais si, par l'avion, nous avons quitté le sol et acquis la vue d'oiseau, nous réalisons, dans le réel, ce qui, jusqu'ici, n'avait été qu'une vue de l'esprit.

Tout l'esprit de nos plans sera illuminé et amplifié par ce nouveau point de vue.

141

"L'oeil est l'outil d'enregistrement."
La Maison des hommes, ***1942.***

If the eye is a "tool for recording," the window is, for Le Corbusier, first of all communication. He repeatedly superimposes the idea of the "modern" window, the lookout window, the horizontal window, with the reality of the new media: "telephone, cable, radios, . . . machines for abolishing time and space." Control is now in these media. The look that from Le Corbusier's skyscrapers will "dominate a world in order" is neither the look from behind the periscope of Beistegui or the defensive view (turned toward itself) of Loos's interiors. It is a look that "registers" the new reality, a "recording" eye. The whole argument of *Précisions* is set up around the opening description of modernity as mass communication:

> **Mechanization has overwhelmed everything.**
>
> ***Communications:*** **in the past, men organized their undertakings at the scale of their legs: time had a different duration. The idea of the world was its great size, without limits. . . .**
>
> ***Interpenetration:*** **one day Stephenson invented the locomotive. They laughed. And as businessmen—the first captains of industry, who will be the new conquistadors—take it seriously, ask for rights-of-way, Mr. Thiers, the statesman who was leading France, intervenes immediately in Parlement, begging the deputies to keep to serious things. "A railroad could never connect two cities. . . ."**
>
> **Came the telegraph, the telephone, steamships, airplanes, the radio, and now television. A word said in Paris is with you in a fraction of a second! . . . Airplanes go everywhere; their eagle eyes have searched the deserts and penetrated the rain forest. Hastening interpenetration, the railway, the telephone unceasingly run the country into the city, the city into the country. . . .**

> ***The destruction of regional cultures:*** **what was held most sacred has fallen: tradition, the legacy of ancestors, local thinking . . . all is destroyed, annihilated. . . .**
>
> **Whiners curse the disturbing machine. Intelligent active persons think: Let us record while there is still time, in photos, films, or tapes, in books, magazines, the sublime evidence of age-old cultures.**[46]

Le Corbusier's architecture is produced by this kind of engagement with the mass media but, as with Loos, the key to his position is in the end to be found in his statements about fashion. Where for Loos the English suit was the mask necessary to sustain the individual in metropolitan conditions of existence, for Le Corbusier this suit is cumbersome and inefficient. And where Loos contrasts the *dignity* of male British fashion with the *masquerade* of women's, Le Corbusier praises women's fashion over men's because it has undergone *change*, the change of modern time.

> **Woman has preceded us. She has carried out the reform of her dress. She found herself at a dead end: to follow fashion and, then, give up the advantages of modern techniques, of modern life. To give up sport and, a more material problem, be unable to take on the jobs that have made woman a fertile part of contemporary production and enabled her *to earn her own living.* To follow fashion: she could not drive a car; she could not take the subway, or the bus, nor act quickly in her office or her shop. To carry out the daily *construction* of a "toilette": hairdo, shoes, buttoning her dress, she would not have had time to sleep. So, woman cut her hair and her skirts and her sleeves. She goes out bareheaded, barearmed, with her legs free. And she can dress in five minutes. And she is beautiful; she seduces us with the charm of her graces of which the designers have**

admitted taking advantage. The courage, the liveliness, the spirit of invention with which woman has revolutionized her dress are a miracle of modern times. Thank you!

And what about us, men? A dismal state of affairs! In our dress clothes, we look like generals of the Grande Armée and we wear starched collars! We are uncomfortable.[47]

While Loos spoke, you will remember, of the exterior of the house in terms of male fashion, Le Corbusier's comments on fashion are made in the context of the furnishing of the domestic interior. The furniture in style (Louis XIV) should be replaced with *equipment* (standard furniture, in great part derived from office furniture), and this change is assimilated to the change that women have undertaken in their dress. He concedes, however, that there are certain advantages to male dressing: "The English suit we wear had nevertheless succeeded in something important. It had *neutralized* us. It is useful to show a neutral appearance in the city. The dominant sign is no longer ostrich feathers in the hat, it is in the gaze. That's enough."[48]

Except for this last comment, "The dominant sign . . . is in the gaze," Le Corbusier's statement is purely Loosian. But at the same time, it is precisely that *gaze* of which Le Corbusier speaks that marks their differences. For Le Corbusier the interior no longer needs to be defined as a system of defense from the exterior. To say that "the exterior is always an interior" means that the interior is not simply the bounded territory defined by its opposition to the exterior. The exterior is "inscribed" in the dwelling. The window in the age of mass communication provides us with one more flat image. The window is a screen. From there issues the insistence on eliminating every protruding element, "de-

Vignolizing" the window, suppressing the sill: "Mr. Vignola is not concerned with windows, but 'between windows' (pilasters and columns). I de-Vignolize with: 'architecture is lighted floors.'"[49]

Of course, this screen undermines the wall. But here it is not, as in Loos's houses, a *physical* undermining, an *occupation* of the wall, but a *dematerialization* following from the emerging media. The organizing geometry of architecture slips from the perspectival cone of vision, from the humanist eye, to the camera angle. It is precisely in this slippage that modern architecture becomes modern by engaging with the media. Given that the media are so frequently identified with the feminine, it is not surprising to find that this slippage is not neutral in gender terms. Male fashion is uncomfortable but provides the bearer with "the gaze," "the dominant sign." Woman's fashion is practical and modern but turns her into the object of another's gaze: "Modern woman has cut her hair. Our gazes have enjoyed the shape of her legs." A picture. She sees nothing. She is an attachment to a wall that is no longer simply there. Enclosed by a space whose limits are defined by a gaze. If for Le Corbusier the woman is the very figure of modernity, the status of that figure remains troubling.

Notes

Archive

1
Heinrich Kulka, *Adolf Loos, das Werk des Architekten,* with a contribution by Franz Glück (Vienna: Anton Schroll, 1931; rpt. Vienna: Löcker, 1979).

2
Cf. Burkhardt Rukschcio, "Adolf Loos Analyzed: A Study of the Loos Archive in the Albertina Graphic Collection," *Lotus International* 29 (1981), p. 100.

3
H. Allen Brooks, "Foreword," *Le Corbusier,* ed. H. A. Brooks (Princeton: Princeton University Press, 1987), p. ix. This book collects the 15 essays first published in *The Le Corbusier Archive,* ed. H. A. Brooks, 32 vols. (New York: Garland Publishing Co.; Paris: Fondation Le Corbusier, 1982–1984). *Le Corbusier Carnets,* 4 vols. (New York: Architectural History Foundation; Paris: Herscher/Dessain et Tolra, 1981–1982). Giuliano Gresleri, *Le Corbusier, Viaggio in Oriente* (Venice: Marsilio Editori; Paris: Fondation Le Corbusier, 1984).

4
Le Corbusier, une encyclopédie, ed. Jacques Lucan, published on the occasion of the exhibition "L'aventure Le Corbusier" in the Centre Georges Pompidou (Paris: Editions du Centre Pompidou, 1987); 66 authors, 144 articles, 231 entries.

5

Le Corbusier and Pierre Jeanneret, *Oeuvre complète*, ed. Willi Boesiger, 8. vols. (Zurich: Girsberger, 1930ff.); vol. 1, 1910–1929; vol. 2, 1929–1934; vol. 3, (ed. Max Bill) 1934–1938; vol. 4, 1938–1946; vol. 5, 1946–1952; vol. 6, 1952–1957; vol. 7, 1952–1965; vol. 8, 1965–1969.

6

Also on the occasion of his birthday, a Festschrift was published with many contributions from his friends, colleagues, and clients: *Adolf Loos, Festschrift zum 60. Geburtstag am 10.12. 1930* (Vienna: Richard Lanyi, 1930).

7

Ludwig Münz and Gustav Künstler, *Der Architekt Adolf Loos*, with an introduction by Oskar Kokoschka (Vienna and Munich: Verlag Anton Schroll, 1964). English translation: *Adolf Loos: Pioneer of Modern Architecture*, with an introduction by Nikolaus Pevsner and an appreciation by Oskar Kokoschka (London: Thames and Hudson, 1966).

8

Burkhardt Rukschcio and Roland Schachel, *Adolf Loos, Leben und Werk* (Salzburg and Vienna, 1982). While this is not the place for a complete reference list, I should also mention as a documentary milestone the special issue of *Bauforum* edited by Johannes Spalt and Friedrich Kurrent on the occasion of the centennial of Loos's birth in 1970, which includes many unpublished documents and photographs. Specifically on the Adolf Loos house in the Michaelerplatz, there is Hermann Czech and Wolfgang Mistelbauer's *Das Looshaus* (Vienna: Löcker & Wögenstein, 1976). More recent publications include: *Raumplan versus Plan Libre*, ed. Max Risselada (Delft: Delft University Press, 1988), *The Architecture of Adolf Loos: An Arts Council Exhibition* (London: Arts Council of Great Britain, 1985), and *Adolf Loos* (Vienna: Graphische Sammlung Albertina, 1989).

9

Adolf Loos, Leben und Werk, pp. 7–9

10

While this house is normally referred to as Maison Jeanneret, it was entirely paid for by Lotti Raaf, who later married Le Corbusier's brother Albert Jeanneret. See Tim Benton, *The Villas of Le Corbusier 1920–1930* (New Haven and London: Yale University Press, 1987), pp. 46ff., and Russell Walden, "New Light on Le Corbusier's Early Years in Paris: The La Roche-Jeanneret Houses," *The Open Hand: Essays on Le Corbusier*, ed. Russell Walden (Cambridge and London: MIT Press, 1977), pp. 116–161.

11

Letter from Le Corbusier to Madame Savoye, 28 June 1931 (Fondation Le Corbusier).

12

"On entre: le *spectacle* architecturale s'offre de suite au *regard;* on suit un itinéraire et les *perspectives* se développent avec une grande variété; on joue avec l'afflux de la *lumière* éclairant les murs ou créant des *pénombres*. Les baies ouvrent des perspectives sur l'extérieur où l'on retrouve l'unité architecturale. A l'intérieur, les premiers essais de polychromie, basés sur les réactions spécifiques des couleurs, permettent le '*camouflage architectural*,' c'est-à-dire l'affirmation de certains volumes ou, au contraire, leur effacement. . . . Voici, vivant à nouveau sous nos *yeux modernes*, des événements architecturaux de l'histoire: les pilotis, la fenêtre en longueur, le toit-jardin, la façade de verre." Le Corbusier, *Oeuvre complète*, vol. 1, p. 60 (emphasis added).

13
"L'architecture arabe nous donne un enseignement précieux. Elle s'apprécie *à la marche*, avec le pied; c'est en marchant, en se déplaçant que l'on voit se développer les ordonnances de l'architecture. C'est un principe contraire à l'architecture baroque qui est conçue sur le papier, autour d'un point fixe théorique. Je préfère l'enseignement de l'architecture arabe. Dans cette maison-ci, il s'agit d'une véritable promenade architecturale, offrant des aspects constamment variés, inattendus, parfois étonnants." Le Corbusier, *Oeuvre complète*, vol. 2, p. 24.

14
Le Corbusier's reference to baroque architecture may be a response to Sigfried Giedion, who positively compared Le Corbusier's house for La Roche to a baroque church: "The way in which the cool concrete walls, alive in themselves, are divided, cut up and dispersed in order to allow new room compartmentalizations has only been known, in a wholly different context, in some Baroque chapels." "The New House" (1926), reprinted in *Le Corbusier in Perspective*, ed. Peter Serenyi (Englewood Cliffs, New Jersey: Prentice-Hall, 1975), p. 33.

15
Walter Benjamin, "The Work of Art in the Age of Mechanical Reproduction," in *Illuminations*, ed. with an introduction by Hannah Arendt, trans. Harry Zohn (New York: Schocken Books, 1969), p. 238.

16
Le Corbusier, "Twentieth Century Building and Twentieth Century Living," *The Studio Year Book on Decorative Art* (London, 1930), reprinted in Risselada, *Raumplan versus Plan Libre*, p. 145.

17
It is curious that Le Corbusier's concept of "walls of light" and the idea of space that it implies are closer, in their material reality, to the space of Mies van der Rohe's architecture than to his own. Le Corbusier's horizontal window is still a window, even if it presupposes a "dematerialized" (non-load-bearing) wall. On the other hand, Mies will write (and nothing could be further from his architecture): "I cut openings into walls where I need them for view or illumination." Mies van der Rohe, "Building," *G*, no. 2 (September 1923), p. 1. Translated in Fritz Neumeyer, *The Artless Word: Mies van der Rohe on the Building Art*, trans. Mark Jarzombek (Cambridge and London: MIT Press, 1991), p. 243.

18

Bruno Reichlin, "Le Corbusier vs De Stijl," in *De Stijl et l'architecture en France,* ed. Yve-Alain Bois and Bruno Reichlin (Brussels: Pierre Mardaga, 1985), p. 98. Reichlin is referring here to Steen Eiler Rasmussen, "Le Corbusier—die kommende Baukunst?," *Wasmuths Monatshefte für Baukunst* 10, no. 9 (1926), p. 381.

19

Le Corbusier, "Twentieth Century Building and Twentieth Century Living," p. 146.

20

Barthes goes on to say: "Since the private is not only our goods (falling under the historical laws of property), since it is also the absolute, precious, inalienable site where my image is free (free to abolish itself) . . . I must reconstitute the division of public and private." Roland Barthes, *La Chambre claire* (Paris: Editions du Seuil, 1980), English translation *Camera Lucida* (New York: Hill and Wang, 1981), p. 98. Translation here slightly different.

21

Friedrich Nietzsche, "On the Uses and Disadvantages of History for Life" (1874), in *Untimely Meditations,* trans. R. J. Hollingdale (Cambridge: Cambridge University Press, 1983), p. 84.

22

Contemporary dictionaries define being *in public* as being "in public view or access." *Random House Dictionary of the English Language,* unabridged edition (New York: Random House, 1966).

23

Cf. Alice Yaeger Kaplan, "Working in the Archives," *Reading the Archive: On Texts and Institutions,* Yale French Studies no. 77 (New Haven: Yale University Press, 1990), p. 103.

24

Nietzsche, "On the Uses and Disadvantages of History," pp. 78–79. Translation here slightly different.

25

Mark Wigley has theorized that the idea of the house is tied up with the idea of digestion, or rather, with the repression of indigestion. See his article "Postmortem Architecture: The Taste of Derrida," *Perspecta* 23 (1986).

26

Adolf Loos, "Die moderne Siedlung," in *Sämtliche Schriften, Adolf Loos,* vol. 1 (Vienna and Munich: Verlag Herold, 1962), pp. 402ff. Loos uses the word "gentleman" in English in the original text.

27

Almost all the scholarship aimed at documenting Loos's life and work is Austrian. See notes 1, 7, and 8 for references.

28
Jacques Lucan, "Avertissement," *Le Corbusier, une encyclopédie*, p. 4.

29
"Historically the various means of communication have competed with one another," writes Benjamin. Maybe it is for that reason that when I read these lines of Lucan I do not think so much of the space of an *encyclopédie*, after all a nineteenth-century form, as of its modern counterpart, computerized information. And I imagine a system that would have included *everything* as the "true museum" that Le Corbusier speaks about, every article on Le Corbusier, good or bad, scholarly or scandalous (and a system to access that information that would have resembled more a supermarket or even a shopping mall than a library). It is this space of the computer that Le Corbusier seems to anticipate, "to envy," when he endorses with enthusiasm the classification methods represented by the filing cabinet.

30
Jonathan Crary, *Techniques of the Observer: On Vision and Modernity in the Nineteenth Century* (Cambridge and London: MIT Press, 1990).

31
Reyner Banham, *A Concrete Atlantis: U.S. Industrial Building and European Modern Architecture* (Cambridge and London: MIT Press, 1986), p. 18.

City

1
Robert Musil, *The Man without Qualities* (New York: Capricorn Books, 1965), p. 12.

2
Wolfgang Schivelbusch in his book *The Railway Journey* (New York: Urizen Books, 1979) compares the world of tourism of the nineteenth century with a department store of landscapes and cities. There is also a novel *The World a Department Store* by Bradford Peck, published by himself in 1900, quoted by Rachel Bowlby in *Just Looking: Consumer Culture in Dreiser, Gissing and Zola* (New York and London: Methuen, 1985), pp. 156–157.

3
"Everything under the same roof" and "fixed price" were the slogans adopted by Aristide Boucicaut for the first department store: the Bon Marché founded by himself in Paris in 1852. "Everything under the same roof" means indifference to "place." In medieval cities, streets have names for what is done in them. "Fixed price" is another form of abstraction. The value of things is no longer dependent on vagaries such as the humor of the merchant at the time of the purchase, the bargaining power of the client, or the time of the day. The distracted perception in the modern city is similar to that in department stores in the way in which buildings pile up and the dazzled state they create. Department stores, on the other hand, create architecture in the disposition of objects. On perception in the big cities see, for example, Ozenfant and Jeanneret, "Formation de l'optique moderne," *L'Esprit nouveau* 21

(1923): "Les modifications du cadre extérieur de notre existence ont réagi profondément, non sur les propriétés fondamentales de notre optique, mais sur l'intensité et la vitesse fonctionnelle de notre vue, sa pénétration, l'extension de sa capacité d'enregistrement, sa tolérance à des spectacles autrefois inconnus (fréquence des images, nouvelles gammes de couleurs en rapports nouveaux dus à l'invention des violentes couleurs chimiques, etc.); il en est de l'éducation de l'oeil comme de celle de l'oreille: un paysan arrivant à Paris est de suite abruti par la multiplicité, l'intensité des bruits qui l'assaillent; il est en même temps comme ébloui par l'apparente cacophonie des images qu'il doit enregistrer avec une vitesse à laquelle il n'est pas entraîné." On perception in department stores see Emile Zola, *Au bonheur des dames* (Paris, 1883), where the disorientation in the department store experienced by the heroine, Denise (a peasant newly arrived in the city), is precisely linked to being lost in a city: "She felt herself lost, she so little in this monster place, in this machine at rest, trembling for fear she should be caught in the movement with which the walls already began to shake. And the thought of the old Elbeuf, black and narrow, increased the immensity of this vast establishment, presenting it to her as bathed in light, *like a city with its monuments, squares and streets*, in which it seemed impossible that she should ever find her way." Emile Zola, *The Ladies' Paradise*, introduction by Kristin Ross (Berkeley and Los Angeles: University of California Press, 1992). The models of Zola's department store were, precisely, the Bon Marché, founded in 1852, and the Louvre, founded in 1855. See Kristin Ross's introduction to *The Ladies' Paradise*, where she also points out that the "illogical layout [of department stores] served to increase customers' disorientation—a disoriented or dazzled customer was more prone to impulse buying" (p. viii). About department stores see also Rachel Bowlby's *Just Looking*, a very important work on the development of early consumer culture and its gender and class implications. About American department stores see M. Christine Boyer, *Manhattan Manners: Architecture and Style 1850–1900* (New York: Rizzoli, 1985).

4
Joris Karl Huysmans, *A rebours* (Paris, 1884).

5
Musil, *The Man without Qualities*, p. 4.

6
Ludwig Wittgenstein, *Tractatus Logico-Philosophicus* (1921), trans. D. F. Pears and B. F. McGuinness, with an introduction by Bertrand Russell (London and Henley: Routledge & Kegan Paul, 1974), proposition 4.115, p. 26.

7
Georg Simmel, "Zur Metaphisik des Todes" (1910). Quoted by Manfredo Tafuri in "The Historical Project," *Oppositions* 17 (1979), p. 60.

8
R. M. Rilke, *Die Aufzeichnungen des Malte Laurids Brigge;* English translation *The Notebooks of Malte Laurids Brigge* (New York: Norton, 1964), p. 15. Translation here slightly different.

9
Sigmund Freud, "'Civilized' Sexual Morality and Modern Nervous Illness" (1908), in *The Standard Edition of the Complete Psychological Works of Sigmund Freud* (London: Hogarth Press, 1953–1974), vol. 9.

10
Karl Kraus, "In dieser grossen Zeit" (1914), translated in *In These Great Times: A Karl Kraus Reader*, ed. Harry Zohn (Manchester: Carcanet, 1984), p. 77.

11
"In the realm of poverty of imagination where people die of spiritual famine without feeling spiritual hunger, where pens are dipped in blood and swords in ink, that which is not thought must be done, but that which is only thought is inutterable." Karl Kraus, *In These Great Times*, p. 71.

12
Hugo von Hofmannsthal, "The Letter of Lord Chandos," originally published in the Berlin newspaper *Der Tag*, 18 and 19 October 1902, with the title "Ein Brief." In Hugo von Hofmannsthal, *Selected Prose*, trans. Mary Hattinger et al., with an introduction by Herman Broch (New York: Pantheon Books, 1952), p. 140.

13
Adolf Loos, "Potemkin City," *Ver Sacrum* (July 1898); English translation in *Spoken into the Void*, trans. Jane O. Newman and John H. Smith (Cambridge and London: MIT Press, 1982), p. 95.

14
Camillo Sitte, *Der Städtebau nach seinen künstlerischen Grundsätzen* (Vienna, 1889); English translation *City Planning According to Artistic Principles*, in George R. Collins and Christiane Crasemann Collins, *Camillo Sitte: The Birth of Modern City Planning* (New York: Rizzoli, 1986), p. 311.

15
Musil, *The Man without Qualities*, p. 3. Translation here slightly different.

16
Ferdinand de Saussure, for example, in his *Cours de linguistique générale* (1916; Paris: Payot, 1972), uses the metaphor of a sheet of paper: "Thought is the front and sound is the back, one cannot cut the front without cutting the back. Likewise in language one can neither cut sound from thought nor thought from sound" (p. 157).

17
Rudolph Schindler, who was a pupil both of the Wagnerschule and of Adolf Loos and who emigrated to America in 1914, wrote: "The distinction between the indoors and the out-of-doors will disappear. The walls will be few, thin and removable. . . . Our house will lose its front-and-back-door aspect." "Care of the Body," *Los Angeles Times*, 2 May 1926, reprinted

in August Sarnitz, *R. M. Schindler, Architect: 1887–1953* (New York: Rizzoli, 1988), pp. 46–47. Moholy-Nagy says in his *The New Vision* (New York, 1947; originally *Von Material zu Architektur,* Munich, 1928): "The new architecture on its highest plane will be called upon to remove the conflict between the organic and artificial, between the open and closed, between the country and city." Theo Van Doesburg, "$-\square+=R_4$," *De Stijl* 6, nos. 6–7 (1924), pp. 91–92: "By the disruption of enclosure [walls] we have abolished the duality between interior and exterior"; van Doesburg, "Tot een beeldende architectuur: de vorm, de plattegrond, ruimte en tijd, symmetrie en herhaling, de kleur, de architectuur als synthese der nieuwe beelding," *De Stijl,* ibid., pp. 78–83: "The new architecture has rendered equal in value 'front' and 'back,' upright, and perhaps also 'upward' and 'downward.'" Frederick Kiesler, pupil and friend of Adolf Loos, takes all of this a step further when he writes: "Let us have no more walls. . . . No walls, no foundations." "Manifest—Vitalbau—Raumstadt—Funktionelle-Architektur," *De Stijl* 6, nos. 10–11 (1924–1925), pp. 141–146.

18

Walter Benjamin, "Karl Kraus" (1931), in *Reflections,* ed. with an introduction by Peter Demetz, trans. Edmund Jephcott (New York: Schocken Books, 1986), p. 239.

19

Hannah Arendt, *The Human Condition* (Chicago: University of Chicago Press, 1955), p. 39.

20

See Jacques Derrida's reading of Saussure in "The Outside and the Inside," in *Of Grammatology,* trans. Gayatri Spivak (Baltimore and London: Johns Hopkins University Press, 1976), pp. 30–44. Also, Geoff Bennington's reading of Derrida in "Complexity without Contradiction in Architecture," *AA Files* 15 (Summer 1987), pp. 15–18.

21

Saussure, *Cours de linguistique générale,* p. 51. Quoted by Derrida in *Of Grammatology,* p. 35; italics as added by Derrida.

22

Saussure, *Cours de linguistique générale,* p. 45; italics added. It also seems strange that Derrida, who has read this text of Saussure so closely, has not picked up this passage where Saussure most radically seems to undermine his own theory: the terminal division between inside and outside, between writing and speech.

23

Adolf Loos, "Architektur" (1910), in *Sämtliche Schriften, Adolf Loos,* vol. 1 (Vienna and Munich: Verlag Herold, 1962), p. 309. The English translation of this text that I am referring to is the one included in the anthology edited by Tim and Charlotte Benton with Dennis Sharp, *Architecture and Design: 1890–1933, An International Anthology of Original Articles* (New York: Whitney Library of Design, 1975). This was the only available translation at the time I originally made this point in an article for *9H,* in 1982. Since then, the editors of that journal have included a complete translation of "Architecture" by Wilfried Wang in the appendix to their catalogue *The Architecture of Adolf Loos: An Arts Council Exhibition* (London: Arts Council of Great Britain, 1985), pp. 104–109, that restores the missing fragments. Except where noted, the translations from "Architektur" used in this chapter are my own.

24
Arguably, the extraordinary deletions from the English translations of Saussure and Loos are not innocent either, and represent the particular thinking about, or even phobia about, the relationship between modern media and space by the culture of the ostensibly faithful, neutral translations. But exactly what in Saussure's and Loos's thinking about photography and space forces such lapses? What is it about the intimate, even just about the thinking about the intimate, that cannot be exposed?

25
Camillo Sitte, *City Planning According to Artistic Principles*, p. 311; italics added.

26
Adolf Loos, "Heimatkunst" (1914), in *Sämtliche Schriften, Adolf Loos*, vol. 1, p. 339.

27
Friedrich Nietzsche, "On the Uses and Disadvantages of History for Life" (1874), in *Untimely Meditations*, trans. R. J. Hollingdale (Cambridge: Cambridge University Press, 1983), p. 78. Translation here slightly different.

28
Musil made a gendered representation of this split when he wrote: "In realizing this, however, Diotima discovered in herself the affliction from which modern man is well known to suffer and which is called civilization. It is a frustrating state of affairs, full of soap, wireless waves, the arrogant symbolic language of mathematical and chemical formulae, economics, experimental research and mankind's inability to live in simple but sublime community. . . . Accordingly civilization meant, for her, everything that her mind could not cope with. And hence too, it had for a long time meant, first and foremost, her husband." *The Man without Qualities*, p. 117.

29
Loos, "Architektur" (1910). Cf. the translation by W. Wang in *The Architecture of Adolf Loos*, p. 108.

30
Georg Simmel, "Fashion," *International Quarterly*, New York (October 1904), p. 130.

31
Adolf Loos, "Ornament und Verbrechen" (1908); English translation as "Ornament and Crime," in *The Architecture of Adolf Loos*, p. 103. Italics added.

32
Adolf Loos, "Die Überflüssigen" (1908), in *Sämtliche Schriften, Adolf Loos*, vol. 1, p. 269.

33

It was Georg Simmel who pointed out, at the beginning of his "Die Grosstadt und das Geistesleben" (1903), that the deepest conflict of modern man (and, one could add, for the same reason the source of all his cultural production) is no longer in the ancient battle with nature (this could be only a metaphor when the limits between city and nature have ceased to exist), but in the one that the individual must fight to affirm the independence and peculiarity of his existence against the immense power of society, in his "resistance to being leveled, swallowed up in the social-technological mechanism." (Trans. as "The Metropolis and Mental Life," in *Georg Simmel, on Individuality and Social Forms*, ed. with an introduction by Donald N. Levine [Chicago and London: University of Chicago Press, 1971], p. 324.)

34

Cf. Hubert Damisch, "L'Autre 'Ich' ou le désir du vide: pour un tombeau d'Adolf Loos," *Critique* 31, nos. 339–340 (August–September 1975), p. 811.

35

Karl Kraus, *Sprüche und Widersprüche* (Munich: Albert Langen, 1909), p. 83.

36

As Janet Wolff has pointed out, the literature of modernity describes the experience of men: "The influential writings of Baudelaire, Simmel, Benjamin and, more recently, Richard Sennett and Marshall Berman, by equating the *modern* with the *public*, thus fail to describe women's experience of modernity." "The Invisible Flâneuse: Women and the Literature of Modernity," *Theory, Culture and Society* 2, no. 3 (1985), pp. 37–48. See also Susan Buck-Morss, "The *Flâneur*, the Sandwichman, and the Whore: The Politics of Loitering," *New German Critique* 39 (Fall 1986), pp. 99–140, where she makes the argument that the most significant female figure of modernity is the whore. In recent years a number of writers have contributed, from different fields, accounts of modernity that focus not just on women's experience of the *private* but on the constructions of gender involved in the very division between public and private. See for example Griselda Pollock, "Modernity and the Spaces of Femininity," in *Vision and Difference* (London and New York: Routledge, Chapman & Hall, 1988), pp. 50–90; Judith Mayne, *Private Novels, Public Films* (Athens and London: University of Georgia Press, 1988); Giuliana Bruno, "Streetwalking around Plato's Cave," *October* 60 (Spring 1992), pp. 111–129. It also should be noted that in architecture, a number of recent studies have contributed to a different vision of modernity, one that is more focused on the transformations of domestic space than of public space. Among them should be mentioned Txatxo Sabater's dissertation on the transformation of the interior of Barcelona with the plan of *Ensanche* of Cerda (a plan traditionally read in purely urbanistic terms): "Primera edad del Ensanche: Arquitectura domestica" (Barcelona, 1989); Georges Teyssot, *The Disease of the Domicile* (forthcoming from MIT Press); and above all Robin Evans's influential articles on the subject, including the much-cited "Figures, Doors and Passages," *Architectural Design* 4 (1978), pp. 267–278.

37

Adolf Loos, "Ornament und Erziehung" (1924), in *Sämtliche Schriften*, vol. 1, pp. 395–396.

38
Loos, "Ornament and Crime," in *The Architecture of Adolf Loos*, p. 100.

39
I am grateful to Todd Palmer for raising this question in a seminar presentation at Princeton University.

40
Adolf Loos, "Underclothes," *Neue Freie Presse* (25 September 1898), translation in *Spoken into the Void*, p. 75. See also "The Leather Goods and Gold- and Silversmith Trades," *Neue Freie Presse* (15 May 1898), translation in *Spoken into the Void*, pp. 7–9.

41
According to Burkhardt Rukschcio, Loos's break with the Secession happened in 1902 when Josef Hoffmann prevented him from doing the interiors for the Ver Sacrum-Zimmer. See B. Rukschcio, "Adolf Loos Analyzed: A Study of the Loos Archive in the Albertina Graphic Collection," *Lotus International* 29 (1981), p. 100, n. 5.

42
Richard Neutra, review of *Adolf Loos: Pioneer of Modern Architecture* by L. Münz and G. Künstler, *Architectural Forum* 125, no. 1 (July–August 1966), p. 89.

43
Adolf Loos, "Foreword to the First Edition," in *Spoken into the Void*, p. 130.

44
Peter Behrens, "The Work of Josef Hoffmann," *Journal of the American Institute of Architects* (October 1924), p. 426.

45
See for example, Adolf Loos, "Die Interieurs in der Rotunde" (1898). English translation "Interiors in the Rotonda," in *Spoken into the Void*, pp. 22–27.

46
Behrens, "The Work of Josef Hoffmann," p. 421.

47
Kraus, "In These Great Times," p. 70.

48
By invented conventions I mean here that they are not socially accepted signs, as linguistic signs or the signs of traditional architecture are. In this sense, the explanation that Behrens feels obliged to give about the "different" in Hoffmann speaks for itself (see following paragraph). In Vienna there was no need for such an explanation, but in a society such as the Anglo-Saxon that had not lost what Loos called "common sense" one had to be given.

49
Behrens, "The Work of Josef Hoffmann," p. 421.

50
Musil, *The Man without Qualities*, pp. 16–17.

51
Aldo Rossi attributes the ostracism Loos suffered as an architect during his life to his "power to irritate": "There is no doubt that these contemporaries of Freud were well aware that 'every joke is a murder.'" Aldo Rossi, introduction to *Spoken into the Void*, trans. Stephen Sartarelli, p. viii.

52
About Josef Hoffmann's career, see Eduard F. Sekler, *Josef Hoffmann: The Architectural Work* (Princeton: Princeton University Press, 1985).

53
Vittoria Girardi, "Josef Hoffmann maestro dimenticato," *L'architettura, cronache e storia* 2, no. 12 (October 1956).

54
On the way, however, something has been lost of what made Loos attractive for the avant-gardes: his destructive character, his relentless taunting of the beaux-arts, arts and crafts, and in general of everything that could be recognized as established and no genuine authority. Loos is of interest today for more than his polemical attitude, for this quality between hermeticism and transparency that is the richness of his message and is also what invites projections. If Aldo Rossi, Kenneth Frampton, José Quetglas, and Massimo Cacciari have something in common when they write about Loos, this is something of what made Loos say to Wittgenstein: "*You are me*."

55
When I originally wrote about this, for an article in *9H* (1982), Hoffmann was being "recovered" from history by the postmoderns. This turned out to be a passing fashion, while the interest in Loos continues.

56
Adolf Loos, "Architektur" (1910). Here I follow the later English translation by W. Wang in *The Architecture of Adolf Loos*, p. 106, which includes this passage.

57
"Ten years ago, at the time of the Café Museum, Josef Hoffmann, who represented the German Werkbund in Vienna, created the interior for the retail shop of the Apollo Candle Factory at the Hof. The work was praised as an expression of our time. Nobody would be of that opinion today. After a period of ten years we know that this was an error, and in ten years more it will be seen clearly that the present-day works of the same tendency do not have anything in common with the style of our days." Adolf Loos, "Kulturentartung" (1908), in *Sämtliche Schriften*, vol. 1, p. 271. There is an English translation in *The Architecture of Adolf Loos*, p. 99. (Translation here slightly different.)

58
In this sense it is interesting to note the early observation of John Ruskin that the purchase of a photograph of a building "is very nearly the same thing as carrying off the palace itself; every chip or stone and stain is there and of course there is no mistake about proportions." From a letter to his father, Venice, October 7, 1845, in the *Works of John Ruskin* (London: George Allen; New York: Longmans, Green, and Co., 1903), vol. 3, p. 210, note 2.

59
Adolf Loos, "Von der Sparsamkeit," compiled by Bohuslav Markalous from various conversations with Loos, *Wohnungskultur* 2/3 (1924). English translation "Regarding Economy," trans. Francis R. Jones, in *Raumplan versus Plan Libre: Adolf Loos and Le Corbusier, 1919–1930*, ed. Max Risselada (Delft: Delft University Press, 1988), p. 139.

60
Marshall McLuhan, *Understanding Media: The Extensions of Man* (New York: McGraw Hill, 1965), p. 4.

61
Adolf Loos, foreword to *Ins Leere gesprochen* (Vienna, 1921). English translation in *Spoken into the Void*, p. 3.

62
Walter Benjamin, "Some Motifs in Baudelaire," in *Illuminations*, ed. with an introduction by Hannah Arendt, trans. Harry Zohn (New York: Schocken Books, 1969), p. 159.

63
McLuhan has noted that this kind of circular reasoning is characteristic of oral societies (*Understanding Media*, p. 26).

64
Susan Sontag, "In Plato's Cave," in *On Photography* (New York: Farras, Straus and Giroux, 1977), p. 4.

65
"What changes must now occur in our way of looking at things, in our notions! Even the elementary concepts of space and time have begun to vacillate. Space is killed by the railways and we are left with time alone. Now you can travel to Orleans in four and half hours and it takes no longer to get to Rouen. Just imagine what will happen when the lines to Belgium and Germany are completed and connected up with their railways! I feel as if the mountains and forest of all countries were advancing on Paris. Even now I can smell the German linden trees." Heinrich Heine, *Lutetia*, cited by Schivelbusch in *The Railway Journey*.

66
Loos, "Architektur" (1910). Cf. the translation by W. Wang in *The Architecture of Adolf Loos*, p. 106.

67

Roland Schachel, notes to Adolf Loos, *Ornamento y Delito, y otros escritos* (Barcelona: Gustavo Gili, 1972), p. 241.

68

Indifferent to the place where it is taken, photography destroys *the thing* (the object loses its aura). In Alain Resnais's film *Last Year in Marienbad,* X shows the woman a photograph that he took of her in the park one afternoon during the previous year, but for her this proves nothing. She says: "Anyone could have taken it, anytime, anywhere." He replies: "A garden, any garden. I would have had to show you the white lace spread, the sea of white lace spread where your body. But all bodies look alike, and all white lace, all hotels, all statues, all gardens. [A pause.] But this garden, for me, looked like no other one. Every day I met you here." Only that which cannot be reproduced—neither the figure nor the garden, but that which the garden *is* for someone, as experience—can still be claimed.

69

Camillo Sitte, *City Planning According to Artistic Principles,* p. 311.

70

Walter Benjamin, "A Small History of Photography," in *One Way Street and Other Writings,* trans. Edmund Jephcott and Kingsley Shorter (London: NLB, 1979).

71

"On planes we don't really travel, we just skip time and space. I once went from New York to Berkeley to make a speech. In the morning I left New York and in the morning I got to Berkeley. I made a speech I had made before, and I saw people I knew. The questions I had already heard, and I gave the same answers as before. Then I came home. I did not really travel." Israel Shenker, "As Traveller," *New York Times,* April 1983.

72

Sigfried Giedion, *Space, Time and Architecture* (Cambridge: Harvard University Press, 1941), p. 321.

73

On the atectonic character of Hoffmann's architecture, see Eduard Sekler, "The Stoclet House by Josef Hoffmann," in *Essays in the History of Architecture Presented to Rudolph Wittkower* (London, 1967).

74

Peter Behrens, "The Work of Josef Hoffmann," p. 422.

75

This kind of space is close to that represented by the Japanese Tateokoshi: "There is such a thing in Japanese architecture as the TATEOKOSHI Plan drawing. In this all surfaces of a space are analyzed as if they were floor plans. The theory is that the person examining them will mentally raise the drawings for the walls to their position in the completed rooms and in this way imagine the way the space will look. In Japanese thought, space is composed of strictly two-dimensional facets. Depth is created by a combination of two-dimensional facets. Time-scales (flows) measure the space between these facets. The basic reason for the use of the word to express both time and space seems to be that the Japanese have understood space as an element formed by the interaction of facets and time." Arata Isozaki, *MA: Space-Time in Japan* (New York: Cooper Hewitt Museum, 1979).

76
Cf. Stanford Anderson, "Peter Behrens and the New Architecture of Germany: 1900–1917," Ph.D. dissertation, Columbia University, published in part in *Oppositions*, nos. 11, 21, and 23. See especially "Modern Architecture and Industry: Peter Behrens and the Cultural Policy of Historical Determinism," *Oppositions*, no. 11 (1977), p. 56.

77
Behrens "argued that fast trains transport us so rapidly that the effective image of the city is reduced to a silhouette. Similarly, our rapid passage through the city precludes any consideration of building details." Anderson, *Oppositions*, no. 23 (1981), p. 76. See also Peter Behrens, "Einfluss von Zeit- und Raumausnutzung auf moderne Formentwicklung," *Deutscher Werkbund, Jahrbuch* (1914), pp. 7–10. And see also "Über den Zusammenhang des baukünstlerischen Schaffens mit der Technik," Berlin, *Kongress für Aesthetik und Allgemeine Kunstwissenschaft 1913, Bericht* (Stuttgart, 1914), pp. 251–265.

78
Loos, "Regarding Economy," in *Raumplan versus Plan Libre*, p. 139.

79
Ibid., pp. 139–140; italics added.

80
Loos, "Architektur" (1910), p. 308; cf. the translation by W. Wang in *The Architecture of Adolf Loos*, p. 106.

81
Loos, "Ornament und Erziehung" (1924), p. 392.

82
Saussure, *Cours de linguistique générale*, p. 23.

83
Adolf Loos, "Das Prinzip der Bekleidung" (1898), in *Sämtliche Schriften, Adolf Loos*, vol. 1, p. 106. English trans. in *Spoken into the Void*, p. 66; translation here slightly different.

84
Jacob Grimm, from the foreword to his German dictionary, as quoted by Loos in the foreword to *Ins Leere gesprochen* (*Spoken into the Void*, p. 2).

85
Loos, "Architektur" (1910), p. 303. Cf. the translation by W. Wang in *The Architecture of Adolf Loos*, p. 104.

86

Karl Kraus, "Nachts" (1918), in *Adolf Loos, Festschrift zum 60 Geburtstag am 10.12.1930* (Vienna, 1930), p. 27.

87

Massimo Cacciari, "Loos-Wien," in *Oikos, da Loos a Wittgenstein* (Rome, 1975), p. 16.

88

Loos, "Ornament und Erziehung" (1924), p. 395.

89

Adolf Loos, "Glas und Ton," *Neue Freie Presse* (26 June 1898); English translation "Glass and Clay," in *Spoken into the Void*, p. 37.

90

Benjamin, "On Some Motifs in Baudelaire," in *Illuminations*, pp. 160, 156.

91

For Bergson, the structure of memory is decisive for experience: "Experience is indeed a matter of tradition, in collective existence as well as private life. . . . It is, however, not at all Bergson's intention to attach any specific historical label to memory. On the contrary, he rejects any historical determination of memory. He thus manages above all to stay clear of that experience from which his own philosophy evolved, or rather, in reaction to which it arose. It was the inhospitable, blinding age of large-scale industrialism. In shutting out this experience the eye perceives an experience of a complementary nature in the form of its spontaneous after-image, as it were." Proust distinguishes between *mémoire volontaire* and *mémoire involontaire:* "Only what has not been experienced explicitly and consciously, what has not happened to the subject as an experience, can become a component of the *mémoire involontaire*." Freud puts the same question in terms of the relationship between memory and consciousness: "Consciousness comes into being at the site of a memory trace." In other words, for Freud "becoming conscious and leaving a memory trace are processes incompatible with each other." In these terms, "consciousness is protection against stimuli," against "shock." Cited in Walter Benjamin, "On Some Motifs in Baudelaire," in *Illuminations*, pp. 157–161.

92

Loos, "Architektur" (1910), p. 317. Cf. the translation by W. Wang in *The Architecture of Adolf Loos*, p. 108.

93

Loos, "Kulturentartung," in *Sämtliche Schriften*, vol. 1, pp. 267ff. English translation: "Cultural Degeneration," in *The Architecture of Adolf Loos*, p. 98; translation here slightly different.

94

Walter Benjamin, "The Work of Art in the Age of Mechanical Reproduction," in *Illuminations*, p. 246, note 8.

95

Ibid., p. 225.

96
Susan Sontag, *On Photography* (New York: Farrar, Straus and Giroux, 1973), p. 72; Benjamin, "The Work of Art in the Age of Mechanical Reproduction," p. 223. I cannot now locate the source of the sentence of Argan.

97
Marcia E. Vetrocq, "Rethinking Josef Hoffmann," *Art in America* (April 1983). Vetrocq is praising here "the continuity between Hoffmann's large and small-scale designs."

98
The similarity with Benjamin's formulation is outstanding, for Loos is also comparing architecture with forms of art that have disappeared, and in particular with tragedy: "It could be said that what produced happiness 5,000 years ago does not succeed in doing so today. A tragedy that in another time would have made us shed tears of emotion today only interests us; a joke of another time will hardly make the muscles of our face move. . . . Tragedy stops being represented, the joke is forgotten. The building stands before posterity," etc. Adolf Loos, "Die alte und die neue Richtung in der Baukunst," *Der Architekt*, Vienna (1898).

99
Benjamin, "The Work of Art in the Age of Mechanical Reproduction," in *Illuminations*, pp. 239–240.

100
Benjamin, "A Small History of Photography," in *One Way Street*, p. 253; translation here slightly different.

101
Walter Benjamin, "Erfahrung und Armut" (1933), in *Gesammelte Schriften* (Frankfurt am Main: Suhrkamp, 1972–1988). It should also be noted that in this extraordinary text Benjamin equates Loos with Le Corbusier, while speaking about the new spaces of glass and steel where it is difficult to leave traces: "houses of glass, displaceable and movable, such as the ones that in the meantime Loos and Le Corbusier have built." Houses of glass, displaceable and movable, Loos (let alone Le Corbusier)? Benjamin's comment confirms the suspicion that Loos's houses, still in the thirties, were known only by hearsay. The text of Loos that Benjamin refers to here is probably "Keramika" (1904).

102
Benjamin, "The Work of Art in the Age of Mechanical Reproduction," in *Illuminations*, p. 250, note 19.

103
Eduardo Cadava, "Words of Light: Theses on the Photography of History," *Diacritics* (Fall–Winter 1992), pp. 108–109. For an analysis of the etymology of the word *experience*, see Roger Munier's response to an inquiry about experience; in *Mise en page*, no. 1 (May 1972), p. 37, cited by Cadava.

104
Benjamin, "Erfahrung und Armut."

105
Benjamin, "The Work of Art in the Age of Mechanical Reproduction," in *Illuminations*, p. 251, note 21.

106
Karl Kraus, "In These Great Times," in *In These Great Times*, p. 73.

Photography

1
Marie-Odile Briot, "L'Esprit nouveau; son regard sur les sciences," in *Léger et l'esprit moderne*, exhibition catalogue (Paris: Musée d'Art moderne de la ville de Paris, 1982), p. 38.

2
I have borrowed the concept of a "shadow line," *linea d'ombra*, from Franco Rella's literary analogy to Joseph Conrad's novel *The Shadow Line*, proposed in "Immagini e figure del pensiero," *Rassegna* 9 (1982), p. 78.

3
Walter Benjamin, "Short History of Photography," translated by Phil Patton, *Artforum* (February 1977), p. 47.

4
Sigmund Freud, "General Theory of the Neuroses," *The Standard Edition of the Complete Psychological Works of Sigmund Freud*, ed. and trans. James Strachey (London: Hogarth Press, 1953–1974), vol. 16, p. 295.

5
Jonathan Crary, *Techniques of the Observer: On Vision and Modernity in the Nineteenth Century* (Cambridge: MIT Press, 1990), pp. 24 and 39.

6
Giuliano Gresleri, *Le Corbusier, Viaggio in Oriente. Gli inediti di Charles-Edouard Jeanneret fotògrafo e scrittore* (Venice: Marsilio Editore; Paris: Fondation Le Corbusier, 1984).

7
Letter of Jean de Maisonseul to Samir Rafi, 5 January 1968. Quoted in Stanislaus von Moos, "Le Corbusier as Painter," *Oppositions* 19–20 (1980), p. 89. According to von Moos, Jean de Maisonseul, later the director of the Musée National des Beaux-Arts in Algiers, was working for the city planner Pierre A. Emery when he was asked to accompany Le Corbusier to the Casbah.

8
See, for example, Malek Alloula, *The Colonial Harem* (Minneapolis: University of Minnesota Press, 1986), about French postcards of Algerian women circulating between 1900 and 1930. And also the review of this and related books by Mieke Bal, "The Politics of Citation," *Diacritics* 21, no. 1 (Spring 1991), pp. 25–45.

9
Von Moos, "Le Corbusier as Painter," p. 89. See also Samir Rafi, "Le Corbusier et les femmes d'Alger," *Revue d'histoire et de civilisation du Maghreb*, Algiers (January 1968).

10
Von Moos, "Le Corbusier as Painter," p. 95.

11
"Chacun rêve légitemement à s'abriter et à assurer la sécurité de son logis. Comme c'est impossible dans l'état actuel, ce rêve, considéré comme irréalisable, provoque une véritable hystérie sentimentale; faire sa maison, c'est à peu près comme faire son testament. . . . *Quand je ferai une maison . . . je mettrai ma statue dans le vestibule et mon petit chien Ketty aura son salon. Quand j'aurai mon toit, etc. Thème pour un médicin neurologue.*" Le Corbusier, *Vers une architecture* (Paris: Editions Crès, 1923), p. 196. The English translation omits the passage here italicized.

12
"It was rape. A fellow architect, a man she admired, had without her consent defaced her design." Peter Adam, *Eileen Gray: Architect/Designer* (New York: Harry N. Abrams, 1987), p. 311.

13
See ibid., pp. 334–335. As Adam points out, no caption of the photographs of the murals published in *L'Architecture d'aujourd'hui* mentions Eileen Gray. In subsequent publications, the house is either simply described as "Maison Badovici" or directly credited to him. In *Casa Vogue* (no. 119, 1981) the house is described as "signed by Eileen Gray and Le Corbusier" and Gray's sofa has become "pezzo unico di Le Corbusier." The first recognition of Gray in architecture since the twenties came from Joseph Rykwert, "Eileen Gray: Pioneer of Design," *Architectural Review* (December 1972), pp. 357–361. But still today Eileen Gray's name does not figure in most histories of modern architecture, including the most recent and, presumably, critical ones.

14
Le Corbusier, *Creation Is a Patient Search* (New York: Frederick Praeger, 1960), p. 203; English translation of *L'Atelier de la recherche patiente* (Paris: Vincent & Fréal, 1960).

15
Ibid., p. 37.

16
Zeynep Çelik, "Le Corbusier, Orientalism, Colonialism," *Assemblage* 17 (1992), p. 61.

17
Victor Burgin, *The End of Art Theory: Criticism and Postmodernity* (Atlantic Highlands, N.J.: Humanities Press International, 1986), p. 44.

18
Ibid., p. 19.

19
Gresleri, *Le Corbusier, Viaggio in Oriente*, p. 141.

20
Le Corbusier, *L'Art décoratif d'aujourd'hui* (Paris: Editions Crès, 1925), pp. 9–11. For the corresponding sketches, see Fondation Le Corbusier A3(6).

21
Roland Barthes, "The Rhetoric of the Image," in *Image-Music-Text*, trans. Stephen Heath (New York: Hill and Wang, 1977), pp. 38–39; original text, "Rhétorique de l'image," *Communications* 1 (1961).

22
Roland Barthes, "The Photographic Message," in *Image-Music-Text*, p. 19; original text, "Le Message photographique," *Communications* 1 (1961).

23
Le Corbusier, *Creation Is a Patient Search*, p. 37.

24
Peter Allison, "Le Corbusier, 'Architect or Revolutionary'? A Reappraisal of Le Corbusier's First Book on Architecture," *AAQ* 3, no. 2 (1971), p. 10.

25
The correspondence between Le Corbusier and Charles L'Eplattenier is in the Fondation Le Corbusier. All quotations here are taken from the letters of 26 February, 29 February, and 2 March 1908. For an extensive commentary on this correspondence, see Mary Patricia May Sekler, *The Early Drawings of Charles-Edouard Jeanneret, 1902–08* (New York: Garland, 1977), esp. pp. 221ff.

26
"Sont fort bien faites, mais que l'effet est pitoyable. Oui, vraiment Perrin et moi avons été renversés de ce que donnait en photographie la belle chose que nous connaissons."

27
"Et nous nous sommes consolés en constatant que de notre stock de photos d'italie, nous n'avions pas une des belles choses architecturales parce que toujours l'effet de ces photographies était dénaturé et offusquant aux yeux de ceux qui avaient vu les originaux."

28
"Voyez l'effet photographique des halls et des chambres à manger (sic!) d'Hoffmann. Que ça a d'unité, que c'est sobre et simple et beau. Examinons de bien de près et analysons: que sont ces chaises? c'est laid, malcommode, barbant et gosse. Ces parois? du gypse tapoté comme il y en a sous les arcades de Padoue. Cette cheminée, un non sense. Et ce dressoir et ces tables et tout? Combien c'est froid, revêche et raide, et comment diable est-ce bâti?"

29
"Le mouvement germain est à la recherche de l'originalité à outrance, en ne s'occupant ni de construction, ni de logique, ni de beauté. *Aucun point d'appui* sur la nature."

30
"Vous nous avez envoyés en Italie pour nous former le goût, aimer ce qui est bâti, ce qui est logique et vous voulez nous obliger à tout ça, parce que des photos font un bel effet sur des revues d'art."

31
Adolf Loos, "Architektur" (1910), in *Sämtliche Schriften*, vol. 1 (Vienna and Munich: Verlag Herold, 1962), pp. 302–318; trans. "Architecture" by Wilfried Wang in *The Architecture of Adolf Loos*, exhibition catalogue (London: Arts Council of Great Britain, 1985), p. 106. It should be noted that an earlier English translation of this famous text omitted this and other relevant passages (see note 23 of chapter 2). On Loos and photography see also chapters 2 and 6 of the present book.

32
Max Horkheimer and Theodor Adorno, *Dialectic of Enlightenment* (New York: Continuum, 1972), esp. the chapter "The Culture Industry."

33
"Et combien la photographie qui est trompeuse déjà quand elle reproduit des surfaces (tableaux), l'est-elle plus encore lorsqu'elle prétend reproduire des volumes." Julien Caron, "Une villa de Le Corbusier, 1916," *L'Esprit nouveau* 6, p. 693.

34
These "painted" photographs are in the Fondation Le Corbusier, Photothèque L2 (1).

35
Stanislaus von Moos, *Le Corbusier: Elements of a Synthesis* (Cambridge: MIT Press, 1979), p. 299.

36
Le Corbusier, *Précisions sur un état présent de l'architecture et de l'urbanisme* (Paris: Editions Crès, 1930), p. 139.

37
I am grateful to Margaret Sobieski for pointing out the "missing" columns of Villa Savoye in a seminar presentation at Columbia University. See Le Corbusier, *Oeuvre complète 1929–1934* (Zurich: Editions Girsberger, 1935), pp. 24–31.

38
Le Corbusier and Pierre Jeanneret, *Oeuvre complète 1910–1929* (Zurich: Editions Girsberger, 1930), pp. 142–144.

39
Colin Rowe has written, "At Garches central focus is consistently broken up, concentration at any one point is disintegrated, and the dismembered fragments of the center become a peripheral dispersion of incident, a serial installation of interest around the extremities of the plan." *The Mathematics of the Ideal Villa and Other Essays* (Cambridge: MIT Press, 1977), p. 12. The blind spot of this brilliant analysis—one that reflects a classical conception of representation and photography—is that Rowe dutifully restored the columns to their place on the plan of Villa Stein vis-à-vis that of Palladio's Malcontenta, as though the way in which Garches was presented in the *Oeuvre complète* was merely a "printing error."

40
Fondation Le Corbusier, Photothèque, L1 (10) 1.

41
Fondation Le Corbusier, B2-15.

42
"La Grèce par Byzance, pure création de l'esprit. L'architecture n'est pas que d'ordonnance, de beaux prismes sous la lumière." Le Corbusier, *Vers une architecture* (Paris: Editions Crès, 1923), p. 130. English trans. by Frederick Etchells, *Towards a New Architecture* (New York: Praeger, 1970), pp. 162–163.

43
Von Moos, *Le Corbusier*, p. 299.

44
Manfredo Tafuri rightly notes that "Le Corbusier did not accept the industrial 'new nature' as an external factor and claimed to enter it as 'producer' and not as interpreter." *Theories and History of Architecture* (New York: Harper & Row, 1976), p. 32. (Originally *Teorie e storia dell'architettura*, Rome and Bari: Laterza, 1969.) In distinguishing "interpreters" and "producers," Tafuri follows Walter Benjamin, "The Work of Art in the Age of Mechanical Reproduction," in *Illuminations* (New York: Schocken, 1968). See also the discussion in chapter 5 below.

45
Among the catalogues in the archives of *L'Esprit nouveau* are those for automobiles by Voisin, Peugeot, Citroën, and Delage; airplanes and seaplanes by Farman and Caproni; trunks and suitcases by Innovation; office furniture by Or'mo, file cabinets by Ronéo; sport and hand traveling bags by Hermès. They include as well a more "extravagant" selection of turbines by the Swiss company Brown Boveri; high-pressure centrifugal ventilators by Rateau; and industrial *outillage* by Clermont Ferrand and Slingsby. The archives also hold department store mail order catalogues from Printemps, Au Bon Marché, and La Samaritaine. See also chapter 4 of this book.

46
Thomas Crow has written that both Clement Greenberg and Adorno "posit the relationship between modernism and mass culture as one of relentless refusal"; and yet "modernism repeatedly makes subversive equations between high and low which dislocate the apparently fixed terms of that hierarchy into new and persuasive configurations, thus calling it into question from within." "Modernism and Mass Culture in the Visual Arts," in *Modernism and Modernity*, ed. Benjamin H. D. Buchloh, Serge Guilbaut, and David Solkin (Halifax, Nova Scotia: The Press of the Nova Scotia College of Art and Design, 1983), p. 251.

47
"Ce livre puise son éloquence dans des moyens nouveaux; ses magnifiques illustrations tiennent à côté du texte un discours parallèle et d'une grande puissance." *Vient de paraître*, publicity brochure for *Vers une architecture*. Fondation Le Corbusier, B2 (15).

48
Stanislaus von Moos, *Le Corbusier*, p. 84. It is also curious to note how, looking at these photographs today, it is the car that appears so "old" while the houses still look "modern."

49
"Cette nouvelle conception du livre . . . permet à l'auteur d'éviter les phrases, les descriptions impuissantes; les faits éclatent sous les yeux du lecteur par la force des images."

50
The same method of thinking the argument through the images is employed for all his books and lectures. For the working material of *Vers une architecture*, see Fondation Le Corbusier, B2 (15).

51
Maxime Collignon, *Le Parténon* and *L'Acropole*, photographs by Frédéric Boissonnas and W. A. Mansel (Paris: Librairie Centrale d'Art et d'Architecture Ancienne, n.d.).

52
Stanford Anderson, "Architectural Research Programmes in the Work of Le Corbusier," *Design Studies* 5, no. 3 (July 1984), pp. 151–158.

53
Bruno Reichlin, "The Pros and Cons of the Horizontal Window," *Daidalos* 13 (1984), pp. 64–78.

54
More precisely, this drawing may have been done when Le Corbusier was in the process of making a *"Special Catalogue L'Esprit Nouveau"* for the Ronéo company. About these catalogues see also chapter 4 of this book.

55
Reichlin, "The Pros and Cons of the Horizontal Window," p. 75.

56
Amédée Ozenfant and Charles-Edouard Jeanneret, *La Peinture moderne* (Paris: Editions Crès, 1925), p. 168.

57
Ferdinand de Saussure, *Course in General Linguistics*, trans. Wade Baskin (New York: McGraw-Hill, 1966), p. 120.

58
Rosalind Krauss, "Léger, Le Corbusier and Purism," *Artforum* (April 1972), pp. 52–53.

59
Raoul Bunschoten, "Wor(l)ds of Daniel Libeskind," *AA Files* 10, p. 79.

60
"The photographic plate in a room illuminated with a horizontal window needs to be exposed four times less than in a room illuminated with two vertical windows." Le Corbusier, *Précisions*, p. 57. About this question see also chapter 7 of the present book.

61
In "The Work of Art in the Age of Mechanical Reproduction," Benjamin studies film techniques as an example of an art in which the reproduction techniques confer a new condition on the artist, the public, and the medium of production. He writes: "In contrast to the magician . . . the surgeon . . . abstains from facing the patient man to man; rather, it is through the operation that he penetrates into him. Magician and surgeon compare to painter and cameraman. The painter maintains in his work a natural distance from reality, the cameraman penetrates deeply into its web. There is a tremendous difference between the pictures they obtain. That of the painter is a total one, that of the cameraman consists of multiple fragments which are assembled under a new law. Thus, for contemporary man the representation of reality by the film is incomparably more significant than that of the painter, since it offers, precisely because of the thoroughgoing permeation of reality with mechanical equipment, an aspect of reality which is free of all equipment. And that is what one is entitled to ask from a work of art." *Illuminations*, pp. 233–234. See also note 44 of this chapter.

62
I am grateful to Kerry Shear for pointing out the paradoxical nature of the Ronéo drawing in a seminar presentation at Columbia University.

63
Le Corbusier, *Almanach d'architecture moderne* (Paris: Editions Crès, 1925).

64
Le Corbusier, *The Decorative Art of Today*, p. 72.

65
Ibid., p. 76n.

Publicity

1
L'Esprit nouveau was published in Paris between 1920 and 1925 by Le Corbusier and the French painter Amédée Ozenfant. Initially the editor of this magazine was the dadaist poet Paul Dermée, but he was dismissed by number 4 amid a polemic among the editorial group that ended up in a court trial. Ozenfant would later write in his memoirs, "Dermée had gotten it into his head to make a dada journal: we eliminated him." The subtitle of the magazine changed significantly coinciding with Dermée's dismissal, from *Revue internationale d'esthétique* to *Revue internationale de l'activité contemporaine*. This change implies a shift from "aesthetics," as a specialized field separate from everyday life, to "contemporary activity," which included not only painting, music, literature, and architecture but also theater, music hall entertainment, sports, cinema, and book design. In relation to Le Corbusier and publicity, see Stanislaus von Moos, *Le Corbusier: Elements of a Synthesis* (Cambridge: MIT Press, 1979), and his later article "Standard und Elite: Le Corbusier, die Industrie und der Esprit nouveau," in Tilmann Buddensieg and Henning Rogge, eds., *Die nützliche Künste* (Berlin, 1981), pp. 306–323; *L'Esprit nouveau: Le Corbusier und die Industrie, 1920–1925*, catalogue of an exhibition in Zurich, Berlin, and Strasbourg, ed. Stanislaus von Moos (Berlin: Ernst & Sohn, 1987); Gladys C. Fabre, "L'Esprit moderne dans la peinture figurative—de l'iconographie moderniste au Modernism de conception," *Léger et l'Esprit moderne 1918–1931* (Paris: Musée d'Art Moderne, 1982), pp. 82–143; Françoise Will-Levaillant, "Norme et forme à travers l'esprit nouveau," *Le Retour à l'ordre dans les arts plastiques et l'architecture, 1919–1925* (Université de Saint-Etienne, 1986), pp. 241–276.

2
At the back of this "found object," the child's school notebook, Le Corbusier wrote: "Ceci est imprimé sur les cahiers des écoles de France/C'est la géométrie/La géométrie est notre langage/C'est notre moyen de mesure et d'expression/La géométrie est la base." A fragment of this image was to find its way into "Nature et création" (*L'Esprit nouveau* 19), an article by Ozenfant and Le Corbusier later reprinted in *La Peinture moderne* (1925). The complete image appears again in *Urbanisme* (1925), reproducing the above comment. The illustrations of an article in *The Autocar*, "The Harmony of Outline," were transplanted into *L'Esprit nouveau* in the form of a photo essay called "Evolution des formes de l'automobile" (*L'Esprit nouveau* 13).

3
The content of these books was first published as a series of articles in *L'Esprit nouveau*, with the exception of the chapter "Architecture ou révolution," which was added to *Vers une architecture*. The *Almanach de l'architecture moderne* was supposed to have been number 29 of *L'Esprit nouveau*, an issue entirely devoted to architecture, but it never appeared.

4
There is never only one reading in Le Corbusier's work. The Rateau ventilator can also be interpreted as a spiral, one of the images that obsesses Le Corbusier throughout his life, and that in modern psychology is bound to the process of individuation. The spiral may be seen

as the expression of a path that goes from life to death to life. The renaissance of man (of the architect) is possible through the death of a part of his previous being. "Architecture or Revolution" could from this point of view also be read as initiating a spiritual-cultural rebirth. Without exhausting the complex significance of the spiral, one might also mention the myth of Daedalus, builder of the labyrinth: "According to an old story . . . he will have been capable of passing a thread through the shell of a snail." Karl Kerenyi, *Labyrinth-Studien* (Zurich: Rhein-Verlag, 1950), p. 47.

5
Theo van Doesburg borrowed some images of silos from *L'Esprit nouveau* for publication in *De Stijl* 4 and 6 (1921). Le Corbusier and Ozenfant wrote to van Doesburg reprimanding him for not crediting *L'Esprit nouveau* as the source of the material. The same photographs of the silos reappeared in Kassak and Moholy-Nagy's *Uj Müveszek Könyve* (Vienna; republished in Berlin as *Buch neuer Künstler,* 1922) and afterward in *MA* (nos. 3–6, 1923). See also Fabre, "L'Esprit moderne dans la peinture figurative," pp. 99–100.

6
Reyner Banham, *A Concrete Atlantis: U.S. Industrial Buildings and European Modern Architecture* (Cambridge: MIT Press, 1986), p. 11.

7
Cf. Marie-Odile Briot, "L'Esprit Nouveau and Its View of the Sciences," *Léger et l'Esprit moderne,* p. 62.

8
Marius-Ary Leblond, *Galliéni parle* (Paris, 1920), p. 53. Cited by Stephen Kern, *The Culture of Time and Space: 1880–1918* (Cambridge: Harvard University Press, 1983), p. 309.

9
The term "machine age" was coined in 1927 with the exhibition organized by the *Little Review* in New York; despite its widespread use, it is hardly an adequate term to characterize the artistic practices of the earlier part of the twentieth century in Europe.

10
"At about the same time that serious artists were discovering in the industrial landscape new religious symbols, businessmen were learning about the power of advertising. To stave off the perils of overproduction, their advertising agencies turned to machine age imagery to stimulate consumption." Alan Trachtenberg, "The Art and Design of the Machine Age," *New York Times Magazine,* 21 September 1986.

11
Reyner Banham, *Theory and Design in the First Machine Age* (New York: Praeger, 1967), p. 221.

12
Le Corbusier-Saugnier, "Les Maisons 'Voisin,'" *L'Esprit nouveau* 2, p. 214. Quoted by Banham, *Theory and Design in the First Machine Age*. Saugnier is the pseudonym used by Ozenfant

when writing about architecture in *L'Esprit nouveau*. As is well known, Le Corbusier is the pseudonym initially chosen by Charles-Edouard Jeanneret for the same purpose.

13

Marie-Odile Briot, "L'Esprit Nouveau and Its View of the Sciences," p. 62.

14

Le Corbusier, *L'Art décoratif d'aujourd'hui* (Paris: Editions Crès, 1925), p. 23.

15

Abraham Moles, in his *Sociodynamique de la culture* (Paris: Mouton, 1968), p. 28, notes: "The role of culture is to provide the individual with a screen of concepts on which he projects his perceptions of the exterior world. This conceptual screen had in traditional culture a rational reticular structure, organized in an almost geometrical fashion . . . we knew how to place new concepts with reference to old ones. Modern culture, mosaic culture, offers us a screen that is like a series of fibers glued together at random. . . . This screen is established by the submersion of the individual in a flux of disparate messages, with no hierarchies of principles: he knows everything about everything; the structure of his thought is extremely reduced." Le Corbusier's constant attempts to classify his knowledge do not exempt his work from this cultural condition described by Moles, but rather make it one of its possible manifestations. The conventionality with which Le Corbusier constructs the table of contents in his books, in an almost nineteenth-century fashion, stands dramatically in opposition to their actual content, which is drawn from all kinds of sources of information and manifested according to the new "visual thinking" strongly indebted to the new condition of printed mass information.

16

Le Corbusier, *L'Art décoratif d'aujourd'hui*, p. 127.

17

Amédée Ozenfant and Charles-Edouard Jeanneret, *La Peinture moderne* (Paris: Editions Crès, 1925), p. i.

18

"The problem I address . . . is not what modernism 'really was,' but rather how it was perceived retrospectively, what dominant values and knowledge it carried, and how it functioned ideologically and culturally after World War II. It is a specific image of modernism that has become the bone of contention for the postmoderns, and that image has to be reconstructed if we want to understand postmodernism's problematic relationship to the modernist tradition and its claims to difference." Andreas Huyssen, "Mapping the Postmodern," *New German Critique* 33 (1984), p. 13. The usual equation of the avant-garde with "modernism" is part of this received view. The "ism" in this sense is particularly telling—it reduces everything to a style. Against this heritage we should indeed try to understand the specificity of the different projects that fall within the modern period—or perform, in Manfredo Tafuri's words, "a thorough investigation of whether it is still legitimate to speak of a Modern Movement as a monolithic corpus of ideas, poetics and linguistic traditions." Manfredo Tafuri, *Theories and History of Architecture*, trans. Giorgio Verrecchia (New York: Harper & Row, 1980; original ed. Rome and Bari, 1969), p. 2.

19

William A. Camfield, "The Machinist Style of Francis Picabia," *Art Bulletin* (September–December 1966).

20

In a 1966 interview with Otto Hahn, Marcel Duchamp makes explicit not only the relation between Mutt and Mott but, perhaps more important, the difference between the attempt to understand the *Fountain by R. Mutt* within a high art tradition and within mass culture:

O.H. To get back to your Readymades; I thought that R. MUTT, the signature on *Fountain*, was the name of the maker, but in an article by Rosalind Krauss, I read: R. MUTT, a pun on the German, Armut, or poverty. Poverty would completely change the meaning of The Fountain.

M.D. Rosalind Krauss? The redhead? That's not it at all. You can contradict it. Mutt comes from Mott Works, the name of a large sanitary equipment manufacturer. But Mott was too close so I altered it to Mutt, after the daily strip cartoon with "Mutt and Jeff," which appeared at the time and with which everyone was familiar. Thus, from the start there was an interplay of Mutt: a fat little funny guy, and Jeff: a tall, thin man. . . . I wanted any old name. And I added Richard [French slang for moneybags]. That's not a bad name for a *pissotière*. Get it? The opposite of poverty. But not even that much, just R. MUTT.

Otto Hahn, "Passport No. G255300," *Art and Artists* 1, no. 4 (London, July 1966), p. 10. For other interpretations of "R. MUTT" see William A. Camfield, *Marcel Duchamp Fountain* (Houston: The Menil Collection, Houston Fine Art Press, 1989), p. 23, note 21.

21

Peter Bürger, *Theory of the Avant-Garde* (Minneapolis: University of Minnesota Press, 1984), p. 52. Bürger also remarks how easily Duchamp's gesture is consumed: "It is obvious that this kind of provocation cannot be repeated indefinitely: here, it is the idea that the individual is the subject of artistic creation. Once the signed bottle drier has been accepted as an object that deserves a place in a museum, the provocation no longer provokes, it turns into its opposite. . . . It does not denounce the art market but adapts to it." Manfredo Tafuri also gives priority to the question of the institution (this time, the institution of architecture). He writes, "one can not 'anticipate' a class architecture; what is possible is the introduction of class criticism into architecture. . . . Any attempt to overthrow the institution, the discipline, with the most exasperated rejections or the most paradoxical ironies—let us learn from Dada and Surrealism—is bound to see itself turned into a positive contribution, into a 'constructive' avant-garde, into an ideology all the more positive as it is dramatically critical and self-critical." *Theories and History of Architecture*, note to the second (Italian) edition.

22

Beatrice Wood, *The Blind Man* 2 (1917). *The Blind Man* was a little magazine that had only two issues and was edited by Marcel Duchamp, Beatrice Wood, and H. P. Roché. As Dawn Ades has put it, "it would be reasonable to suppose that its main purpose was to publicize *Fountain*."

23

Cf. Le Corbusier, *L'Art décoratif d'aujourd'hui*, p. 57.

24

Adolf Loos, "Die Überflüssigen" (1908), in *Sämtliche Schriften*, vol. 1, pp. 267–268.

25

Le Corbusier, *L'Art décoratif d'aujourd'hui*, p. 77.

26

Reyner Banham, *Theory and Design in the First Machine Age*, p. 250.

27

Beatrice Wood, *The Blind Man* 2 (1917).

28

Adolf Loos, "Die Plumber," *Neue Freie Presse* (17 July 1898). English translation in *Spoken into the Void*, trans. Jane O. Newman and John H. Smith (Cambridge and London: MIT Press, 1982), p. 46; translation here slightly different.

29

Walter Benjamin, "Karl Kraus," in *Reflections*, ed. with an introduction by Peter Demetz, trans. Edmund Jephcott (New York: Harcourt Brace Jovanovich, 1979), p. 260.

30

Fondation Le Corbusier, A1 (7), 194.

31

Fondation Le Corbusier, A1 (17), 1.

32

Letter of Le Corbusier to Michelin, 3 April 1925, in Fondation Le Corbusier, A2 (13). Cited in Stanislaus von Moos, "Urbanism and Transcultural Exchanges, 1910–1935: A Survey," in H. Allen Brooks, ed., *The Le Corbusier Archive*, vol. 10 (New York: Garland, 1983), p. xiii.

33

Roberto Gabetti and Carlo del Olmo, *Le Corbusier e L'Esprit nouveau* (Turin: Giulio Einaudi, 1975), p. 6. A dossier titled "Demandes et offres d'études de projets et de construction à la suite des visites au Pavillon," Fondation Le Corbusier, A1 (5), contains all these letters.

34

Letter to Ateliers Primavera, in Fondation Le Corbusier, A1 (10).

35

Documents in Fondation Le Corbusier, A1 (18). See also Gabetti and del Olmo, *Le Corbusier e L'Esprit nouveau*, pp. 215–225.

36

Documents in Fondation Le Corbusier, A1 (17), 105.

37

Tafuri, *Theories and History of Architecture*, p. 141.

Museum

1

The exhibition "Modern Architecture: International Exhibition" opened at the Museum of Modern Art on February 10, 1932. It was installed in five rooms at 730 Fifth Avenue, and included models, photos, plans, and drawings mainly from Frank Lloyd Wright, Walter Gropius, Le Corbusier, J. J. P. Oud, Mies van der Rohe, Raymond Hood, Howe & Lescaze, Richard Neutra, and the Bowman Brothers. These architects were the only ones whose works appeared in the catalogue accompanying the show, *Modern Architecture: International Exhibition*, by Henry-Russell Hitchcock, Philip Johnson, and Lewis Mumford (New York: MoMA, Plandome Press, 1932; 5000 copies printed; rpt. New York: Museum of Modern Art and Arno Press, 1969). The exhibition traveled throughout the United States for over seven years. It is usually referred to as "The International Style Exhibition" because of the book *The International Style: Architecture since 1922* (New York: Norton, 1932) by the curators of the show, Henry-Russell Hitchcock and Philip Johnson. The content of the book and the catalogue do not coincide. For additional information see Suzanne Stephens, "Looking Back at Modern Architecture: The International Style Turns Fifty," *Skyline* (February 1982), pp. 18–27, Helen Searing, "International Style: The Crimson Connection," *Progressive Architecture* (February 1982), pp. 89–92, Richard Guy Wilson, "International Style: The MoMA Exhibition," in the same issue, pp. 93–106, and above all the recent book by Terence Riley, *The International Style: Exhibition 15 and the Museum of Modern Art* (New York: Rizzoli and Columbia Books of Architecture, 1992).

2

Philip Johnson, interviewed by Peter Eisenman, *Skyline* (February 1982), p. 15.

3

Hitchcock and Johnson, *The International Style*, pp. 33, viii–ix.

4

Johnson interview, *Skyline*, p. 14.

5

Hitchcock and Johnson, *The International Style*, pp. 80–81.

6

Ibid., pp. 12–13. "New Building for the New Age" includes Saarinen, Mendelsohn, Tengbom, Dudok. . . . "If we have added the Romanesquoid Stuttgart Railway Station, a cubistic house from the rue Mallet-Stevens, a concrete church by the brothers Perret, and the neo-Barocco-Romanesque Town Hall of Stockholm, we will have nearly a complete list of the modern European buildings most familiar . . . and admired by the large majority of American architects." "Poets in Steel" is concerned with skyscrapers: "Romanesque, Mayan, Assyrian, Renaissance, Aztec, Gothic, and specially Modernistic. . . . No wonder that some of us who have been appalled by this chaos turn with the utmost interest and expectancy to the International Style."

7

Riley, *The International Style*, p. 10.

8

Alfred H. Barr, Jr., "Modern Architecture," *The Hound and Horn* 3, no. 3 (April–June 1930), pp. 431–435. Cited in Riley, *The International Style*.

9

Letter of Philip Johnson to Ms. Homer H. Johnson, Berlin, 21 July 1930, Johnson Papers. Cited in Riley, *The International Style*.

10

"Revised Exhibition Proposal," 10 February 1931, in Riley, *The International Style*, appendix 2, p. 219.

11

Letter of Johnson to Bowman Brothers, 22 May 1931, Museum Archives, MoMA, New York. Cited in Riley, *The International Style*, pp. 42, 47.

12

Lewis Mumford, "Housing," in *Modern Architecture: International Exhibition*, pp. 179–184.

13

Alfred H. Barr, preface to *The International Style*, p. 15.

14

Ibid., pp. 15–16.

15

Hitchcock and Johnson, *The International Style*, p. 31.

16

Le Corbusier, *My Work* (London, 1960), p. 51. The lectures given on this tour formed the basis of his book *When the Cathedrals Were White: A Journey to the Country of Timid People* (New York: Reynal and Hitchcock, 1947).

17

Le Corbusier, *L'Art décoratif d'aujourd'hui,* p. 127.

18

André Malraux, "The Museum without Walls," in *The Voices of Silence* (Garden City, N.Y.: Doubleday, 1953).

19

"Lettre de Paris," undated manuscript, Fondation Le Corbusier, A1 (16). The document is part of the *L'Esprit nouveau* archives. The argument is so close to that of *L'Art décoratif d'aujourd'hui* as to suggest a possible 1924–1925 date.

20

Le Corbusier, *L'Art décoratif d'aujourd'hui,* p. 17.

21

André Malraux, "The Museum without Walls," pp. 13–14.

22

Walter Benjamin, "The Work of Art in the Age of Mechanical Reproduction," in *Illuminations,* ed. with an introduction by Hannah Arendt, trans. Harry Zohn (New York: Schocken Books, 1969), p. 225.

23

"Fresque," *L'Esprit nouveau* 19. The question of the poster (*l'affiche*) will be taken up again in *L'Esprit nouveau* 25, where P. Boulard, alias Le Corbusier, writes in "Actualités": "Le tumulte est dans les rues. Le Bûcheron pavoise au Boulevard Saint-Germain. En dix jours, le cubisme, sur un kilomètre, s'étale et est présenté au populaire." The posters that Le Corbusier was here admiring were those of Cassandre. However, he did not know at the time, or did not acknowledge, their authorship. Instead he wrote to the company the posters were advertising, Le Boucheron, in an effort to obtain a publicity contract for *L'Esprit nouveau*. See letters of 6 and 14 June 1924, in Fondation Le Corbusier, A1 (17). Of course, Cassandre's posters were not "art" for Le Corbusier, but one more instance of the beautiful objects the industrialized everyday life was producing. More about this subject in A.H., "L'Affiche," in *L'Esprit nouveau: Le Corbusier und die Industrie, 1920–1925,* ed. Stanislaus von Moos (Berlin: Ernst & Sohn, 1987), p. 281.

24

"L'art est partout dans la rue qui est le musée du présent et du passé." Le Corbusier, *L'Art décoratif d'aujourd'hui,* p. 189.

25

Ibid., p. 182.

26

Cf. Manfredo Tafuri, *Theories and History of Architecture,* trans. Giorgio Verrecchia (New York: Harper & Row, 1980), p. 32. The passage from Benjamin that Tafuri refers to is "The

Work of Art in the Age of Mechanical Reproduction," p. 233. Tafuri finds in this passage a principle by which to identify the distinctive features of the twentieth-century avant-gardes. It is interesting to note that he includes Marcel Duchamp among those who perpetuate the figure of the artist-magician. *Theories and History of Architecture*, p. 32. See also chapter 3, note 61, above.

27
James Johnson Sweeney, "A Conversation with Marcel Duchamp . . . ," interview at the Philadelphia Museum of Art, constituting the sound track of a 30-minute film made in 1955 by NBC. Quoted in Arturo Schwarz, *The Complete Works of Marcel Duchamp* (New York: Abrams, n.d.), p. 513.

28
Stanislaus von Moos, *Le Corbusier: Elements of a Synthesis* (Cambridge: MIT Press, 1979), p. 302.

29
Le Corbusier 1910–1965, edited by W. Boesiger and H. Girsberger (Zurich: Les Editions d'Architecture, 1967), pp. 236–237.

Interior

1
Walter Benjamin, "Paris, Capital of the Nineteenth Century," in *Reflections*, trans. Edmund Jephcott (New York: Schocken Books, 1986), pp. 155–156.

2
"Loos m'affirmait un jour: 'Un homme cultivé ne regarde pas par la fenêtre; sa fenêtre est en verre dépoli; elle n'est là que pour donner de la lumière, non pour laisser passer le regard.'" Le Corbusier, *Urbanisme* (Paris, 1925), p. 174. When this book was published in English under the title *The City of To-morrow and Its Planning*, translated by Frederick Etchells (New York, 1929), the sentence read: "A friend once said to me: 'No intelligent man ever looks out of his window; his window is made of ground glass; its only function is to let in light, not to look out of'" (pp. 185–186). In this translation, Loos's name has been replaced by "a friend." Was Loos "nobody" for Etchells, or is this just another example of the kind of misunderstanding that led to the mistranslation of the title of the book? Perhaps it was Le Corbusier himself who decided to erase Loos's name. Of a different order, but no less symptomatic, is the mistranslation of "laisser passer le regard" (to let the gaze pass through) as "to look out of," as if to resist the idea that the gaze might take on, as it were, a life of its own, independent of the beholder.

3
The perception of space is produced by its representations; in this sense, built space has no more authority than do drawings, photographs, or descriptions.

4

Ludwig Münz and Gustav Künstler, *Der Architekt Adolf Loos* (Vienna and Munich, 1964), pp. 130–131. English translation: *Adolf Loos, Pioneer of Modern Architecture* (London, 1966), p. 148: "We may call to mind an observation by Adolf Loos, handed down to us by Heinrich Kulka, that the smallness of a theatre box would be unbearable if one could not look out into the large space beyond; hence it was possible to save space, even in the design of small houses, by linking a high main room with a low annexe."

5

Georges Teyssot has noted that "the Bergsonian ideas of the room as a refuge from the world are meant to be conceived as the 'juxtaposition' between claustrophobia and agoraphobia. This dialectic is already found in Rilke." G. Teyssot, "The Disease of the Domicile," *Assemblage* 6 (1988), p. 95.

6

There is also a more direct and more private route to the sitting area, a staircase rising from the entrance of the drawing room.

7

"Under Louis-Philippe the private citizen enters the stage of history. . . . For the private person, living space becomes, for the first time, antithetical to the place of work. The former is constituted by the interior; the office is its complement. The private person who squares his account with reality in his office demands that the interior be maintained in his illusions. This need is all the more pressing since he has no intention of extending his commercial considerations into social ones. In shaping his private environment he represses both. From this spring the phantasmagorias of the interior. For the private individual the private environment represents the universe. In it he gathers remote places and the past. His drawing room is a *box in the world theater*." Walter Benjamin, "Paris, Capital of the Nineteenth Century," in *Reflections*, p. 154. Emphasis added.

8

This calls to mind Freud's paper "A Child Is Being Beaten" (1919), where, as Victor Burgin has written, "the subject is positioned both in the audience *and* on stage—where it is both aggressor *and* aggressed." Victor Burgin, "Geometry and Abjection," *AA Files*, no. 15 (Summer 1987), p. 38. The *mise-en-scène* of Loos's interiors appears to coincide with that of Freud's unconscious. Sigmund Freud, "A Child Is Being Beaten: A Contribution to the Study of the Origin of Sexual Perversions," in *Standard Edition of the Complete Psychological Works of Sigmund Freud* (London: Hogarth Press, 1953–1974), vol. 17, pp. 175–204. In relation to Freud's paper, see also Jacqueline Rose, *Sexuality in the Field of Vision* (London, 1986), pp. 209–210.

9

Münz and Künstler, *Adolf Loos*, p. 36.

10
See note 7 above. There are no social spaces in the Benjaminian interior. He writes: "In shaping his private environment he [the private person] represses both [commercial and social considerations]." Benjamin's interior is established in opposition to the office. But as Laura Mulvey has noted, "The workplace is no threat to the home. The two maintain each other in a safe, mutually dependent polarisation. The threat comes from elsewhere: . . . the city." Laura Mulvey, "Melodrama Inside and Outside the Home" (1986), in *Visual and Other Pleasures* (London: Macmillan, 1989), p. 70.

11
In a criticism of Benjamin's account of the bourgeois interior, Laura Mulvey writes: "Benjamin does not mention the fact that the private sphere, the domestic, is an essential adjunct to the bourgeois marriage and is thus associated with woman, not simply as female, but as wife and mother. It is the mother who guarantees the privacy of the home by maintaining its respectability, as essential a defence against incursion or curiosity as the encompassing walls of the home itself." Laura Mulvey, "Melodrama Inside and Outside the Home."

12
Münz and Künstler, *Adolf Loos*, p. 149.

13
Jacques Lacan, *The Seminar of Jacques Lacan: Book I, Freud's Papers on Technique 1953–1954*, ed. Jacques-Alain Miller, trans. John Forrester (New York and London: Norton, 1988), p. 215. In this passage Lacan is referring to Jean-Paul Sartre's *Being and Nothingness*.

14
There is an instance of such personification of furniture in one of Loos's most autobiographical texts, "Interiors in the Rotunda" (1898), where he writes: "Every piece of furniture, every thing, every object had a story to tell, a family history." *Spoken into the Void: Collected Essays 1897–1900*, trans. Jane O. Newman and John H. Smith (Cambridge: MIT Press, 1982), p. 24.

15
This photograph has only recently been published. Kulka's monograph (a work in which Loos was involved) presents exactly the same view, the same photograph, but without a human figure. The strange opening in the wall pulls the viewer toward the void, toward the missing actor (a tension that the photographer no doubt felt the need to cover by literally inserting a figure). This tension constructs the subject, as it does in the built-in couch of the raised area of the Moller house, or the window of the *Zimmer der Dame* overlooking the drawing room of the Müller house.

16
Adolf Loos, *Das Andere*, no. 1 (1903), p. 9.

17
Kenneth Frampton, from a lecture at Columbia University, Fall 1986.

18
It should also be noted that this window is an exterior window, as opposed to the other window, which opens into a threshold space.

19
The reflective surface in the rear of the dining room of the Moller house (halfway between an opaque window and a mirror) and the window in the rear of the music room "mirror" each other, not only in their locations and their proportions but even in the way the plants are disposed in two tiers. All of this produces the illusion, in the photograph, that the threshold between these two spaces is virtual—impassable, impenetrable.

20
Letter from Kurt Ungers to Ludwig Münz, quoted in Münz and Künstler, *Adolf Loos*, p. 195. Emphasis added.

21
Christian Metz, "A Note on Two Kinds of Voyeurism," in *The Imaginary Signifier* (Bloomington: Indiana University Press, 1977), p. 96.

22
Adolf Loos, "The Principle of Cladding" (1898), in *Spoken into the Void*, p. 66 (emphasis added). Loos is explicitly referring here to Semper's concept of space as cladding, borrowing even the term "principle of cladding" from Semper. Aside from this instance, the influence of Semper on Loos can be found throughout Loos's theories and could perhaps be traced back to his studies in the Technische Hochschule in Dresden where he was an auditor in 1889–1890. Gottfried Semper taught at this school from 1834 to 1848 and left an influential theoretical legacy.

23
Franco Rella, *Miti e figure del moderno* (Parma: Pratiche Editrice, 1981), p. 13 and note 1. René Descartes, *Correspondance avec Arnauld et Morus*, ed. G. Lewis (Paris, 1933): letter to Hyperaspistes, August 1641.

24
Adolf Loos, "The Principle of Cladding" (1898), in *Spoken into the Void*, p. 66. Compare Semper's statement: "Hanging carpets remained the true walls, the visible boundaries of space. The often solid walls behind them were necessary for reasons that had nothing to do with the creation of space; they were needed for security, for supporting a load, for their permanence, and so on. Wherever the need for these secondary functions did not arise, the carpets remained the original means of separating space. Even where building solid walls became necessary, the latter were only the inner, invisible structure hidden behind the true and legitimate representatives of the wall, the colorful woven carpets." Gottfried Semper, "The Four Elements of Architecture: A Contribution to the Comparative Study of Architecture" (1851), in *Gottfried Semper: The Four Elements of Architecture and Other Writings*, trans. Harry Francis Mallgrave and Wolfgang Herrmann (Cambridge: Cambridge University Press, 1989), p. 104.

25
José Quetglas, "Lo Placentero," *Carrer de la Ciutat*, nos. 9–10, special issue on Loos (January 1980), p. 2.

26
Adolf Loos, "Architecture" (1910), trans. Wilfried Wang, in *The Architecture of Adolf Loos* (London: Arts Council of Great Britain, 1985), p. 106.

27
See in this respect Loos's use of the word "effect" (*Wirkung*) in other passages. For example in the fragment of "The Principle of Cladding" quoted above, the "effect" is the "sensation" that the space produces in the spectator, the feeling of "homeyness" in a house.

28
Richard Neutra, *Survival through Design* (New York: Oxford University Press, 1954), p. 300.

29
Adolf Loos, "Ornament und Erziehung" (1924), in *Sämtliche Schriften*, vol. 1, p. 392.

30
Adolf Loos, "Architecture," p. 106. Emphasis added.

31
This window, the only "picture" window to appear in Loos's work, points to the difference in his work between architecture in the context of the city and in that of the countryside (the Khuner villa is a country house). This difference is significant not only in terms of architectural language, as often discussed (Gravagnuolo, for example, talks of the differences between the "whitewashed masterpieces"—the Moller and Müller houses—and the Khuner villa, "so vernacular, so anachronistically alpine, so rustic"; see Benedetto Gravagnuolo, *Adolf Loos* [New York: Rizzoli, 1982]), but in terms of the way the house sets itself in relation to the exterior world, the construction of its inside and outside.

32
In the photograph of the dining room of the Moller house, the illusion that the scene is virtual, that the actual view of the dining room is a mirror image of the space from which the view is taken (the music room), thus collapsing both spaces into each other, is produced not only by the way the space is framed by the opening but also by the frame of the photograph itself, where the threshold is made to coincide exactly with the sides of the back wall, making the dining room into a picture inside a picture.

33
"The deepest conflict of modern man is not any longer in the ancient battle with nature, but in the one that the individual must fight to affirm the independence and peculiarity of his existence against the immense power of society, in his resistence to being levelled, swallowed up in the social-technological mechanism." Georg Simmel, "Die Grosstadt und das Geistesleben" (1903), English translation "The Metropolis and Mental Life," in *Georg Simmel: On Individuality and Social Forms*, ed. Donald Levine (Chicago, 1971), p. 324.

34
George Simmel, "Fashion" (1904), in ibid, pp. 313ff.

35
Adolf Loos, "Ornament and Crime" (1908), trans. Wilfried Wang, in *The Architecture of Adolf Loos*, p. 103.

36
Adolf Loos, "Architecture," p. 107.

37
Adolf Loos, "Heimat Kunst" (1914), in *Sämtliche Schriften*, vol. 1, p. 339.

38
One of the ways in which the myth of Loos as an author is sustained is by privileging his writings over other forms of representation. Critics legitimize observations on buildings, drawings, and photographs by the use of written statements by the architect. This practice is problematic at many levels. Critics use words. By privileging words they privilege themselves. They maintain themselves as authors (authorities). This convention is dependent on the classical system of representation, which I am here putting in question.

39
Münz and Künstler, *Adolf Loos*, p. 195.

40
Gravagnuolo, *Adolf Loos*, p. 191. Italics added.

41
Ibid. Italics added.

Window

1
For other interpretations of these photographs of Le Corbusier's villas presented in the *Oeuvre complète*, see Richard Becherer, "Chancing It in the Architecture of Surrealist Mise-en-Scene," *Modulus* 18 (1987), pp. 63–87; Alexander Gorlin, "The Ghost in the Machine: Surrealism in the Work of Le Corbusier," *Perspecta* 18 (1982); José Quetglas, "Viajes alrededor de mi alcoba," *Arquitectura* 264–265 (1987), pp. 111–112; Thomas Schumacher, "Deep Space, Shallow Space," *Architectural Review* (January 1987), pp. 37–42.

2
A copy of this movie is in the Museum of Modern Art, New York. About the movie see J. Ward, "Le Corbusier's Villa Les Terrasses and the International Style," Ph.D. dissertation, New York University, 1983, and by the same author, "Les Terrasses," *Architectural Review* (March 1985), pp. 64–69. See also Becherer, "Chancing It in the Architecture of Surrealist

Mise-en-Scene." Becherer compares Le Corbusier's movie to Man Ray's *Les Mystères du Château du dé* of 1928, which uses as setting the Villa Noailles by Robert Mallet-Stevens.

3

Mary McLeod, "Charlotte Perriand: Her First Decade as a Designer," *AA Files* 15 (1987), p. 6.

4

Pierre-Alain Crosset, "Eyes Which See," *Casabella* 531–532 (1987), p. 115. Should we remind the reader that Le Corbusier lost the sight of his left eye in 1918: separation of the retina while working at night on the drawing "La Cheminée"? See Le Corbusier, *My Work*, trans. James Palmes (London: Architectural Press, 1960), p. 54.

5

See chapter 6, note 2, above.

6

"Un tel sentiment s'explique dans la ville congestionnée où le désordre apparaît en images affligeantes; on admettrait même le paradoxe en face d'un spectacle natural sublime, trop sublime." Le Corbusier, *Urbanisme* (Paris: Crès, 1925), pp. 174–176.

7

Le Corbusier refers to Hugh Ferriss in his book *La Ville radieuse* (Paris: Vincent, Fréal, 1933), where a collage of images contrasting Hugh Ferriss and the actual New York with the Plan Voisin and Notre-Dame is accompanied by the caption: "The French tradition—Notre Dame and the Plan Voisin ('horizontal' skyscrapers) versus the American line (tumult, bristling, chaos, first explosive state of a new medievalism)." *The Radiant City* (New York: Orion Press, 1986), p. 133.

8

Charles de Beistegui interviewed by Roger Baschet in *Plaisir de France* (March 1936), pp. 26–29. Cited by Pierre Saddy, "Le Corbusier chez les riches: l'appartement Charles de Beistegui," *Architecture, mouvement, continuité,* no. 49 (1979), pp. 57–70. On this apartment, see also "Appartement avec terrasses," *L'Architecte* (October 1932), pp. 102–104.

9

"L'électricité, puissance moderne, est invisible, elle n'éclaire point la demeure, mais actionne les portes et déplace les murailles." Roger Baschet in the interview with Charles de Beistegui, *Plaisir de France* (March 1936).

10

Le Corbusier, *L'Art décoratif d'aujourd'hui* (Paris: Crès, 1925), p. 79.

11

Pierre Saddy, "Le Corbusier e l'Arlecchino," *Rassegna* 3 (1980), p. 27.

12

"Appartement avec terrasses," *L'Architecte* (October 1932).

13

Peter Blake, *The Master Builders: Le Corbusier, Mies van der Rohe, Frank Lloyd Wright* (New York: Alfred A. Knopf, 1961), p. 60.

14

Manfredo Tafuri, "*Machine et mémoire:* The City in the Work of Le Corbusier," in *Le Corbusier*, ed. H. Allen Brooks (Princeton: Princeton University Press, 1987), p. 203.

15

Le Corbusier, *Urbanisme*, p. 176.

16

See also chapter 3 above.

17

Le Corbusier, *Précisions sur un état présent de l'architecture et de l'urbanisme* (Paris: Vincent, Fréal, 1930), pp. 57–58. Emphasis added.

18

Le Corbusier, *Précisions*, pp. 132–133.

19

Ibid., pp. 136–138. Emphasis added.

20

This erasure of the front (despite the insistence of traditional criticism that Le Corbusier's buildings should be understood in terms of their facades) is a central theme of Le Corbusier's writings. For example, about the project for the Palace of Nations in Geneva he wrote: "Alors, me dira-t-on inquiet, vous avez construit des murs autour ou entre vos pilotis afin de ne pas donner l'angoissante sensation de ces gigantesques bâtiments en l'air? Oh, pas du tout! Je montre avec satisfaction ces pilotis qui portent quelque chose, qui se doublent de leur reflet dans l'eau, qui laissent passer la lumière sous les bâtiments *supprimant ainsi toute notion de 'devant' et de 'derrière' de bâtiment*." *Précisions*, p. 49 (emphasis added).

21

Of course, it does not mean that these images represent literally the *itinerary* of the house, as Tim Benton seems to understand when he attempts to reconstruct the *promenade* with the help of a cameraman, and of course does not succeed. See Tim Benton, "Le Corbusier y la promenade architecturale," *Arquitectura* 264–265 (1987), p. 43. The essence of film is the montage, not the linear narrative. About Le Corbusier's relationship with Eisenstein and his thought see Jean-Louis Cohen, *Le Corbusier et la mystique de l'URSS* (Brussels: Pierre Mardaga Editeur, 1987), p. 72

22

Lawrence Wright, *Perspective in Perspective* (London: Routledge and Kegan, 1983), pp. 240–241; Luis Fernandez-Galiano, "La mirada de Le Corbusier: hacia una arquitectura narrativa," *A&V, Monografias de Arquitectura y Vivienda* 9 (1987), p. 32. One should also note the relation between the form of representation employed in these houses and the way Le Corbusier constructs the manuscripts of his books or the notes for his lectures, where the line of thought can be followed through a string of images representing the ideas. See also chapter 3 above.

23
"Je savais que la région où l'ont voulait construire comportait un secteur de 10 à 15 kilomètres de coteaux bordant le lac. Un point fixe: le lac; un autre, la vue magnifique, frontale; un autre, le sud, frontal également./ Fallait-il tout d'abord rechercher le terrain et faire le plan d'après le terrain? Telle est la méthode courante. J'ai pensé qu'il valait mieux faire un plan exact, idéalement conforme à l'usage qu'on en espérait, déterminé par les trois facteurs déjà énoncés. Ceci fait, partir, plan en poche, à la recherche d'un terrain avantageux." Le Corbusier, *Précisions*, p. 127.

24
Ibid., p. 230.

25
Le Corbusier, *Une petite maison* (Zurich: Editions d'Architecture, 1954), pp. 8, 5.

26
Ibid., pp. 22–23.

27
"Aujourd'hui, la conformité du sol avec la maison n'est plus une question d'assiette ou de contexte immédiat." Le Corbusier and François de Pierrefeu, *La Maison des hommes* (Paris: Plon, 1942), p. 68. It is significant that this and other key passages of this book were omitted in the English translation, *The Home of Man* (London: Architectural Press, 1948).

28
Le Corbusier, *The Radiant City*, p. 224.

29
In *Précisions* he writes (p. 62): "La rue est indépendante de la maison. La rue est indépendante de la maison. Y réfléchir." It must be noted that it is the street that is independent of the house and not the other way around.

30
About the association of the notion of spectacle with that of dwelling, see Hubert Damisch, "Les Tréteaux de la vie moderne," in *Le Corbusier: une encyclopédie* (Paris: Centre Georges Pompidou, 1987), pp. 252–259. See also Bruno Reichlin, "L'Esprit de Paris," *Casabella* 531–532 (1987), pp. 52–63.

31
Le Corbusier and François de Pierrefeu, *The Home of Man*, p. 87.

32
Le Corbusier, *The Radiant City*, pp. 223–225.

33
Cf. Damisch, "Les Tréteaux de la vie moderne," p. 256.

34
Le Corbusier and François de Pierrefeu, *The Home of Man*, p. 87.

35
Le Corbusier, *The Radiant City*, p. 224.

36
Le Corbusier, *Précisions*, p. 56.

37
The etymology of the English word *window* reveals that it combines *wind* and *eye*. As Georges Teyssot has noted, the word combines "an element of the outside and an aspect of innerness. The separation on which dwelling is based is the possibility for a being to install himself" (G. Teyssot, "Water and Gas on All Floors," *Lotus* 44 [1984], p. 90). But in Le Corbusier this installation splits the subject itself, rather than simply the outside from the inside. Installation involves a convoluted geometry that entangles the division between interior and exterior, between the subject and itself. This etymology of *window* is also cited by Ellen Eve Frank in *Literary Architecture* (Berkeley: University of California Press, 1979), p. 263.

38
Le Corbusier, *Précisions*, p. 136.

39
It is not a casually placed cup of tea that we find, but an "artistic" arrangement of objects of everyday life, as in the kitchens of Savoye and Garches. We may speak here of "still lifes" more than of domesticity.

40
Luigi Pirandello, *Si gira*, quoted by Walter Benjamin in "The Work of Art in the Age of Mechanical Reproduction," in *Illuminations* (New York: Schocken Books, 1969), p. 229.

41
Benjamin, "The Work of Art in the Age of Mechanical Reproduction," p. 230.

42
Le Corbusier, *Précisions*, p. 78.

43
Le Corbusier and François de Pierrefeu, *The Home of Man*, p. 100.

44
Paul Virilio, "The Third Window: An Interview with Paul Virilio," in *Global Television*, ed. Cynthia Schneider and Brian Wallis (New York and Cambridge: Wedge Press and MIT Press, 1988), p. 191.

45
Le Corbusier and François de Pierrefeu, *The Home of Man*, p. 125.

46
"Le machinisme a tout bouleversé:
les communications: auparavant les hommes organisaient leurs entreprises à l'échelle de leurs jambes: Le temps avait une autre durée. La notion de la terre était de grandeur, sans limite. [. . .]
l'interpénétration: un jour Stevenson inventa la locomotive. On rit. Et comme des gens d'affaires prennent cela au sérieux, demandent des concessions, M. Thiers, l'homme d'Etat qui conduisait la France, intervient instamment au Parlement, suppliant les députés de s'occuper d'autres choses plus sérieuses: 'Jamais un chemin de fer [. . .] ne pourra relier deux villes . . .'!
Sont venus le télégraphe, le téléphone, les paquebots, les avions, la T.S.F. et voici la télévision. Un mot lâché de Paris est chez vous en une fraction de seconde! [. . .] Les avions vont partout; leur oeil d'aigle a fouillé le désert et a pénétré la forêt vierge. Précipitant l'interpénétration, le fer, le téléphone font couler sans arrêt la province dans la ville, la ville dans la province . . .
l'anéantissement des cultures régionales: ce que l'on croyait être le plus sacré: la tradition, le patrimoine des ancêtres, la pensée du clocher, [. . .] est tombé [. . .]
Les pleurnicheurs invectivent la machine perturbatrice. Les actifs intelligents pensent: *enregistrons* pendant qu'il est temps encore, par la photo, le cinéma ou le disque, par le livre, le magazine, ces témoignages sublimes des cultures seculaires."
Le Corbusier, *Précisions*, pp. 26–27. English translation from *Precisions: On the Present State of Architecture and City Planning*, trans. Edith Schreiber Aujame (Cambridge: MIT Press, 1991), pp. 25–27.

47
Le Corbusier, *Précisions*, pp. 106–107.

48
Ibid., p. 107.

49
"M. Vignole ne s'occupe pas des fenêtres, mais bien des 'entre-fenêtres' (pilastres ou colonnes). Je dévignolise par: *l'architecture, c'est des planchers éclairés*." Ibid., p. 53. English translation from *Precisions*, p. 51.

Illustration Credits

Page 18: Postcard from the Archives of the New York Stock Exchange.

Page 19: Postcard. Photograph by Paul Strand.

Pages 22, 34, 53, 235, 236, 237, 239, 241, 242, 246, 247, 249, 253, 254, 256, 258, 259, 261, 262, 268, 272, 275: Courtesy Graphische Sammlung Albertina, Vienna.

Pages 24, 81, 257: From *Berggasse 19: Sigmund Freud's Home and Offices, Vienna 1938* (New York: Basic Books, 1976). Photographs by Edmund Engelman.

Page 25: From *Karl Kraus Briefe an Sidonie Nadherny von Borutin 1913–36* (Munich: Kösel Verlag, 1974).

Pages 29, 30: From Hans Weigel, *Karl Kraus.*

Page 36: From Heinrich Kulka et al., *Adolf Loos* (Vienna, 1931).

Page 45: From B. Rukschcio and R. Schachel, *Adolf Loos* (Salzburg and Vienna, 1982).

Pages 48, 49: Reproduced from period postcards.

Page 52: From Klaus Wagenbach, *Franz Kafka: Pictures of a Life* (New York: Pantheon Books, 1984).

Page 54: Origin unknown.

Pages 55, 59, 60: Hoffmann Estate.

Page 58: Archive E. F. Sekler.

Page 62: From Z. P. Alexander, *Iron Horses: American Locomotives 1829–1900* (New York: W. W. Norton, 1968).

Page 63: From Sigfried Giedion, *Space, Time and Architecture* (Cambridge: Harvard University Press, 1941).

Page 74: From *Das Andere* 2 (1903).

Page 78: Still from Dziga Vertov, *The Man with the Movie Camera* (1928–1929).

Page 79: From Jonathan Crary, *Techniques of the Observer: On Vision and Modernity in the Nineteenth Century* (Cambridge: MIT Press, 1990).

Page 85: Courtesy Musée du Louvre.

Pages 86, 87, 89, 97, 99, 110, 113, 126, 127, 129, 135, 137, 138, 162, 163, 215, 227, 230, 284, 288, 294, 295, 299, 300, 308, 309, 313, 316, 317, 320, 321, 331: © 1993 ARS, New York / SPADEM, Paris.

Page 92: From Malek Alloula, *The Colonial Harem* (Minneapolis: University of Minnesota Press, 1986).

Pages 93, 94: From Giuliano Gresleri, *Le Corbusier, Viaggio in Oriente* (Venice: Marsilio Editori; Paris: Fondation Le Corbusier, 1984).

Pages 96, 98, 121: From Le Corbusier, *L'Art décoratif d'aujourd'hui* (Paris: Editions Crès, 1925).

Page 102: From Mary Patricia May Sekler, *The Early Drawings of Charles-Edouard Jeanneret 1902–1908* (New York: Garland Publishing, 1977).

Page 103: From *Dekorative Kunst* 7 (1903–1904).

Page 105: From Le Corbusier, *L'Atelier de la recherche patiente* (Stuttgart: Gerd Hatje, 1960).

Pages 106, 108, 109, 112, 142, 143, 150, 166, 167, 174, 182, 189, 198, 214, 216, 218: From *L'Esprit nouveau* (issue numbers and dates as noted in captions).

Page 115: From Le Corbusier, *Précisions* (Paris: Editions Crès, 1930).

Pages 116, 120, 122, 144, 145, 146, 147, 149, 151, 152, 155, 158, 168, 178, 179, 186, 188, 196, 197, 199, 222, 224: Courtesy Fondation Le Corbusier.

Pages 117, 125, 154, 161, 164: From Le Corbusier, *Vers une architecture* (Paris: Editions Crès, 1923).

Page 123: From Le Corbusier, *Une maison, un palais* (Paris: Editions Crès, 1928).

Pages 131, 285, 286, 287, 328: From *L'Architecture vivante* (1929–1931).

Page 132: From Sigfried Giedion, *Mechanization Takes Command* (New York: W. W. Norton, 1969).

Pages 157, 165, 169: From *L'Illustration* (issues as noted in captions).

Page 172: From *Art Bulletin*, September-December 1966.

Pages 191, 193: From Le Corbusier, *Almanach de l'architecture moderne* (Paris: Editions Crès, 1925).

Pages 205, 208: Courtesy Museum of Modern Art, New York.

Pages 223, 225, 228: © 1994 ARS, New York / ADAGP, Paris.

Pages 240, 245: From Ludwig Münz and Gustav Künstler, *Adolf Loos: Pioneer of Modern Architecture* (London: Thames and Hudson, 1966).

Page 243: From Max Risselada, ed., *Raumplan versus Plan Libre* (Delft: Delft University Press, 1988).

Page 251: From *Der Architect*, no. 22 (1922).

Page 263: From Lynn Haney, *Naked at the Feast: A Biography of Josephine Baker* (New York: Dodd, Mead & Company, 1981).

Pages 266, 267: From Amédée Ozenfant, *Foundations of Modern Art* (1931).

Page 278: From *Das Interieur* (1901).

Pages 290, 291, 292: Stills from *L'Architecture d'aujourd'hui* (1929).

Page 298: From *AA Files* 15 (1987), courtesy Charlotte Perriand.

Page 302: From *L'Electricité à la maison* (Paris: Compagnie parisienne de distribution d'électricité, c. 1930).

Pages 304, 305, 307, 310: From *L'Architecture* (1932).

Pages 324, 325: From Le Corbusier, *La Ville radieuse* (Paris: Vincent, Fréal, 1933).

Index